Xenophon's Other Voice

Also available from Bloomsbury

American Anabasis, Tim Rood
Military Leaders and Sacred Space in Classical Greek Warfare, Sonya Nevin
The Thucydidean Turn, Benjamin Earley
Xenophon, Fiona Hobden

Xenophon's Other Voice

Irony as Social Criticism in the 4th Century BCE

Yun Lee Too

BLOOMSBURY ACADEMIC
LONDON • NEW YORK • OXFORD • NEW DELHI • SYDNEY

BLOOMSBURY ACADEMIC
Bloomsbury Publishing Plc
50 Bedford Square, London, WC1B 3DP, UK
1385 Broadway, New York, NY 10018, USA
29 Earlsfort Terrace, Dublin 2, Ireland

BLOOMSBURY, BLOOMSBURY ACADEMIC and the Diana logo
are trademarks of Bloomsbury Publishing Plc

First published in Great Britain 2022
This paperback edition published 2023

Copyright © Yun Lee Too, 2022

Yun Lee Too has asserted her right under the Copyright, Designs and
Patents Act, 1988, to be identified as Author of this work.

For legal purposes the Acknowledgements on p. viii constitute an extension
of this copyright page.

Cover design: Terry Woodley
Cover images © Pictorial Press Ltd / Alamy Stock Photo
and Chronicle / Alamy Stock Photo

All rights reserved. No part of this publication may be reproduced or transmitted in
any form or by any means, electronic or mechanical, including photocopying,
recording, or any information storage or retrieval system, without prior permission
in writing from the publishers.

Bloomsbury Publishing Plc does not have any control over, or responsibility for, any
third-party websites referred to or in this book. All internet addresses given in this book
were correct at the time of going to press. The author and publisher regret any
inconvenience caused if addresses have changed or sites have ceased to exist,
but can accept no responsibility for any such changes.

A catalogue record for this book is available from the British Library.

Library of Congress Cataloging-in-Publication Data

Names: Too, Yun Lee, author.
Title: Xenophon's other voice : irony as social criticism in the 4th century BCE / Yun Lee Too.
Description: New York : Bloomsbury Academic, 2021. |
Includes bibliographical references and index.
Identifiers: LCCN 2021018840 (print) | LCCN 2021018841 (ebook) |
ISBN 9781350250529 (hardback) | ISBN 9781350250543 (ebook) |
ISBN 9781350250550 (epub)
Subjects: LCSH: Xenophon–Criticism and interpretation. | Irony in literature.
Classification: LCC PA4499 .T66 2021 (print) | LCC PA4499 (ebook) |
DDC 938/.007202—dc23
LC record available at https://lccn.loc.gov/2021018840
LC ebook record available at https://lccn.loc.gov/2021018841

ISBN: HB: 978-1-3502-5052-9
PB: 978-1-3502-5053-6
ePDF: 978-1-3502-5054-3
eBook: 978-1-3502-5055-0

Typeset by RefineCatch Limited, Bungay, Suffolk

To find out more about our authors and books visit www.bloomsbury.com
and sign up for our newsletters.

Contents

Preface	vii
Acknowledgements	viii
Introduction	1

Part One   Socrates on Athens

1 Xenophon's *Apology*: The Death of Socratic Irony; the Birth of Xenophontic Irony — 21

2 The *Memorabilia*: Remembering Truth and Lies about Socrates — 31

3 Partying Life (Away) in Xenophon's *Symposium* — 45

4 The Economies of Pedagogy in the *Oeconomicus*: Xenophon's Wifely Didactics — 61

Part Two   Xenophon on Athens

5 The Critique of the Sophists in *On Hunting* — 81

6 Xenophon on Equine Culture — 93

7 Xenophon's *Poroi* or 'Ways and Means'? — 105

Part Three   The Rest of Greece

8 Why Xenophon's *Hiero* Is not a Socratic Dialogue — 119

9 Spartan Disappointments — 131

10 The *Hellenica* and the Irony of War — 151

Part Four   Persia

11 Xenophon's *Cyropaedia*: Disfiguring the Pedagogical State — 169

12 Coming Home? The *Anabasis* as Community — 187

Concluding Thoughts	207
Notes	215
Bibliography	237
Greek Index	251
Index	253

Preface

In the summer of 1992 I had finished my dissertation on Isocrates and I went to chat with Professor Donald Russell, who had been my examiner. During the course of the conversation he made the observation that 'Even more interesting than Isocrates is Xenophon'. Holding onto that thought, I went on to publish two essays on Xenophon – 'The Pedagogical State and the Disfigurement of Power in Xenophon's *Cyropaedia*' in Too and Livingstone (eds), *Pedagogy and Power: Rhetorics of Classical Learning*, Cambridge, 1998), pp. 282–302 and 'The Economies of Pedagogy: Xenophon's Wifely Didactics', *Proceedings of the Cambridge Philological Society* 47 (2001), pp. 65–80; both of which are included in this book. I began working further on the subject of Xenophon four years ago, when I returned to thinking about my conversation with Donald and his comment on the author. I have now read the complete surviving works of Xenophon and indeed found every one of his works to be very interesting; not necessarily more so than Isocrates is, but intriguing in their own right!

I would like to thank Eleni-Melina Tamiolaki for her intellectual support during my work on this project. I am also grateful to the readers of my manuscript as their criticisms and suggestions have made this a much better book. I also want to state here that it has been an absolute pleasure working with the editorial team at Bloomsbury. I must express my heartfelt thanks to Georgie Leighton for having faith in my project and for her considerable patience in seeing this book through to a contract, and also to Alice Wright for her understanding of what I am attempting to achieve with this book and for believing in it. Thanks also to Lily Mac Mahon for support during the publication process, and to Aidan Cross for his splendid work copy-editing the manuscript.

To the memory of the late Donald Russell and his astute observations about literature, and especially Greek prose, I dedicate this volume.

Acknowledgements

'The Economies of Pedagogy in the *Oeconomicus*: Xenophon's Wifely Didactics' is reprinted with permission from *Proceedings of the Cambridge Philological Society* 47 (2001), 65–80. Copyright @2001 by Yun Lee Too.

All rights reserved.

'Xenophon's *Cyropaedia*: Disfiguring the Pedagogical State' is reprinted with permission in an updated form from its earlier incarnation: 'The Pedagogical State and the Disfigurement of Power in Xenophon's *Cyropaedia*', in Too and Livingstone (eds), *Pedagogy and Power: Rhetorics of Classical Learning*. Cambridge: Cambridge University Press, 1998, 282–302. Copyright @1998 by Yun Lee Too.

All rights reserved.

Introduction

I

Xenophon's Other Voice: Irony as Social Criticism in the 4th Century BCE is the title of my study on Xenophon, and it is a title bound eventually to provoke. *Xenophon's Other Voice* implies that there are two voices in the author's work, as indeed I maintain there are: one ostensible at the level of the literal text, which is available to everyone, while the sub-title designates the other voice, which is less obvious to the reader – indeed, an ironic one. Certainly, I acknowledge the presence of irony in Xenophon, and this is the chief provocation of my volume because some scholars doubt its presence in the text of Xenophon, while others, who acknowledge its existence, have invested so much in the term 'irony' as far as the author is concerned that 'irony' has become distorted in its meaning. Indeed, Xenophon is an author who has attracted so much interest at the end of the twentieth century and the beginning of the twenty-first at least partly because of irony and the implications of reading ironically.

Irony has generated the most impassioned response to Xenophon, and it traditionally divides readers into at least two main camps. First, there are those who wish to see irony in the author as indicative and productive of an ideology that is ultra-conservative in contemporary terms – so, for instance, women are to be denigrated; classics are considered exclusive to a wealthy elite from a prestigious educational background; society must assume conservative values and 'smart' people are the bearers of this ideology. As Annabel Patterson notes, in this mode of reading, irony is a tool of exotericism.[1] The readers who take this tack tend to be 'Straussians' following Leo Strauss, the most influential proponent of this way of reading Ancient Greek texts (and I believe that I have been called a Straussian for seeing irony in Xenophon even though I do not at all subscribe to this ideology). It would seem that being a Straussian gives one a licence to read almost anything one wants into Xenophon because one can take recourse to a hidden meaning in the text, which one may always conveniently find even if it is not there at any level. There are other scholars – including Tuplin, Dillery, Tatum, and Morrison – who assign ironic readings to Xenophon in a much more moderate way and without the shackles of a particular ideology.[2] On the other side, there are those who regard Xenophon as incapable of irony, as in the case of Søren Kierkegaard,[3] Gregory Vlastos,[4] or to a lesser extent, Vivienne Gray, although she wavers in being willing to see a very weak form of irony in various leaders in the *Hellenica* whom Xenophon only regards as 'seeming to be …' rather than actually being what they seem to be.[5] In his work *The Concept of Irony with Continual Reference to Socrates*, which was submitted as a dissertation to the University of Copenhagen in 1841, Søren Kierkegaard did not see Xenophon as producing an ironic Socrates. The Socrates he saw in Xenophon was lacking, deflated and therefore somewhat disappointing.[6] Kierkegaard found that Xenophon was interested in Socrates as a representative of finitude and the useful, that is of the non-ironic, whereas Plato saw Socrates as ironic and a representative of the good, the beautiful and the true.[7] For Xenophon, Socrates was ignorant although not wholly so because he *knew* that he was ignorant. Irony is extremely muted in Xenophon, but this ignorance was enough to keep the ancient philosopher ironically afloat, as far as the nineteenth-century author was concerned. Kierkegaard writes in *The Concept of Irony* of the Xenophontic Socrates having 'observations [which] are altogether run-of-the-mill'.[8] He did not look elsewhere in Xenophon for irony.

After Kierkegaard there are others who try to ignore the irony in Xenophon (and after Leo Strauss, the conservatism that irony entails).[8] Vivienne Gray, who has published a great deal of widely read material on Xenophon, seems to be in agreement with Kierkegaard when she offers 'straight' readings of the Xenophontic texts. In her view the *Cyropaedia* is straightforwardly about the Persian monarch's 'successful government of eastern kingdoms (1.1.1–6)', while the *Oeconomicus* is about Ischomachus running his household well and profitably.[9] Gray reads these texts straight, that is, at face value. Elsewhere, in her view Xenophon supports forms of government which are non-democratic, just as Isocrates does.[10] Nonetheless, it is the case that Gray fortunately relents somewhat on irony in her introduction to her 2010 edited volume on Xenophon, when she proposes to see irony in the author's 'images of power'.[11] I observe that Michael Flower also sidesteps the issue of irony in his volume *A Cambridge Companion to Xenophon*.[12]

II

My approach to Xenophon stands apart from either of these two main approaches to the author. I significantly observe that in the introductions to his translations of the *Anabasis* and *Hellenica*, George Cawkwell indicated that all is not as it seems to be in the text of Xenophon. He suspected that something was afoot in this author. Cawkwell declared that 'But though plain, he [Xenophon] is never transparent' in writing of the Persian expedition in 1951, and warned in his translation of the *Hellenica* in 1966 that one must read 'between the lines' and refuse to believe all that one reads in this work.[13] Cawkwell does not name irony in the works of Xenophon but to all intents and purposes he describes it, while Louis André Dorion observes that the word εἰρωνεία does not appear in Xenophon, but he is willing to accept with Strauss a subversive Socrates.[14] I accept irony in the author but I want to change quite radically the parameters of the treatment of irony. I decisively move away from the issue of Xenophon's supposed and projected ideology as assumed by Straussians. Instead, I suggest that irony is a feature of the presentation, gesturing at inconsistencies in the text, which serve to achieve the author's goal, namely, the social criticism of the fourth-century world and its institutions.

There is another good reason for Xenophon to conceal his actual political position and views through irony. If we believe Athenian authors of the fourth century BCE, Athens was a noisy, fractious place where certain people often spoke publicly in the lawcourts and in the Assembly (cf. e.g. Isocrates, *On the Peace* pp. 129–30; *Antidosis* p. 38). It was populated by troublemakers, such as Lysimachus, Teisias, Callimachus and Cleon, in addition to other orators and sophists too numerous to name. These individuals, the 'new politicians', as Robert Connor has named them,[15] would argue minor court cases on matters of finance and of wrongs against their opponents, offering specious speeches on political topics and topical concerns, and their often rambunctious audiences were misled by pleasure (cf. Thucydides 3.38.7 and 3.40.2–3); jostling one another, they would cheer on their favourites or shout down those they did not like.[16] Athens was a chaotic and disorderly place where business was conducted through the spoken word, and where the mob's favour decided policy and legal outcomes.

As far as conservative authors such as Xenophon were concerned, the new politician was responsible for the loss of power and respect for speaking in public in the fourth century. Public oratory was the manipulation, seduction and hoodwinking of a mob too stupid to know when someone was taking advantage of them or seeking their own furtherance at the expense of the community. Speaking was, moreover, an aspect of πολυπραγμοσύνη or meddling in civic affairs, for instance, concerning oneself with lawsuits where one has no business for one's own personal and selfish gains.[17] Another individual, Isocrates, had constructed for himself an authority that was oppositional and counter-cultural. His small voice marked him as an ἀπράγμων, a figure who, at a slightly earlier time criticized by Thucydides' Pericles for his indifference to affairs of the city in the 'Funeral Oration' (2.40.2), now possessed an authority and respectability which derived precisely from the fact that he was unlike the 'new politicians' and the sycophants of the recent past and present. Isocrates' μικροφωνία or 'small voice' that left him unable to orate was part of a larger complex rhetoric of civic identity. Like the (generally disingenuous) *topos* 'unaccustomed as I am to public speaking', it was a plea which derived its power from the implication that the speaker was a political innocent quite distinct from the busybodies who frequented the assembly and lawcourts. Μικροφωνία and its variants thus articulated the elitist's rejection of the civic ideal of the right to public speech in a phonocentric Athens,[18] providing the citizen with an excuse to be exempt from public and political life as it was currently being conducted.

Because not all public discourse needed to be spoken from the orator's platform, Xenophon pursued another, more exclusive one.[19] As a conservative elitist, a member of a minority privileged by wealth, status and education, he preferred to live his life apart from the commonality of Athens. In this sense, he would have been to a greater or lesser extent a 'quiet Athenian'.[20] He himself avoided the places of public speech and sought ways of expressing himself as such apart from public speech. Accordingly, Xenophon, along with other fourth-century authors such as Isocrates, Plato and Thucydides, turned to the written word, which was the medium of the privileged few – as public literacy stood, according to William Harris, at only ten to fifteen per cent of the population.[21] One might note that even literary documents inscribed on stele or placed in the Metroon might not have been intended to be read by the many so much as to signify that the document was a public one, that is, potentially available to all even if in reality it was not.[22] With the majority of the population unable to read or without any facility or familiarity with letters, Xenophon chose literary expression as the manner in which he independently created an authoritative voice for himself. He sought the attention of the few, inevitably educated and wealthy like himself, and their approbation through the medium of writing, which was the preferred means of communication by which the elite could distinguish itself.

III

But how do we understand irony? To begin to answer these questions I must first consider that irony was initially embodied in the εἴρων in ancient Greek drama. The εἴρων was one of three stock figures in Greek Old Comedy, and his role was to bring about, by understatement or modest speech and self-deprecation, the downfall of his opponent – the braggart, or ἀλαζών – who regarded himself more highly than he should and who was an impostor. (The third character was the βωμολόχος or buffoon, who served to express wit in often crude language and who frequently addressed the audience.) The εἴρων was a figure thus who showed illusions and delusions for what they were – the ἀλαζών was misguided about his status in society – and made this known to the audience. He was a character with a greater or heightened knowledge than that held by the braggart and sought to communicate this knowledge through his understated discourse. Aristotle supports this characterization of the braggart and the εἴρων in the *Nicomachean Ethics*. At 1108a21–2 he states that ἀλαζονεία and the ἀλαζών are concerned to exaggerate, while εἰρωνεία and the εἴρων tend to diminish or are inclined to the lesser (cf. ἐπι τὸ ἔλαττον). According to Aristotle, the truth is a middle state between exaggeration and the lesser (*NE* 1108a20).

But according to Xenophon and Plato, it would seem that truth rested rather with the εἴρων, for it is an understatement which reveals the deception under which others live and which displays the truth to those who are willing to perceive it. Plato's Socrates plays the εἴρων in the philosopher's dialogues, which is why we speak of 'Socratic irony'.[23] Socrates feigns ignorance and humility in order to expose the delusions of his interlocutors. Irony is an understated, non-assertive way for an individual – the teacher? – to get his point across to his audience – the student? And where the Platonic Socrates was concerned, its method is very particular. The teacher feigns ignorance about, or at least does not state outright, the point or the teaching he is trying to communicate to the student and the student eventually comes to a realization of the point or the teaching through subtle prompts or on his own with indirect help from the teacher – because in the Platonic schema, learning is simply remembering as a consequence of hints and clues, i.e. *anamnesis*. The teacher may also contradict his literal words either explicitly or by understatement, and in the contradiction lies the more significant teaching. After all, Quintilian writes that irony is a figure of speech in which the opposite of what is said is to be understood, *in utroque enim contrarium ei, quod dicitur, intellegendum est* (*I. O.* 9.2.44). The recognition of irony requires a perspective of superior knowledge or awareness to be gained by the viewer. The teaching is thus student-driven and more effective for being so.

For example, the Platonic Socrates greets the rhapsode Ion, who has just come from the contest of Asclepius in Epidaurus (530a), and he engages him in conversation about the poets, while pretending to be completely ignorant of poetry. Socrates gets Ion to agree that knowledge of poetry and knowledge of what the poetic concerns are one and the same so that the rhapsode and the general have the same knowledge and the good rhapsode is a good general, although the converse is not necessarily true (541a). Thus, according to the false knowledge that Socrates feigns, because Ion is the best rhapsode, he must also be the best general and greatly desired by a city like Ephesus (541d). In the end, Ion is forced to admit that he is after all not a great general and that his knowledge of Homer only comes through divine inspiration (542a–b). Irony requires Socrates to be disingenuous about what he knows to be the truth; namely, that Ion is rather stupid and ignorant of the material of poetry, and so his supposed 'ignorance' ideally leads his interlocutor into a realization of what is actually the case.

Socrates is a figure in several of Xenophon's works: the *Memorabilia*, the *Apology*, the *Symposium* and the *Oeconomicus*, where he has conversations with other Athenians of the day. There is irony in these texts, which is far from surprising in light of the presence of the philosopher, who is the subject supposed to know and also the subject who indeed does know, among his less enlightened interlocutors or community. Just having Socrates present and speaking in the text of Xenophon suggests a discrepancy of knowledges, a discrepancy that leads to an ironic situation, but irony does not always require the presence of the philosopher. Irony does not always or inevitably require the explicit presence of Socrates or Plato. To be ironic the work simply requires an individual to supply the presence of an ironic teacher, who may be implicit. Xenophon, the narrator (rather than, say, Xenophon, the character, in the *Anabasis*), who is generally not characterized as a presence in the text but remains invisible and omniscient, offers his narrative and then drops the remarks and comments which undermine everything that he is seeming to affirm up to that point. And the irony can occur anywhere in the work, whether at its beginning, as in the case of the *Agesilaus*, where, for instance, Xenophon announces that there were signs that Agesilaus should be the king at his birth but refuses to offer any justifications for this, and then goes on to state that he enriched his friends in war in what appears to be a rather corrupt manner (1.18), or at the end, as in the *Constitution of the Spartans*, where we learn in the penultimate chapter that Lycurgus' legislative reforms had no effect on latter day Sparta as its citizens were greedy for money, and they now seek power without endeavouring to rule others well (chapter 14). Irony can also occur throughout the work as in the case of *On the Cavalry Commander*, where the cavalry appears less interested in war and in the physical exertion necessary to train for war than in its appearance and wealth. Accordingly, the final chapter of the work proposes that Athens is better off with a well-trained mercenary cavalry that is partly foreign. Equine culture at Athens is deeply flawed. Irony may also be extratextual in the sense that the reader knows a fact which lies outside the text that undermines the ostensible narrative: so, e.g. the fabulously wealthy Critias was known to have died extremely poor (*Symposium*), the wife of Ischomachus, who may be Chrysilla, slept with Critias (*Oeconomicus*), and silver, the great resource of Athens, actually diminishes the city-state's wealth by supporting the war effort (*Poroi*).

I maintain the simplest and most encompassing articulation of irony for this study, namely that it occurs when there are differences of thought and perception about a matter. Yet irony is not an argument or a debate because it does not take recourse to the explicit; irony occurs when matters are different from the way most people think that they are or should be, and this difference is perceived by someone or some others, who only implicitly suggest that this is the case and allow others to also perceive the alternative view but do not widely publicize the difference of perception. In this sense, irony is, as Wayne Booth (see below) suggests, elitist. The author Xenophon is the individual who sees differently in the corpus, and while his corpus is potentially available to all, his ideal audience is one that also comes to view reality as he does.

Plato and Xenophon, like other intellectuals of their class and their era, used writing as the means by which they articulated their views apart from the vocal mass. Their irony is a literary irony, which was something that a reading audience could perhaps best entertain because it had the ability to reconsider and revisit that bit of the text which did not quite sit properly with the rest and which pointed to another, alternative reality, whereas once the oral text was spoken it had passed away. The audience of the literary text may read (or have the text read to them), having the leisure to reflect on the disjunctions of knowledge between the ironic philosopher, i.e. Socrates, or narrator (as in the case of Xenophon) and his unknowing or less knowing interlocutor(s) or actors in the text. Socrates is the εἴρων whom these authors report upon and who thus makes these writers themselves in turn ironic in reporting his conversations and discussions. Accordingly, one cannot always take Plato and Xenophon at face value but must always read between the lines, although not as in a Straussian reading, which insists on one consistent interpretation – actually a paraphrase – of the text, which generally runs counter to and despite what is actually written, and which imposes a subsequent ideology on much earlier texts.²⁴

For the Greeks, irony (εἰρωνεία) was often regarded as saying the opposite of what one means. Where irony (εἰρωνεία) is concerned, one looks for incongruities, for a mismatch between what is outwardly said and what is actually intended. Irony is a double writing and it admits a double audience (who will include characters internal to the work and individuals receiving the work as a read or performed text), one which perceives what is said at face value and does not understand the literary figure of the irony, and another, which is aware that more is going, that the sense is other than and lies beneath the surface of what is explicitly said.²⁵ In effect, I maintain the simplest and most encompassing articulation of irony for this study, namely that it occurs when there is a mismatch of thought and perception about a certain matter: irony involves different parties to a situation at different levels of knowledge.²⁶ Yet irony is not an argument or a debate because irony does not take recourse to the explicit; irony occurs when matters are different from the way most people think that they are or should be, and this difference is perceived by someone or some others (e.g. the author, one of his characters, a member/members of the audience), who suggest(s) that this is the case and allow(s) others to also perceive the alternative view, but does not widely publicize the difference of perception. The author Xenophon is the individual who sees differently in the corpus, and while his corpus is potentially available to all, his ideal audience is one that also comes to view reality as he does and indeed comes into view as *his* audience. The audience is 'in' – it gets the irony – or 'out' – it does not get the irony.²⁷ I suggest thus that irony is the ideal figure of speech for an elitist such as Xenophon to employ, determining a divide between an audience that will not properly understand what the author seeks to convey – the mass – and an audience that will understand more deeply – an elite, which is probably educated and able to read.

I suggest that there is indeed irony in Xenophon without agreeing with Straussian readings of the text. Furthermore, I propose that there is a politics implicit in εἰρωνεία, which is quite separate from Strauss' neo-conservative ideology. Wayne Booth suggests that Kierkegaard offers an interesting comment of how irony is involved in elitism. Booth comments, 'For Kierkegaard, irony looks down, as it were, on plain and ordinary discourse immediately understood by everyone; it travels in an exclusive incognito … [It] occurs chiefly in the higher circles as a prerogative belonging to the same category as that *bon ton* requiring one to smile at innocence and regard virtue as a kind of prudishness.'²⁸ Hierarchical as it must be, irony involves its producer and the individual who perceives it in a complicity of superiority. These individuals see what others cannot see due to their lack of social position or to their ignorance and this is what makes irony so subversive. The readers who do not perceive irony are excluded from this superiority. Strauss, misguided in other respects, can correctly observe that irony is a 'noble dissimulation of one's worth, one's superiority' and is 'peculiar to the superior man',[29] acknowledging the superiority of the author he reads. And, indeed, irony implies that the ironist knows best and is therefore superior. Irony lies in dissembling what one says with a view to intending something different from what is said, as Socrates, with whom irony is most often associated, frequently did in the Platonic dialogues.[30]

I show that Xenophon's works themselves contain deliberate discrepancies which suggest that we should read them in ways that stand apart from received tradition, which, apart from Leo Strauss and his followers, has tended not to recognize irony. I am saying that irony is prevalent – indeed, it is present to a greater or lesser extent in every genuine work – in the Xenophontic corpus. The author's position is that things in the fourth century are not as most people perceive them to be. And the presence of irony perhaps explains why Xenophon, as Jacqueline de Romilly has observed, is not an author who focussed on facticity to the point that, she notes, historical fiction derives its origin from this author. It is not the facts themselves but the reading of the representations that matters most.[31] Irony enables Xenophon to be a critic of the societies around him, whether they be Athens or Sparta or Persia, and the politics they sustain, without openly denigrating these societies. As an author, he is a commentator on human nature and behaviour in these societies, writing for the social and intellectual elite, who have the capacity to receive his critique. And this is why, I suggest, the *Constitution of the Athenians* is a pseudo-Xenophontic text rather than an authentic work (see 'Concluding Thoughts'). This text openly criticizes Athenian culture throughout, without any sense that the criticism is being hidden or concealed. Accordingly, the work declares that Athens chooses bad men to rule and does wrong to other Greeks (1.1), Athens no longer practises gymnastics (1.13), and so on and on. The tone of the work does not change at all, so what the reader experiences is an unabated, negative rant.

IV

The realization of an ironic presence in Xenophon's works is very significant for how one might read them in terms of their generic distinctions. It means that one does not take genre as the chief consideration that controls how one might approach the texts. This also entails that one cannot read the historical works of Xenophon separately from the philosophical or fictional works inasmuch as the first group of works require understanding of a method set out or, at the very least, implied by the latter. Whether one is reading about individuals encountering Socrates, or others making money, riding horses, being generals, the specificities of what they are doing is less important than their understanding about what they think they are doing. Xenophon is engaging with a misinformed and deluded world and wishes to make this known to his readers. Irony becomes an overarching concern and a unifying methodology for reading.

But approaching ancient texts through a distinction between historical, philosophical and fictional work may in any case be somewhat anachronistic, something that is in keeping with our contemporary understanding of literary categories.[32] If Aristotle had written about prose, which is a much more recent literary form, he would also have considered the modes and objects of imitation for this type of literature. He might offer as categories historical and philosophical writing; fiction comes into existence at a much later date. But as far as concerns poetry and prose, the fact is that fully formed generic thinking only came about, as Mary Depew and Dirk Obbink observe,[33] in the seventeenth century. In her book *Genres in Dialogue: Plato and the Construct of Philosophy* (Cambridge: 1996), Andrea Nightingale takes the view that Plato works to abstract philosophy as a separate genre from other forms of prose.[34] In other words, Plato does his best to construct a distinct type of writing, i.e. philosophy, where no distinct notion of philosophy necessarily existed before.

In Ancient Greece, genre was conceived somewhat differently from the way it is conceived now. Form determined the categorizations of literature, and so there were three main genres in Greek literature: poetry, tragedy and prose. Within these genres there were sub-categories, so that poetry might contain epic, tragedy and lyric. Scholars often turn to Aristotle's *Poetics* on the assumption that the philosopher offers authoritative, because philosophical, thoughts on the question of genre. What one finds in the *Poetics* is an acknowledgement of the existence of epic poetry (ἐπιποίεα), tragedy (ἡ τῆς τραγῳδίας ποίησις), comedy (κωμῳδία) and dithyramb (ἡ διθυραμβοροτική). Aristotle is concerned with these forms of literature as modes of imitation and observes that they differ in the medium, the objects and the mode of imitation (1447a13–18). But I would argue that what the philosopher says about poetic literature is not to be taken as prescriptive of that literary form, for after all the philosopher is merely making observations about the forms of poetic writing. G. Most observes that what Aristotle says about tragedy is neither 'normative' nor 'descriptive'.³⁵ The *Poetics* is a far from exhaustive treatment of poetic genre in any sense of the word 'exhaustive' and perhaps a sign of this is that it does not mention prose, even as a counterpoint to poetry.

Isocrates is another author of the fourth century who demonstrably downplays what we would identify as generic distinctions. In the *Antidosis* at sections 45–6 Isocrates observes that there are as many types of prose as of verse. Some people may have dedicated their energies to writing about the genealogies of demigods, others to studies of the poets, others to histories of wars and still others have concerned themselves with dialogue and are called dialecticians. There are many more types of prose, which the rhetorician elects not to mention here. But there is one other prose form that he mentions here: public discourse concerned with Hellas and with affairs of state. This is political discourse, which he privileges above all other forms of prose as being most aesthetically pleasurable and most useful to society.³⁶ All generic categories are rendered insignificant with regard to λόγος πολιτικός, and so are essentially nullified in the Isocratean scheme of things.

Nonetheless, I maintain that the chief distinction in literary categories is between poetry and prose because these literary forms are so distinct and different in form, and so as far as the fourth century BCE was concerned, Xenophon is a prose writer, like Herodotus, Isocrates, Plato and Thucydides and so on, and he is certainly not a poet. The appearance of the poet Simonides in the *Hiero*, I argue, implicitly shows the difference between the poetic world and the prose world. That he writes what we classify as philosophy or history is not (to) the point and he may not have thought in these terms in any case. This is a good reason to read the Socratic works together with those dealing with the history of Greece and Persia, rather than as distinct types of literature and as dealing with distinct topics, for they are after all by the same author. Certainly, W. E. Higgins and John Dillery do this to some degree, with the former declaring that he reads 'Xenophon *qua* Xenophon' and the latter in rejecting the view that the historical Xenophon must be separated from the philosophical Xenophon.³⁷

Disregarding generic categories of work sets me apart from most of the prior scholarship on Xenophon, which tends to concern itself with the historical *or* the philosophical Xenophon, with a separation of the works of Xenophon according to different formal categories.³⁸ The scholars who are foremost concerned with Xenophon as an historical or political author show their concern above all with the *Anabasis*, the *Hellenica*, the works on the Athenian and Spartan constitutions. They include among their number Christopher Tuplin,³⁹ who collects a variety of articles by different scholars on historical topics concerning Xenophon in his 2004 collection, Robin Lane Fox,[40] W. E. Higgins,[41] Stephen Hirsch,[42] and Robin Waterfield.[43] John Dillery, whose foremost concern is the *Anabasis* and *Hellenica*, is less historically bound than other scholars for he reads them also in the context of the *Memorabilia*, the *Cyropaedia*, the *Agesilaos* and the *Constitution of the Spartans*.[44] He observes that other scholars who observe generic distinctions keep Xenophon the historian quite apart from the Xenophon who is concerned with philosophy.[45] He notes that in the *Cambridge History of Classical Literature* this approach is well demonstrated by Immerhwahr and Connor's chapter on Xenophon as historian and by Sandbach's chapter on Xenophon as philosopher.[46]

Then, there are the scholars who are interested above all in Xenophon as a student of Socrates, and as a Socratic, showing their concern foremost with the *Oeconomicus* and the *Memorabilia*. Among their number are L.-A. Dorion,[47] D. Morrison,[48] G. Danzig,[49] Paul van der Waerdt,[50] the idiosyncratic and perhaps notorious Leo Strauss,[51] Strauss' disciple Thomas Pangle,[52] and J. K. Anderson[53] (to some degree). For the most part, their Xenophon is a distinct author who takes on the socio-historical Greek city-state to offer his insights on reality – or what these scholars regard 'reality' to be, as in the case of the Straussians – in an Athens which is the hotspot of intellectual activity and inquiry. It is of course with this scholarship that irony has been a major concern and filter through which to read Xenophon.

There is a third group of scholars, who are interested in Xenophon as a writer of fiction, being concerned foremost with the *Cyropaedia* even though this might also be claimed to be historico-political work. Here I might mention James Tatum,[54] Bodil Due[55] and Deborah Gera.[56]

In *Xenophon: Ethical Principles and Historical Enquiry* (Leiden: 2012), Hobden and Tuplin present essays which are concerned with philosophical and historical topics in Xenophon and do something to suggest that the division between philosophy and history may be bridged, even if by only juxtaposing studies in these different 'fields'. Vivienne Gray brings all three areas of study concerning Xenophon together in her 2010 collection of essays, entitled quite simply *Xenophon*. She collects essays on the social aspects of Xenophon as in his work and on homosexuality, on Socrates, on the historical works, which she identifies as the *Anabasis* and the *Hellenica*,[57] and on the *Cyropaedia*, which she has identified as the 'mirror of princes'.[58] With the exception of Christopher Nadon's *Xenophon's Prince: Republic and Empire in the Cyropaedia*,[59] which sets forth a political agenda completely influenced by Strauss, the readers concerned with Xenophon as a writer of historical fiction are apolitical in their analyses, unaffected by various ideologies which originate with contemporary rather than fourth-century BCE thought.

V

I assert that I am concerned foremost with Xenophon as an ironic author, and not as individually and separately a historian, a philosopher or an author of prose fiction, although I acknowledge that much valuable scholarship has been done on separate aspects of the author's writings. Xenophon is at once all of these things and none of them in that he deals with the material of what we currently regard as history, philosophy and fiction. Yet because he is an ironic author, the subjects of his works are not as important as his method. In fact, he produces an alternative narrative within the text, one which exists side by side with the ostensible non-ironic narrative but is nonetheless more authoritative than the latter. What we see and get in Xenophon is a difference between what the speaker thinks he says and what his interlocutor, a wiser figure, might say or do, and between intentions and actualities where both characters are involved in a situation. Irony indeed has its authorities and its own authority is even greater than the ostensible narrative precisely because it undermines and flies in the face of this power. Irony is subversive, offering an alternative perspective on what is otherwise assumed to be the case. But it is important that irony be distinguished from a recent mode of reading that has been prevalent since the middle of the twentieth century. This is the Straussian 'reading between the lines'[60] which so many scholars, such as Higgins, have pursued and which takes often forced liberties with the text.[61] 'Reading between the lines' presumes an elite audience and a generalist audience, with the former able to perceive more – the ironic reading – in the text, because he (the Straussian reader is ideally a 'he') ascribes to a particular ideology, and the latter only able to see the ostensible text. Yet Xenophontian irony is present for the attuned reader, who now comprises the 'in' group, to perceive, whether or not this reader is part of that (Straussian) elite.

Xenophon is teaching or instructing through his writing, and perhaps teaching is above all the purpose of writing in the fourth century BCE. After all, Thucydides, the teacher, is a paramount figure in the political arena. Pericles implicitly depicts himself as a good teacher in his defence in Book 2 of the *History*. In this speech he states that the individual who knows (ὅ τε γὰρ γνούς) but cannot teach clearly (μὴ σαφῶς διδάξας) is no different from someone who does not have the capacity to discern (εἰ μὴ ἐνεθυμήθη), while the person who has knowledge and the ability to communicate this knowledge, but is not favourably disposed towards the city, would be of no use to it (2.60.6). The general is someone who has knowledge and is also favourably disposed to the city, for he is also a 'lover of the city' (φιλόπολίς), as the citizen should ideally be (2.60.5), and he, moreover, is incorruptible (χρημμάτων κρείσσων) (60.5).

Where his audience is concerned, Pericles 'teaches' that intellect and understanding are a strategy for coping with the Athenians' present predicament. ἡ σύνεσις, that is understanding, makes courage more secure because it places less trust in hope, which is actually without any true strength and which the plague defeats (cf. 2.62.5). It relies on knowledge (cf. γνώμη) derived from actual circumstances and allows one to despise the enemy due to foresight (ἡ πρόνοια). Pericles makes a distinction between the confidence which proceeds from lack of learning (ἀπὸ ἀμαθίας) and good fortune and the contempt which results from trusting in γνώμη and which defeats the opponent (2.62.4). In the latter part of the oration, the speaker reinforces the emphasis on knowledge when he urges his audience to consider its future benefits rather than the present misfortune (cf. 2.64.6). What such anticipation involves and relies upon is a recollection of Athens' greatness in the past. If Pericles had spoken of the courageous actions of the ancestors in the Funeral Oration, he is now obliged to invoke the lasting memory of the state's greatest name among all peoples, the numerous lives spent and the labours undergone in war, the superlative power possessed until recently, the rule of most of Greece and its previous wars (2.64.3; cf. 2.61.4).

Thucydides treats Pericles as a political teacher in order to present his own teaching indirectly as pedagogy for the state of Athens. Pericles is the ideal pedagogue for the city-state and Thucydides follows his example by elucidating his teaching through his own writing.

Furthermore, there is another self-styled civic teacher of the fourth century in Isocrates, whose *Antidosis* is all about the standing of the teacher in ancient Athens and of the city as premier teacher of the Greek world as it seeks to defend its author of the charge that he was a greedy and corrupt sophist. In section 224 of this speech the author names the various and varied regions from which his students originate, and he makes the point that Athens, due to his teaching, is literally the teacher of the rest of Greece and of the civilized world. Teaching is a significant and privileged activity at classical Athens, which perhaps explains the antipathy of the more traditional members of society to the sophists, who only purport to provide instruction in skills which advantage the bearer of them and who engage in teaching for their own ends and profit. At 293–5 in this speech, the specific point of Athens' cultural standing is made again, when the rhetorician presents the city as a 'teacher (διδάσκαλος)' of the rest of the world in oratory and its instruction. This sentiment is also articulated at 4.48–50 and at Thucydides 2.41.1, where Pericles describes Athens as the teacher of Greece in order to declare her power and pre-eminent position in the Greek world in the 'Funeral Oration'. At 9.50 the author notes that many of the Cypriot tyrant's citizens go to be educated in Greece as a result of philhellenism. Isocrates characterizes the political speech in which he claims the superiority of Athens, the *Panegyricus*, as political teaching (cf. διδάσκειν) at *Antidosis* 58.

But the *Antidosis* is also a speech which manifests itself as pedagogy. At *Antidosis* 60, Isocrates stresses the identity of the present speech as a teaching to his audience-jury, who are cast in the role of students. And what he is teaching about is his value to the city as a teacher of rhetoric against the background of the sophists, who are fraudulent teachers.

VI

One might ask why teaching is such a privileged mode of discourse in the fourth century? I answer this question by suggesting that Xenophon, Thucydides, Isocrates and other conservative prose writers at this time are teaching in opposition to the sophists, who sell their skill at instruction in any number of skills apparently to make their students successful in life. At *Antidosis* 56, for instance, Isocrates notes that the professional teachers damage the civic community. They are supposedly intellectual itinerants, travelling throughout the Greek world in search of audiences and pupils to sell their wares to, although many settled in Athens. The sophists make exaggerated promises which feature in their iconography to discredit them (cf. e.g. *Antidosis* 178 and *Against the Sophists*). In part, because they are figures without any long-standing ties or loyalties to the community they have entered, their teaching is potentially disruptive and destructive of the community. As far as Isocrates is concerned, the teacher-student relationship should be not just a monetary one. It is ideally far more, with teacher and pupils becoming as kin, perhaps as father and sons. This emotive leaving of a mentor by young protégés has its closest analogy in the poetry of Sappho, who is often regarded as a 'schoolmistress' (cf. 94 LP), while in Plato one reads of the state's laws as teachers and nurturing parents at *Crito* 54b3–d1.

At *Hippias Major* 282c–d Socrates makes a distinction between the past generation of wise men, who did not charge for dispensing wisdom, and the current generation of sophists, who make huge profits for passing on their apparent wisdom. Sophists are extremely mercenary and offer little for what they take. Indeed, Xenophon himself offers a potent critique of the sophists in the last chapter, 13, of the *Cynegeticus* or *On Hunting* and at various places in the *Memorabilia*. The first text begins by criticizing the professional teachers for not leading students to virtue but rather concerning themselves with words and language (13.1–2). The sophists above all seek their own advantage and not those of the people they purport to help (13.10). At *Memorabilia* 1.6.13 Socrates accuses Antiphon of prostituting wisdom in offering wisdom to those who are willing to pay for it.[62]

Teaching assumes the ignorance of one party, the student, and the enlightenment of the other, the teacher. It is thus akin to the ironic situation, which assumes the lack of foresight and knowledge of one or more parties, and the knowledge and insight of the εἴρων. Xenophon is at once teacher and εἴρων. What is ultimately produced from the irony of Xenophon's text, that is to say, what he teaches, is a critique of his world and times (and sometimes of an earlier era as in the case of the *Hiero* and the *Cyropaedia*). I observe that each of Xenophon's works focuses on a different aspect of his world: the object of the author's ironic treatment changes and is particular to the text that treats it. Indeed, the *Cyropaedia* has something to offer about leadership: the *Oeconomicus* is concerned with household management and organization and the role of the woman in this, while the *Cynegeticus* deals with the training of the young Athenian man, as does the *Memorabilia*. Each work is discrete from others in respect of the irony it treats, although two works may deal with the same irony. For instance, *On Horsemanship* and *On the Cavalry Commander* show up equine culture in fourth-century Athens and are therefore treated in the same chapter in this volume, while the *Agesilaus* and the *Constitution of the Spartans* both expose shortcomings in Laconic history and government and therefore are also discussed together.

I intend to examine the writings of this author to recover that parallel narrative which is embedded within the ostensible narrative and in the process to offer a very different Xenophon from the one that has come down to us in some two thousand years. Avoiding the strictures of 'genre' and in an effort to produce different juxtapositions of the works, which may stimulate productive readings, I have organized my discussion according to the geographical places that the author is critiquing. I am first concerned with the depiction of irony at Athens. I begin with Xenophon's depiction of Socratic irony. I consider the *Memorabilia*, the *Apology*, the *Symposium* and the *Oeconomicus*, where Socrates is the central figure and has conversations with other Athenian figures of the day. Then, I deal with non-Socratic irony at Athens, with the author's takedown of hunting in *On Hunting*, his critique of equine culture in *On Horsemanship* and *On the Cavalry Commander* and his harsh examination of the culture of civic wealth in the *Poroi*.

The next major section of the book concerns Xenophon's portrait of other parts of Greece. 'Spartan Ironies' deals with Lycurgus' reforms to the Lacedaimonian state and the subsequent failure to maintain them so that Sparta begins to resemble contemporary Athens in *On the Constitution of the Spartans*. This chapter also goes on to consider the shortcomings of Agesilaus in the work named for him. While appearing to commend the Lacedaimonian leader, the *Agesilaus* actually reveals his failings in military affairs and in the governance of his state. *Hiero* depicts a conversation between the praise poet Semonides and the Syracusan tyrant in order to denigrate the former and his apparent 'wisdom' as well as the rather self-obsessed Hiero. The *Hellenica* is a long work which deals with events of the Peloponnesian War following on from Thucydides' *History* but continuing until the Battle of Mantinea in 362 BCE. It portrays war between the various Greek city-states, but with a view of revealing the pointlessness of this state of affairs. The *Hellenica* is an implicit and ironic appeal for peace, implicitly urging a panhellenic position to which Xenophon moves in light of the events of the conflict.

The third and final section of the book concerns Persia, and it looks first at the upbringing and reign of the elder Cyrus (a.k.a. the Great) in the *Cyropaedia*. The long narrative reveals shortcomings in the education of the young Cyrus, which eventually result in the ruler conducting his reign through appearance and showmanship. In a society where knowledge is knowledge of how to rule, the failure of education leads to the downfall of Cyrus' line. In the *Anabasis* the early death of Cyrus the Younger in battle requires the Greeks on the Persian expedition to return home and implicitly transforms them from being a military force into a panhellenic civic community, which is more ideal as far as Xenophon is concerned and of which the author becomes the leader. I suggest that the *Anabasis* is a work that defines Persia by emphatically insisting upon a Greek ideal of unity.

Part One

Socrates on Athens

1

Xenophon's *Apology*: The Death of Socratic Irony; the Birth of Xenophontic Irony

Death often brings about a new birth, and this brief chapter is about the death of a certain form of irony – Socratic irony – which is the preface for the creation of a new irony: Xenophontic irony. It concerns the individual who engaged in irony, Socrates, his trial and his death in 399 BCE. When the work was actually written is uncertain according to Gabriel Danzig, but it was composed clearly long after the event it portrays.[1] In this chapter, I suggest that examining the death of Socrates and Socratic irony is a necessary in-road into an analysis of irony within the corpus of Xenophon because it confronts the most obvious, and thus the most illustrative, case of the phenomenon. Irony in the fourth century BCE is often 'Socratic irony' and this is because the philosopher Socrates is a figure who attempts to remedy human ignorance with knowledge, with the result that the ignorance which is so central to irony is an essential element to the Socratic drama.

Socrates identifies instances of ignorance and attempts to correct them with the truth, although the interlocutors generally fail to recognize their own failures to know the truth and this is where the irony lies. The point of Socratic – and indeed, any – irony is that things are indeed different from the way the majority of people think they are. The structure of the Socratic method is important because ignorance, as distinct from knowledge, is the hinge upon which irony depends and one can therefore expect the Socratic dialogues of Xenophon to be rife with ironies. This is because the philosopher is wise and dispenses his knowledge accordingly whereas his interlocutors are ignorant and unknowing. This is certainly the case with the *Apology*, a dialogue which Danzig extensively examines together with Plato's *Apology* for evidence of what he mistakenly sees to be Socrates' largely non-ironic behaviour in court.[2]

I approach the *Apology* with the view that it is perhaps the most obviously ironic of Xenophon's texts, with the irony resting in the difference between the knowing exhibited on the one hand by the philosopher and the ignorance exhibited on the other by his accusers and the jury, who constitute his audience at the trial. The irony is distinctly Socratic in that the philosopher simply has to articulate the truths he perceives and knows to an unknowing and unenlightened audience for there to be the gap in knowledge which constitutes irony. The *Apology* features the philosopher and his accuser Meletus at odds over Socrates' piety: is he an atheist, as the prosecutor Meletus claims due to the latter's lack of knowledge of what true piety is, or is Socrates rather a follower of the gods, as seems to be the case according to Socrates in his adherence to τὸ δαιμόνιον or the Divinity? Irony stands behind major historical events – here the death of Socrates – and this will be a chapter about a brief work which reveals a very apparent irony, one in which Socratic irony is silenced, and sets the scene for irony in other texts, both Socratic and non-Socratic, in the corpus.

I

According to Xenophon, this *Apology* seeks to hand down to posterity how Socrates thought about his own defence and his own death. As L. R. Shero has noted, Xenophon deals with Socrates before, during and after his trial, whereas Plato only treats the trial itself.[3] Danzig argues that the work attempts to absolve Socrates of his rather incompetent showing in court,[4] as he seems rather arrogant at times[5] and does not really seek to address the charges against himself. Elsewhere, Danzig suggests that Socrates is actually arranging his own suicide,[6] but I offer that to view the text in this way misses the whole point of what Xenophon is trying to suggest. Kierkegaard is more to the point when he states that the *Apology* demonstrates what a scandalous injustice it was for the Athenians to sentence Socrates to death,[7] while Ralkowski argues that a city corrupted by greed and by rhetoric resulted in the philosopher's condemnation.[8] But even so, I suggest that Xenophon's emphasis is placed elsewhere. The author states that the philosopher regarded death as more desirable than life, a fact not known to other writers on the trial and on the death of Socrates, and so, his bold defence seems ill-considered, even rather thoughtless to his audience (ὥστε ἀφρονεστέρα αὐτοῦ φαίνεται εἶναι ἡ μεγαληγορία, 1). This may explain why Xenophon chooses a wider perspective for the trial than Plato.[9] Danzig notes that Socrates does nothing to counter the death sentence at the trial, unlike Plato's Socrates[10] – he does not offer a penalty for his supposed crime or seek to escape from prison at his friends' urgings (cf. 23) – but this is not surprising given the philosopher's view that death is to be more desired at his stage than life is. The Xenophontic Socrates is willing to go to his death to avoid the debilitations that come with old age (6 and 8), whereas the

Platonic Socrates sees the death as the outcome of his divine mission to keep philosophizing. So, in the case of the Xenophontic Socrates, the misunderstanding that the author attempts to confront the audience with has to do with why Socrates died when he did: it was not so much the decision of the jury as it was Socrates' own wish to end his life due to the inconveniences of old age and a sense that he had already done as much as he could in trying to shake Athens and her citizens from their mistaken assumptions about how to live their lives. This the in-crowd already understands. Nonetheless, his μεγαληγορία or loftiness of speech is appropriate to his character.

But it is precisely in the gap between Socrates' behavior in the lawcourt and what others perceive to be the case that I suggest the chief irony of this work lies. Piero Pucci, however, sees the main irony as lying in the fact that the city wants money and glory, which Socrates is not at all interested in.[11] I, however, argue that the concern is primarily with the understanding of the gods and their role in human life, something that is a recurring theme in Xenophon's writings in general. At section 22 the author states that he has not concerned himself with reporting the whole trial but rather he has focussed on the fact that the philosopher sought to keep clear of committing any act of impiety and of wrong-doing towards his fellow man. That is to say, in Xenophon's portrayal, Socrates emerges as a righteous man. The misperception of Socrates by others includes most obviously the prosecutors at the trial, the audience of the trial and possibly, the readers of the *Apology*, who, as Xenophon's audience, may often fail to perceive the truth that the author is attempting to convey.

II

Socratic texts are generally reported discourse so it is difficult to approach Socrates directly. Certainly, the narrator of the text is usually absent, and indeed, the *Apology* is a second-hand reported narrative. The existence of the Xenophontic text is due to the attendance of Hermogenes, son of Hipponicus, who reports accurately the events he perceived at the trial and death of Socrates. Xenophon was absent at the time of these events, marching as a Greek mercenary with the Ten Thousand, an event which is recorded in the *Anabasis*, but, according to him, his account of the trial seeks to reconcile Socrates' lofty speech (cf. μεγαληγορία) and his resolve. Other writers have failed to do this so that his lofty speech seems to be rather senseless (ἀφροντεστέρα) (1). According to Xenophon's mediated report, one learns that Hermogenes is in danger of making the same mistake as the other writers on the trial have done. Hermogenes is struck by Socrates talking about everything other than the trial and asks the philosopher if he should not be rather thinking about his defence.

The Platonic Socrates in the end suggests a thirty minae fine for himself (Plato *Apology* 38b), whereas the Xenophontic Socrates did no such thing and did not allow his friends to propose a punishment because this would suggest that he was guilty of the charges. In response, the philosopher declares that he has spent his whole life preparing to defend himself and that he has been free of any wrong-doing, which is the main substance of his defence (3). But Hermogenes observes that sometimes the innocent are condemned to death, while the guilty are acquitted (4). Socrates counters this observation by giving the first strong indication of his piety. He declares that his divine sign has prevented him from even thinking about his defence on two occasions and thereby demonstrates that he is obedient to the gods. He supposes that this means that God thinks it better for him to die now, especially since he has lived a good life, having been righteous to both God and man (4–5). Furthermore, being sentenced to death allows him to avoid the frailties of old age – poor vision, less keen hearing, slower learning and forgetfulness (6). The execution through poison is a relatively easy way to die (7). Dying at this point in his life means that Socrates will avoid illness and the troubles of old age (8).

This introduction to the trial underscores the irony of the charge presented in section 10 of the *Apology*. Socrates' accusers have charged him with not believing in the gods worshipped by the state, with the introduction of new gods and with the corruption of the young, accusations which are also mentioned in the *Memorabilia* (10; *Mem.* 1.1). Yet the philosopher has been seen – even by his accuser Meletus – offering sacrifices at the communal festivals and at public altars and this is evidence that he worships the gods worshipped also by the state (11). The evidence persuasively suggests that Socrates has a considerable regard for the gods, and Shero sees Xenophon as relying on the common knowledge of Athens' citizens to prove that Socrates was religious.[12] This point is corroborated in the *Memorabilia* at 1.2. As for the charge of worshipping new gods, this is due to a misperception. Socrates argues that the divine has a voice which others acknowledge as coming through the cries of birds, through the utterances of men, through thunder or through the oracle at Delphi. Accordingly, his 'voice' is not out of keeping with normal religious observance. Where others call the source of prophecy 'birds', 'utterances', 'chance meetings' or 'prophets', he calls his the 'divine' thing (τοῦτο δαιμόνιον) and thereby, he argues, he shows more profound religious feelings than those who ascribe the gods' power to birds (13).

The god has revealed to him many counsels that he has given to his friends and on no occasion have they been found to be mistaken (13). The 'divinity' is thought by Xenophon to be responsible for the charge of worshipping new deities elsewhere (*Mem*. 3). The jurors do not accept what Socrates says, as the outcome of the trial proves (14). They ironically fail to see that the philosopher indeed worships the gods. But Socrates has even more to say regarding the oracle at Delphi, which nominates him the freest, most just and wise man of all (14). The jurors are in a turmoil, disbelieving what the philosopher has said about τὸ δαιμόνιον (14) and then, about the words of the Delphic oracle. And it is at this point that the philosopher confronts the irony of the situation most patently. He asks if they know (ἐπίστασθε) of anyone else to be less a slave to bodily appetites than he (16); or of anyone who is freer than he, for he accepts no gifts or money from anyone? Moreover, do they know of anyone who is more just than he for he does not want what others have? He states that he is furthermore a wise man for continuing to want to learn what is good (16). The Athenians are obviously ignorant of Socrates' piety and thus, the philosopher finds himself on trial for impiety. Moreover, Socrates leads such an exemplary life that he cannot be accused of corrupting the youth by his actions, as he claims to Meletus at section 19 of the speech. As far as receiving the obedience of students to himself rather than to their parents, Socrates argues that this is because he is regarded as an expert on education (21). Likewise, people do not seek the advice of their families in medical matters, or in issues of war, but rather they seek out the advice of experts (20). The trial is clearly to be regarded as a consequence of the Athenians' ignorance about who the philosopher is or what he does in his life.

Xenophon does not relate any further arguments from the trial but observes that the philosopher knew it was clearly his time to die (22). Section 23 relates the concern of Plato's *Crito*, which deals with the events following Socrates' conviction and his refusal to escape. Sections 24–25 of the *Crito* further emphasize the irony which underlies the trial. The prosecutors have failed to show that Socrates does not believe in the state gods and moreover, that he has corrupted the youth of the state. They have lied, perjuring themselves in instructing the jury to vote as they did (24). Socrates gains comfort from the fact that he is to be unjustly executed while his accusers will gain a bad reputation for killing him (26). To one of his followers, Apollodorus, who laments the state of affairs, namely that Socrates is being led to death unjustly, the philosopher asks if the former would prefer him to be executed justly (28).

A further irony consists in Anytus, one of the prosecutors, walking by with pride because he has managed to convict the philosopher. What we know of

Anytus suggests a political motive for the prosecution of Socrates. The son of Anthemion, Anytus came from a prosperous family of tanners, and he himself became a powerful, upper-class politician in Athens. He was, however, not born elite but a member of the nouveaux riches and became a supporter of the democratic movement, which was opposed to the Thirty Tyrants.[13] Furthermore, Anytus' profile fits that of the meddling orators of a class slightly lower than the aristocrats, who populated classical Athens and caused much political and social mayhem. Xenophon displays Socrates as a man of the people inasmuch as he has been righteous towards the gods and his fellow man (5), and he worships the gods of the state, although perhaps not as other citizens do (12-13). But it is the case that Socrates gives himself away as something of an elitist, even someone with oligarchical leanings. He continually emphasizes the privileges and favours he has received from the gods and men (9, 15), but above all, he insists on having taught his students what are in effect the aristocratic virtues of piety, sobriety, moderation and a willingness to undertake pains, which involves discipline (19). Those who read the corpus with a democratic bias would miss these aristocratic references, but they show up the author as an individual with a strong upper-class bias. Xenophon is perhaps ironically promoting an elitist Socrates as a hero of the people against his more obviously democratic accuser, Anytus.

Socrates states that Anytus does not know that whoever does the more beneficial and noble deeds is truly the victor (29). Socrates has done a far better thing by educating the young. The author Xenophon adds an observation from his perspective of a subsequent time, which has him corroborate the philosopher's observation that the son of Anytus will live a life of disgrace and vice (30). He notes that it is the case that the son of Anytus, even though he seemed educable, never ceased to drink day or night and so turned out worthless to himself, to his friends and to his city (31). The prosecutor Anytus has died and gained a bad reputation for his son's mistaken upbringing and his own hard-heartedness (31). Socrates has received the best death possible for himself, avoiding the difficulties of old age (32-3).

Xenophon concludes the *Apology* by noting that he cannot forget the philosopher and in remembering him, that he cannot refrain from praising him. If anyone who is concerned with virtue has met anyone more helpful than Socrates, he is to be regarded as most blessed (ἐκεῖνον ἐγω τὸν ἄνδρα ἀχιομακαριστότον νομίζω, 34). To be μακάριος is to be deemed happy because the gods regard you well. Therefore, it is implied that to learn virtue from Socrates is tantamount to a divine blessing and that Socrates is like the gods when he instructs in virtue. That is the major irony which the Athenians do not get but which the sympathetic reader is directed to.

III

It would appear then that the *Apology* is an obviously ironic text in these respects. The Athenians do not understand Socrates or his piety at all and convict him of not believing in the gods, which they believe in. Socrates regards death as a blessing at his age but has offered his whole life as a defence. He has been pious and even at death follows the lead of the god, choosing to die rather than to live. In fact, Danzig chooses to see Socrates as 'an arrogant man gloating at the prospect of an easy death.'[14] This is the death of Socratic irony, of the truths *spoken* by the philosopher, which his audience fails to see or to comprehend. But the end of Socratic irony allows for the creation of a Xenophontic irony, which is distinct from the Socratic because it is *literary* rather than oral. Where Socrates engaged only in conversational interactions, Xenophon is a writer, who presents what he perceives to be truth against a backdrop of ignorance. Furthermore, he has a reading audience that to a greater or lesser degree is supposed to be in on the irony. Xenophon had a favourable bias towards the philosopher Socrates if only in recognizing a discrepancy between what is and what appears to be the case, that is, if only in recognizing that the world is an ironic place. So in the case of the *Apology*, one group of actors – the Athenian citizens – is unaware or ignorant of what is the case, and another group – the philosopher, his friends, his followers, and those who write about him – Xenophon and Plato, for instance – are at least party to the truth of the matter and attempt to instruct this first group, often to no avail. So Xenophontic irony owes its origins to Socratic irony and seeks through the literary text to achieve irony's goal of instructing the unenlightened mass.

Irony is clearly pedagogical for, when recognized, it demonstrates the ignorances that plague the rest of the world. Socrates realizes his position with the gods – he needs to be obedient to them – and his followers understand this, but the majority of the Athenians fail to recognize this, regarding his piety as impiety and execute him as a consequence. Their view of the gods is flawed or, at least, incomplete and so, their whole understanding of religious observance, not to mention of justice, is faulty. The point of an ironic discourse or text is that it is gently instructive for the reader, nudging him to accept the truth through a realization of the ignorance of others.

IV

Irony depends very much on context. The right sort of people have to be present with the wise interlocutor. That wise interlocutor may be the omniscient narrator, e.g. Xenophon, for irony is especially operative when there is omniscience. Narratives can therefore be the scenario for irony. Ideally but not necessarily, the players have to be unlearned and unlearning so that there remains a gap between their unknowledge and the knowledge of the wise interlocutor, Socrates and his author, Xenophon. Irony may be present but it depends ultimately upon the reader to perceive it. It is like a picture, usually comprised of dots, in which another picture or design is hidden. When that other picture is not perceived, one has a certain view of the whole; when that other picture is distinguished, one then has a very different view of the whole, as two pictures. These, accordingly, are the workings of irony, one picture and then another, quite different one.

I suggest that the *Apology* has a further and larger point to make. Irony must exist because the multitude of people in any community remain unknowing, while only a few are, or become, aware of what reality actually is. The *Apology* demonstrates that Athenians as a whole are unable to perceive an obvious fact: Socrates was indeed pious, obeying his τὸ δαιμονίον, as he himself attempted to make plain to the court. The jury were unable and refused to perceive that the divine thing was as much a god as anything else they normally acknowledged as such, whether these were the screechings of birds or the entrails of animal sacrifices, which they read. Socrates just has to be himself to be ironic. Yet beyond this, I suggest that Xenophon is making a more general point about the differing levels of knowledge that constitute irony. Most of the people in the world will not perceive the truth, and therefore, they are caught up in the ignorance that makes them subject to the ironic. Remarkably, Xenophon simply has Socrates state the facts about his life and beliefs: irony involves no shifts in tone or perspective.

Perhaps Xenophon is suggesting that most of his readers will refuse to see the truth that is evident and before their eyes, preferring to go along with the generally accepted lies that he perceives to constitute life and reality in classical Greece. The *Apology* is as much about the misperceptions that resulted in the trial, condemnation and death of Socrates as it is about the all-present and all-pervasive misperceptions of the realities that Xenophon presents to his audience. The work is thus a re-enactment of the irony experienced in the trial of Socrates in the works of Xenophon. Thus, the death of Socrates and his irony gives birth to Xenophon as writer and his more complex ironies.

V

Socrates is a figure who sets the scene for irony as someone who knows whereas those around him do not know. Socratic irony is thus often merely underlying a situation where the philosopher is present. Socrates knows the larger external reality of how things are and ideally should be, whereas his interlocutors are ignorant of this larger reality and remain cocooned by their wealth and privilege in their worlds of materialism and celebrity/notoriety. So completely wrapped up in this world of appearances are they that they cannot be taught or learn from the philosopher. (Indeed, in the *Oeconomicus*, as we shall see, Ischomachus purports control over his household whereas in reality he does not have as much authority as he thinks and is misguided in its management (Chapter 4). Socrates attempts to make Ischomachus aware of his shortcomings but with no success.)

This initial chapter is an investigation into Socratic irony. It would appear that Socrates, with his differing understanding of the world and life, just has to be present among other people for irony to exist. Baker reports that scholars have seen Xenophon's Socrates to be 'trivial and commonplace'; he does not make the profound arguments and statements that Plato's Socrates does.[15] Baker's analysis follows on from Søren Kierkegaard, who comments that 'Finally, with respect to irony, there is not one trace of it in Xenophon's Socrates'.[16] But irony only requires differing levels of knowledge to come into being: Socrates knows more while his interlocutors know far less, if at all, and this constitutes the ironic. This is the essence of Socratic irony as represented by Xenophon. It is the basis for Xenophontic irony, which as we shall see has to be much more assertive and startling because it is the audience of the text, rather than interlocutors within the text, who have to be shaken out of their ignorances.

2

The *Memorabilia*: Remembering Truth and Lies about Socrates

After the *Apology*, the *Memorabilia* seeks to vindicate Socrates by demonstrating the mistaken nature of the charges that he did not believe in the state's gods and that he corrupted the young through recollections of the philosopher in conversation with a number of youthful and prominent Athenians at the time. It is not an obviously ironic work at every turn but it is overall an ironic text, as we shall see, in a fashion that is Socratically ironic as far as Xenophon is concerned: Socrates does not have to change his mode of conversation or drop stunning and surprising observations in his speech (which is, as we shall see, what Xenophon typically does) but simply has to be himself and has to state what he regards as truths against the misunderstanding of his interlocutors to create an ironic situation. What is distinctive about the *Memorabilia* is Xenophon's presence and observations regarding the interactions with the interlocutors, which introduce the author as a commentator on the social scenario in the fourth-century BCE world. It is a work of memorialization, and the best mode of analysis for this text seems to be simply recollection and summary of what has been written.

I

Book 1 of the *Memorabilia*, I suggest, rehearses the argument of the *Apology*, replaying the trial against Socrates and the defence against the philosopher. The beginning of the work recites the operative charges against the philosopher: namely, that he was guilty of rejecting the gods accepted by the state and he corrupted the youth of Athens (1.1.1). What is notable about the presentation of these charges is that they are framed by the perception of the author, Xenophon: he wonders what could have persuaded the Athenian people to condemn the philosopher to death. In the *Apology* there is a distance between the narrator and the events presented as the events are mediated through the perceptions of others, who may not have been so favourably disposed to the philosopher. Xenophon states that other people have written (γεγράφασι) about Socrates but they have not been clear (τοῦτο οὐ διεσαφήνισαν) that death was preferable to life for the philosopher (*Apology* 1.1). The *Apology* seeks to clear up misperceptions and non-perceptions which have been conveyed by other writers, whereas the *Memorabilia* presents us with a Socrates who, the author claims, is directly and accurately encountered by the author.

The *Memorabilia* begins by directly responding to, and refuting, the charges brought against the philosopher. The author declares that Socrates did indeed acknowledge the state's gods, continually offering sacrifices to them at the altars of the state's temples and using divination. Xenophon concludes that the philosopher's references to his deity must have been responsible for the charge regarding strange deities (1.1.2). Indeed, he believed no differently from others who used divination (1.1.3) and the divinity gave him advice so that it either helped those who followed it or caused those who disregarded it to regret what they had done (1.1.4). Those who intend to govern and control a house or city require the guidance provided through divination (1.1.6). And Xenophon is adamant that Socrates lived visibly and in the open, talking every day to whichever people might listen, and he was never seen to offend against the gods or against piety and religion in word or deed (1.1.10).

Xenophon also attacks the charges against Socrates brought by Aristophanes in his comedy, the *Clouds*. Socrates, the author asserts, did not deal with the nature of the universe, as so many others have done (1.11). He argued that it was absolute foolishness to deal with such matters and it was beyond the reach of human intellect to solve the problems that such speculations raised (1.1.1.13). Socrates was of the view that one must deal instead with human problems (cf. 1.1.12, 11.15–16). Rather his concerns were with questions that affected human beings, such as what is godly or ungodly? what is beautiful? ugly? just? unjust? what is prudence? madness? courage? cowardice? what is a state? a statesman? government and a governor? (1.1.16). Socrates was concerned with humans' relationships to the gods and to each other: he was a social being. Such knowledge helped to make a gentleman (καλὸς κἀγαθός), while in his opinion ignorance of these matters was slavishness (ἀνδραποδώδης). Moreover, it is ignorance of these matters which Xenophon ascribes to the jury's decision to kill Socrates (1.1.17). The author concludes the first chapter of the first book by observing that the philosopher thought the gods were omniscient as they knew everything humans said and did (1.1.19) and that Socrates, far from being an atheistic freethinker, was a truly religious man.

The second chapter in Book 1 addresses the well-known and major charge against Socrates of corrupting the young. It begins by observing that the philosopher very strictly controlled his desires and appetites (1.2.1). So rather than leading others into impiety, he showed them that controlling themselves (cf. ἑαυτῶν ἐπιμελῶνται) would make them gentlemen (cf. καλοὺς κἀγαθούς) (1.2.2). He hoped that those who spent time with him would imitate him (1.2.3) and so he took care of his body (1.2.4) and did not seek money (1.2.5). Refusing fees for teaching in fact ensured Socrates' freedom, since fee-taking in contrast obliged one to speak to whomever one took money from (1.2.6). Socrates could not have corrupted anyone unless he corrupted in order to foster virtue (1.2.8). Against the accuser who said that he taught his companions to despise the established laws because he criticized the appointment to office by lot, the philosopher argued that it was considered unsatisfactory to appoint by lot to other professions, such as pilot, builder or flautist, and so, it would be even more disastrous to appoint by lot in government. Such action would lead the young to despise the constitution and make them violent (1.2.9). Here again as in the *Apology*, however, is a suggestion that Socrates held aristocratic assumptions, which would lead to curtailing opportunities in political life for those who were not well-born and so, assumedly, not well-endowed with the qualities that would make a leader.

Socrates' accuser had observed that two of the most violent and well-born young men of the time, Critias and Alcibiades, were associates of the philosopher (1.2.12). This may have been the case but the author observes that the two youths only did so to improve their speech and actions (1.2.15). They were using Socrates and would have preferred to die rather than actually follow his lifestyle and principles (1.2.16). Being with the philosopher meant that the two sought to be prudent (cf. σώφρων) while they were with him (1.2.18) but as soon as they left him, one, Critias, turned to lawlessness and the other, Alcibiades, neglected himself and let himself go as he was pursued for his beauty (1.2.24). Mark Ralkowski argues that the politics of Athens was ultimately to blame for Alcibiades' later misdoings.[1] Socrates was thus not responsible for leading these two youths astray, as they were already inclined to do no good (1.2.26) and they were completely out of sympathy with the philosopher (1.2.39 and 47). And Socrates cannot be held to blame for evil that was not in him (1.2.28). This is the obvious irony of the trial: the Athenians do not see things for what they really are as they misunderstand the nature of the philosopher's associations with some of his young associates.

Critias and Alcibiades are bad associates but at 1.2.48 Xenophon tells us of good associates, Criton, Chaerephon, Chaerecrates, Hermogenes, Simmias, Cebes,

Phaedondas and others, who never did evil nor invited criticism in their youth or in their old age. This demonstrates that Socrates' teaching in itself is not responsible for how his associates turn out, as their outcome is due to the sort of person that the interlocutor actually and originally is. It would seem that nature and proclivity prevail over nurture in Socratic pedagogy.

Furthermore, Critias is one of thirty tyrants who retaliated against the philosopher because the latter had publicly commented on the tyrant falling for Euthydemus (1.2.30). As a consequence, Critias drafted a law which made it illegal to teach the art of words, which was an art generally attributed to philosophers (1.2.31). Accordingly, Socrates was forbidden to speak with anyone under the age of thirty (1.2.35).

In the conversation that is reported with Charicles, Xenophon gives us a key insight into what Socratic irony is. Following on from the prohibition of Socrates speaking to individuals under thirty, the philosopher asks if he is even forbidden to speak to a young man to ask him the price of an item if he is under thirty. Charicles then says that he may and observes that Socrates tends to ask questions when he very well knows the answers to them, ἀλλὰ τοι σύγε, ὦ Σώκρατες, εἴωθας εἰδὼς πῶς ἔχει τὰ πλεῖστα ἐρωτᾶν (1.1.36). Socrates feigns ignorance of what he knows to be the case, as any ironist indeed does. Charicles draws attention to the structure of Socratic irony, observing the gap in knowledge between Socrates and his interlocutors: the former knows the truth while the latter is unaware of it and probably remains unaware even after speaking with the philosopher, as Critias and Alcibiades did. And because Charicles is not one of Socrates' inner circle and later became one of the Thirty Tyrants (cf. *Hellenica* 2.3.2), he also remains ignorant even after his interaction with Socrates. He is perhaps commenting unknowingly and ironically (as far as the more enlightened audience members are concerned) on his own lack of knowledge and understanding in relation to the philosopher's knowledge and understanding. Alternatively, the interlocutor may simply agree to what Socrates says as he says it, appearing to realize his own lack of wisdom. This constitutes the ironic situation where Socrates is concerned: the philosopher simply has to speak to other individuals and their ignorance or delusion has to be recognized by an audience, for instance and more probably, the reader of Xenophon's text. That is why the Thirty wish Socrates to stay away from discussing topics such as holiness and justice (1.2.37), the very topics which explain the irony underlying the philosopher's trial and death sentence.

Indeed, Xenophon concludes the second chapter of the first book of the *Memorabilia* by observing that Socrates did far more to enhance the reputation and name of Athens than even Lichas did for Sparta and that he improved his associates when they left him (1.2.61). The author points out that, accordingly, he deserved honour rather than death for his contributions and it is the case rather that thieves, highwaymen, cutpurses, robbers of temples and kidnappers are rather the individuals who deserve death (1.2.62). Thus, the author seeks to exonerate Socrates of the charges that he rejected the gods – he was indeed pious – and that he corrupted the youth – he actually made them better than he initially found them to be (1.2.64).

II

The following chapters of Book 1 detail Socrates' piety and modest behaviour in an attempt to refute the charge that he could have corrupted the young. He prayed for good gifts (1.3.2); he gave sacrifices, albeit humble ones (1.3.3); he had regard for the warnings given by the gods (1.3.4); he was frugal in food and drink (1.3.5); he was restrained at dinner parties (1.3.6); he advocated self-control in sexual matters (1.3.9–14). As for piety, in 1.4 Xenophon has Socrates convince the irreligious dwarf Aristodemus of the need to have regard for the gods and divination. The philosopher, the author remarks, kept his companions from impiety, injustice and baseness through his conversation with them (1.4.19). He taught about self-control (ἐγκράτεια), rejecting a predilection to vice and excess for military leaders, teachers and masters of slaves (1.5.1–3).[2] Self-control he declared to be the foundation stone of virtue, and all that virtue might enable – e.g. a good life or strong leadership, which Straussians particularly focus on[3] (1.5.4). Socrates' own mastery of ἐγκράτεια was demonstrated in his control of his bodily passions and in his refusal to give in to desire for money (1.5.6). In a conversation with Antiphon the sophist, who seeks to draw the philosopher's companions away from him, Socrates declares that to have no wants is divine and to have as few as possible is close to the divine, with the result that luxury and extravagance do not and cannot characterize him as a philosopher (1.6.10).

Book 2 continues with Socrates teaching young men about self-control in matters of food, drink, sex, sleep and endurance of cold and heat (2.1.1). This leads the philosopher to discuss whether it is better to rule or be ruled, considering that those who wish to rule must provide for the needs of others as well as their own needs (e.g. 2.1.8). From 2.1.21 Socrates seeks to instruct Aristippus, who seems to have a huge appetite for food (2.1.1). The questioning here produces a discourse about ἐγκράτεια or self-control, because controlling hunger is aimed at the individuals who are being trained to rule, from whom Aristippus emphatically excludes himself (2.1.1 and 2.1.9). There is no apparent irony in this interaction because there is no self-deception on the part of the interlocutor, who does not seek self-improvement or knowledge in any case. Irony is a condition, it would seem, of the individual who mistakenly aspires to better things.

Socrates subsequently relates Prodicus' famous allegory of vice and virtue, with the former characterized as one plump, soft and well-adorned female, and the latter presented as a woman who is modest, sober and wearing white. Each of these beings attempts to attract Heracles to themselves. Vice tempts him with softness and lack of hardship in his life (2.1.23–5) and reveals her own identity as either 'happiness' or 'vice' (2.1.26). Virtue then addresses Heracles, stating that he will do high and noble deeds if he follows her, but he must toil to accomplish these deeds (2.1.27–8). The path of virtue brings one fame and true happiness (2.1.33). The content of this discourse is intended to demonstrate again that Socrates is only to be identified with virtue and not with the excess and extravagance that some of the associates, e.g. Critias and Alcibiades, have been identified with. If Socrates associates with the well-born members of Athenian society, he also rejects the behaviours associated with them, calling into question what it means to be a privileged member of society (as we shall see to be the case in the *Symposium*).

Socrates discourses on the value of friendship at 2.4 and on the behaviours required to maintain it, namely generosity and support (2.4.6). In 2.5 he considers the value of a friend; at 2.6 he treats the topic of how to go about winning a good friend with Critoboulus. Socrates speaks of the importance of avoiding the greedy (2.6.3), those who pursue bodily pleasure (2.6.5) and rogues (2.6.20). He suggests that Critoboulus must first himself be good in order to find a good friend who is a gentleman (2.6.28).

Book 3 deals with Socrates helping those who wished to earn distinctions in the city to gain the honours they sought (3.1.1). This makes the point that the philosopher was concerned with the well-being of the city and its people. The topic is generalship, and it is raised by Dionysidorus' arrival in Athens to teach the art of warfare. Whereas Dionysidorus has instructed a young man in tactics (3.1.5), Socrates speaks of the need to furnish the troops with the correct equipment and of the need for the general to have the right qualities of character (3.1.6). At 3.6 we meet Glaucon, who wants to be prominent in the state even though he is only twenty (3.6.1–2). Socrates teaches him that he must benefit the state (3.6.3), but Glaucon's shortcomings quickly become evident. In order to enrich the state one may go to war with an enemy and in order to do so one has to know one's own strength and that of the enemy. Glaucon reveals that he does not know the naval and military strength of either (3.6.9). The irony is that the interlocutor is sorely lacking in knowledge of the state and does not even know about the resources provided by the silver mines (3.6.12).

Socrates ends his conversation by advising the interlocutor to gain knowledge about what he intends to manage (3.6.18). Glaucon is so ignorant that the irony existing between him and the philosopher is so obvious as to nearly be unremarkable. Book 3 ends with observations of Socrates' actions with food and drink that reveal him to be truly and completely moderate regarding his behaviour with both. At banquets he asked for small contributions to be shared so that those who brought more would also share their contributions (3.14.1), while when he sees a diner eating meat without the bread, which is an obvious overindulgence, he draws attention to this fact in his conversation so that the diner eventually eats some bread with his meat (3.14.2–5). In this way, he calls the young man back to a more moderate diet. Yet, the earlier conversation with Aristippus, which stresses the need for the individual intending to rule to show moderation in their appetite, shows up Glaucon's unsuitability for leadership. Furthermore, and perhaps more significantly, this situation has the larger ironic function of allowing the reader to realize how mistaken the charges against the philosopher were: he was a moderate and virtuous citizen, who deserved to be celebrated rather than condemned to death.

III

At the beginning of the last book in the *Memorabilia*, 4, the author notes that Socrates was useful in all sorts of circumstances and in all ways (4.1.1). This final book of the *Memorabilia* attempts to reject the ironically mistaken views of Socrates that led to his death sentence: the philosopher is just and promotes justice according to his conversation with the sophist Hippias (4.4); he made his companions useful, as illustrated by a conversation with Euthydemus (4.5); he taught his companions to speak well by coming to knowledge of what they were speaking about, once more as demonstrated by talking to Euthydemus (4.6); and he advised them to become familiar with a subject regarding which they were well-educated (4.7).

Xenophon discusses the philosopher's view on education, particularly the view that those with greater natural abilities most need education (4.1.3).

Education will ensure that such individuals are excellent and useful, while lack of education will make them evil and mischievous (4.1.4). Socratic irony is evident in the last section of the chapter as it addresses the wealthy who think that they have no need of education. Wealth and materialism are quite distinct from knowledge and understanding. But this is precisely the mistaken view that creates the ironic gap: people are actually foolish in thinking they can distinguish between what is good and useful and what is not (4.1.5).

Irony is also evident in Socrates' interaction with Euthydemus, who thinks he has received the best education and regards himself as being wise. The latter has collected works of poets and sophists so that he regards himself as being wise beyond his contemporaries (4.2.1). The stage is set for irony as Euthydemus is clearly mistaken about his learning and wisdom and is about to encounter the wise Socrates. The philosopher characteristically seeks to shift the conceited youth from his current thinking and position: he wishes to 'move' (κινεῖν) him (4.2.2). He asks Euthydemus if it is the case that given those who wish to be good at their respective arts require teachers, then surely those who wish to control the state cannot learn this skill of their own accord? Socrates wants to make the point also familiar from Plato's writings that teaching, which results in *anamnesis*, that is, a recollection of what one already knows from a prior time, is very necessary for the cultivation of any virtue. Euthydemus prefers not to engage with the philosopher but affects wisdom by remaining silent (4.2.6). Socrates disingenuously praises the youth for his collection of books with the result that the latter (wrongly!) thinks he is on the path to wisdom (4.2.9). The irony that becomes apparent here is the youth misunderstanding the philosopher's false praise and continuing to believe that his books contain actual wisdom and knowledge. Socrates then proceeds to engage in an *elenchos*, the question and answer that more certainly leads to understanding and in doing so, ultimately leaves the interlocutor confused and in doubt about his own opinions (cf. 4.2.19). Indeed, Euthydemus, having regarded himself as a student of philosophy, now realizes that he can answer none of the philosopher's questions (4.2.23). He does not even know himself, as it transpires in the *elenchos*, and he has to ask Socrates how he may begin to know himself (4.2.30). Self-knowledge is of course a priority in Socratic thought, and the end result of the encounter is that Euthydemus realizes he must spend as much time as possible with Socrates so that the philosopher does not worry about him, unlike others who avoid the latter and are regarded by him as 'blockheads' (βλακοτέρους).

What begins as a clearly ironic situation with Euthydemus regarding himself as learned and wise ends well with the interlocutor's mistaken beliefs cast aside.

But this situation highlights the larger irony of the state believing that Socrates corrupted the young. On the contrary, he brought them to a realization of their ignorances and limitations. He actually educated them to the good. In fact, in the following section, Socrates is depicted teaching Euthydemus to be respectful of the gods and thus also refuting another of the charges against the philosopher, namely impiety (4.3.2). Euthydemus learns that it is best to do as the gods ordain (4.3.16).

IV

The final chapter of the *Memorabilia* is the final word on the injustice of Socrates' death penalty and it shows the complete irony of killing the philosopher when death is not really a punishment for him and when he did not deserve for the state to execute him in any case. Certainly, he was old enough that death was naturally imminent and in dying sooner, he avoided the discomforts and inconveniences of old age (4.8.1 and 4.8.8). The jury may have been wrong to convict him (4.8.5), but they also ironically have helped him to a more comfortable, because quicker, death. It is furthermore the case that the Athenians who condemned the philosopher will have to bear the shame and bad reputation for doing so (4.8.9–10). Through their lack of knowledge about what Socrates actually did and how he contributed to the life of the city, the jury has very wrongly condemned the philosopher to death and in this ignorance committed the greatest irony possible: they executed someone who should rather have been rewarded for his contributions to the state. And the very last section of the work lists these positive actions: he was religious (rather than impious, as the charge held), he helped those he conversed with (rather than corrupted them, which was what the prosecutor Meletus maintained), he exercised such self-control that he always chose the better option, and he was a good teacher of virtue and gentleness (4.8.11).

V

The *Memorabilia* is an ironic work in the Socratic sense of irony. Some people know the truth, that is the way things actually are, namely Socrates and his close associates, including the author Xenophon Meanwhile others, namely the interlocutor(s), who exemplify the whole city of Athens, live in a deluded state and in a world of images and false aspirations. The gap, which the reader is ideally to perceive, constitutes the situation in which irony occurs.

And the *Memorabilia* is also a very interesting text for the role that the narrator, Xenophon, is given to play in it. Xenophon is a follower of Socrates and is present in the background at the majority of the interactions that Socrates has with his interlocutors in this work. We see him grow into his role as witness of irony from a situation of ignorance because he is willing to learn from the philosopher. The narrator shows up at 1.3.8–9 not as the one telling of the events surrounding Socrates, but as one of those keeping company with Socrates, who poses a question to him after it is heard that Critoboulus has kissed Alcibiades' good-looking son. The philosopher asks Xenophon if he regarded Critoboulus as sober rather than rash, and prudent rather than thoughtless or risk-taking (1.3.9). Xenophon agrees with the first view of Critoboulus but is then immediately asked to regard the latter as hot-headed and thoughtless, the sort of individual who would jump into a ring of fire because he kissed Alcibiades' son.

The Xenophon within the narrative is not yet the wise and sober individual who writes the text, but he is still young and needing Socrates' instruction as he admits that he too would have kissed Alcibiades' handsome son (1.3.10). To this response Socrates declares that his interlocutor would lose his liberty, becoming a slave to his infatuation, and would spend large sums of money on the object of his concern (1.3.11). Xenophon thus learns the consequences of a kiss at 1.3.12 and in the following section of the work is advised by the philosopher to flee any handsome face, while Critoboulus is told to spend a year away in order to recover from his infatuation. And that is how Xenophon learns about the philosopher's views of bodily appetites, as he tells us from his more mature and better-informed position as narrator of the *Memorabilia*.

At 2.7.1 Xenophon states that he will reveal what he knows about Socrates helping individuals who find themselves in distress due to their ignorance (cf. δι' ἄγνοιαν). Ignorance is of course the condition which is essential to irony and the advice of the philosopher establishes that gap between knowing and unknowing that the audience, most immediately Xenophon within the action of the dialogue, and less immediately, the reader, perceives as irony. Here Aristarchus is having a problem after the revolution with his women-folk coming to him and with no means to support them (2.7.2). Socrates asks how it is that Ceramon can provide for himself and his family while saving enough to be a rich man, while Aristarchus, who is wealthy, fears starving to death (2.7.3). The philosopher has his interlocutor believe that he is better than Ceramon and his kinsfolk simply because they are gentlefolk – and therefore do nothing – and the latter are artisans (2.7.4–7). Yet in reality Ceramon's family do useful work, and therefore can keep themselves while Aristarchus' family are a drain on him (2.7.9). Thus, Socrates persuades Aristarchus to take a loan and have his womenfolk engage in work involving wool (2.7.11). The philosopher dispels his interlocutor's ignorance where work, social class and wealth are concerned so that he and his family can become self-sufficient.

Xenophon narrates his presence also at a conversation that Socrates had with Euthydemus regarding the importance of prudence towards the gods (4.3.2). The author declares 'I was there myself (ἐγὼ . . . παρεγενόμην)'. Remember that Euthydemus is someone who quite wrongly believes himself intelligent, having acquired the works of poets and sophists (4.2.1), so this misbelief creates a situation where Socratic irony must exist given the distance between one person's (Socrates') knowledge and another's (Euthydemus') ignorance. Socrates begins by asking his interlocutor to consider how the gods have made provisions for humanity's needs, giving light and dark, food, water, fire and seasons so that Euthydemus has to admit that the gods satisfy our needs (4.3.9) and eventually relents into thinking that he must thank the gods for their assistance to mankind (4.3.15). Because Euthydemus takes on the teaching that Socrates offers with regard to the gods, the irony of the situation is gradually diminished. The self-assured interlocutor is humbled into accepting that the gods must be regarded and thanked.

Xenophon is assumedly present at all the interactions related in the *Memorabilia*. Indeed, one may assume that the interactions are reported precisely because Xenophon is present at them and then writes them down later. Observing these interactions constitutes the author's own education into wisdom and perceptiveness. He has grown from being an impressionable youth, initially quite similar to some of Socrates' interlocutors, but very different in that he is nonetheless very open to Socratic wisdom and insight. (We shall find that Xenophon is similarly both present in the *Anabasis* as the narrator and as an actor in the events of the march, who grows into the later knowing self through observation of events.) As a consequence, he becomes a mature and insightful observer of the society around him and its inhabitants. What this means is that in retrospect the reader realizes the narrative voice introduced at 1.1 is an authoritative one. Indeed, this is the voice of an author in his middle to later years, as the *Memorabilia* was supposedly written after 371 BCE following the Spartan defeat at Leuctra (cf. 3.5). If Xenophon was born circa 430 BCE, he would have been in his very late 50s or early 60s, and so he would have been the fully mature author that we know him as in other works, such as the *Cyropaedia*, a text of an apparently experienced author concerning the Persian king Cyrus which was written, it seems, around 370 BCE.

As one of Socrates' associates, Xenophon becomes a 'subject-supposed-to-know'; he understands the way things truly and actually are – the injustices, the lack of understanding and foresight in others, and so on. Due to the conversations he observed, Xenophon knows that Socrates was a pious individual (1.1.2) and that he gave his associates good counsel, rather than corrupting them (1.1.5). He is thus a presence who enables irony, which he does by reporting it, as in the *Memorabilia*, the *Apology* and the *Symposium*, and which he must do in the absence of Socrates, the subject who does truly know. The dialogues in the text are stagings of irony, for the narrator, as an associate who has learned well from the philosopher, writes of the truth and of others' failures to see and understand the truth to an audience which is enlightened or is becoming enlightened to the truth as a consequence of reading the work which Xenophon has written, while the rest of Athens remains unknowing and ignorant of what constitutes reality.

It is important to observe that the *Memorabilia* foregrounds an irony of hindsight at least as far as the author is concerned. The title of the work in Greek is ἀπομνημόνευματα, which may be translated as 'memoirs'. The *Memorabilia* is a narrative of sayings and doings which occurred in the past and are now being recalled for the present and future. Thus, one may understand the text as implicitly dramatizing a process whereby the narrator has come to know in the present because he experienced the past in the past. He may have known how things were – that is, deluded and false, although Socrates' interlocutors failed to recognize this – or he may not have initially known, and only later come to this knowledge. Accordingly, these experiences have produced realizations about the events perceived or subsequent to them. Hindsight, which constitutes the narrative of the *Memorabilia*, is the knowledge offered to contemporary Athens so that it has the capacity to come to a realization of reality as Xenophon has done.

VI

I suggest that the *Memorabilia* has a double aim. First of all and most obviously, it seeks to absolve from the charges brought by the accusers the philosopher Socrates, who was pious rather than impious and who taught his associates to be good and useful people in the city, as far as the reading audience was concerned. Secondly and less patently but no less significantly, the work offers an aetiology of Xenophon's role as narrator of the life of Socrates and of the author's subsequent role as observer of his times. The narrator, initially inexperienced and untaught by the wise Socrates, grows into the role of perceptive and wise observer of human actions and character. He becomes the author Xenophon, who will offer his perceptions of the Greek and non-Greek, that is barbarian/Persian, worlds, which are out of sorts with the understanding that most people in the world have of social and political interactions and behaviours and of human nature in general. A few, ideally the reading audience of Xenophon's works, will perceive the difference between the author's views and those of the many and it is this difference which constitutes Xenophontic irony.

3

Partying Life (Away) in Xenophon's *Symposium*

In the *Symposium* we are confronted with a more or less amicable drinking party with entertainment at the house of Callias, which Socrates attends with some reluctance (*Symposium* 1.7). Callias is holding the party for his *eromenos* or beloved Autolykos, who has won the pankration in the Panathenea in 422 BCE. As a work concerned with Socrates, the *Symposium* presents itself as a critique of the social elite at Athens in the fourth century. As I read this dialogue in this chapter, the *Symposium* suggests that the individuals prominent at the parties and in the milieu of the city-state are mistaken in what they take to be their priorities in life. They are the unknowing and ignorant persons who are implicitly shown up by the philosopher Socrates so that the dialogue is underpinned by their lack of awareness, which is cast in stark relief by Socrates' wisdom.

I

Xenophon, the omniscient narrator, begins the *Symposium* with the observation that what καλοὶ καγαθοὶ do when they are having fun (cf. τά ἐν ταῖς παιδιαίς) is as worthy of recollection as the deeds that they do when they are being serious (cf. τὰ μετὰ σπουδῆς) (1.1). The occasion of the drinking party, or in fact any drinking party, is cast as fun and Xenophon, who now functions as omniscient but invisible narrator, seeks to relate what happened at the gathering held by Callias. And Callias is characterized as a καλὸς καγαθὸς, a very wealthy, upper class gentleman, and all that this characterization implies – rich, seeking after status, politically ambitious, exclusive and so on.[1] The deeds of the καλοί καγαθοί excite interest and curiosity among the less privileged Athenians but also among themselves. They are the subject of gossip and perhaps speculation. Yet in a Socratic dialogue they are the setting for irony. What the social and financial elite of Athens do and say tends to be unenlightened with respect to the truth and what the philosopher Socrates stands for, and the latter will attempt to show them that this is the case.

Callias and the philosopher have a chance meeting in the dialogue. Callias is going home through the Piraeus with his beloved Autolycus, who has just won the pancratium in the Greater Panathenaia, and with Autolycus' father, Lycon. It is significant that Lycon was one of the prosecutors at Socrates' trial (cf. Plato *Apology* 24a), so that this group of individuals is somewhat dangerous. In common with the chance meeting that leads to Plato's *Republic* (cf. 327a), he then catches sight of Socrates and some of his followers, namely Critobulus, Hermogenes, Antisthenes and Charmides. Callias extends a dinner invitation to the men he has just met, declaring that he would rather have at his party individuals whose hearts have been purified (by philosophy) than generals, cavalry commanders and those aspiring to public office (1.4). Callias *seems* to articulate a view of company that is desirable and in keeping with Socrates' own. The philosopher, however, responds by noting that Callias makes fun of him because the latter has rather thrown in his lot with the sophists.

Callias is the unknowing and unenlightened host who, as we learn from Plato, as a consequence of his extreme wealth has spent more money to learn from the sophists than anyone else (cf. Plato *Apology* 20a). In the current text, Socrates observes that his host-to-be has paid out much money to Protagoras, Gorgias, Prodicus and many others, in other words to all the best known sophists, while he and his companions are (wrongly!) viewed as individuals who work perhaps amateurishly at philosophy (αὐτουργούς) (1.5). Yet knowing what we do of sophists – that they are purveyors of only *apparent* knowledge and skills – Callias' position as a student of these intellectuals, supposedly the brightest and best in town, and as a member of the extremely wealthy set at Athens, sets him up to be a subject who does not know and fails to learn.

Paying money to Gorgias, Prodicus and the like in order to learn from them was a serious non-starter as far as Xenophon was concerned. Gorgias, Prodicus and others like them were sophists, professional teachers, who sought payment for what they taught. In fact, for the sophists greed was the chief motivating factor in what they did and their teachings were generally inconsequential or specious. 'Sophist' (σοφιστής) was a debased form of σοφός, 'wise man' and likewise, the knowledge, if it even was knowledge, that the sophist purported to dispense was equally demeaned. In the *Euthydemus* Plato's Socrates describes Euthydemus and Dionysodorus as 'advertising themselves' (cf. 273e5). Yet the magnitude of their *epangelma*, their advertisement or claim to be able to teach virtue well and quickly, raises serious doubts about their credibility (cf. 273d8–9 and 274a3–4). At *Memorabilia* 1.2.7 Socrates displays his amazement that individuals promised virtue and charged fees for supposedly providing them with virtue, although it is the case that he can cite Prodicus' account of *Heracles at the Crossroads* at *Memorabilia* 2.1. Xenophon's insistence that Socrates 'advertised' no such thing is supported by a number of the Platonic dialogues (cf. Meno 95b–c).[2]

In *Against the Sophists* Xenophon's near contemporary Isocrates censures the sophists for their exaggerated claims to teach. The sophists put out inflated advertisements, which invariably become unfulfilled promises. Isocrates' work is an anatomy of the unfulfilled promise. It attacks individuals who announce themselves as teachers but have no knowledge of what they supposedly teach and also who write 'Arts of Rhetoric' (τεχνήν ῥητορικήν) and argue ignorant of their supposed expertise. *Against the Sophists* is specifically directed against four identifiable groups of professional intellectuals. In sections 3–8 the rhetorician faults those who promise to make their students virtually immortal as a result of their teaching, especially of moderation and virtue. Outwardly, they play down the importance of money and profit but actually charge fees and even request deposits, which are entrusted to a third party for safe-keeping (4–5). By requiring a deposit, the sophists betray their own promises to be able to teach moral virtue, particularly justice, because the deposit suggests that they mistrust the students whom they teach to pay for their lessons (5). At sections 9–18 Isocrates faults the professional teachers who promise instruction in political speeches, the discourse he reserves for himself (9; cf. *Antidosis* 46–7). He complains that these individuals have created an 'art' or 'skill' (τεχνήν) which consists in drawing people by cheap fees and big boasts (9). Yet such teachers themselves produce speeches which are far worse than those made up on the spot by mere amateurs or lay people. Furthermore, these teachers advocate an art of speech which lacks flexibility (12–14) and they instruct students who have no innate talent or potential to succeed (15).

In section 19 of *Against the Sophists* Isocrates deals briefly with two different groups of sophists. He first makes mention of a recent group of professional teachers who boast about their methodological approach to pedagogy but who will, he predicts, show their ineffectiveness like the individuals criticized in sections 9–14 (cf. 19). The second group of unnamed sophists, the 'rest' (λοποί) produced treatises or manuals (τεχναί) which promised to teach the art of litigation. The treatise writers misrepresent the art of logography and dicanic pleading, which for the most part deals with private litigation (cf. *Panathenaicus* 11), as λογός πολιτικός, the discourse which Isocrates defines as dealing with matters of public or 'national' concern, and thus become instructors of political meddling and greed (20).[3]

Accordingly, Callias paying money to sophists is clearly Callias allowing himself to be cheated by the professional teachers and immersing himself in a world of deception and illusion. He has fallen for the scam put forth by the sophists: they seek money for wisdom that is only apparent. The wisdom he purports to be able to utter is false or mistaken knowledge, falsely validated by the sophists' mercantilism. The fact that he calls Socrates and his friends 'amateurs' as a term of denigration reveals his ignorance, for it is precisely Socrates' amateurism, his refusal to involve money in his teaching, that proves his knowledge so valuable and valid. Socrates takes knowledge away from economics. Yet, for Callias, a high price makes something valuable even if it is without value. A further and very apparent irony is that Callias lives in a world uninformed by philosophical wisdom, and mistakenly regards himself as learned and wise. Accordingly, Callias boasts that he has been hiding his ability to say many wise things and to give long and wise speeches, and so he would now like the opportunity to show that he is worth taking seriously (cf. ἐπιδείξω ὑμῖν ἐμαυτὸν πάνυ πολλῆς σπουδῆς ἄξιον ὄντα, 1.6). Later Callias promises to display his wisdom (σοφία) and does so, as he thinks, at 3.4 where he declares that he takes pride in his ability to make men better (βέλτιους). Clearly, Callias is not a teacher but blows his own trumpet in a way that discredits him. Antisthenes asks if it is by teaching a manual trade or by teaching a virtue, only to be told by Callias that he instructs in the latter (3.5).

All the while, Socrates plays the εἰρών, appearing modest and refusing initially to accept the dinner invitation extended by Callias (cf. 1.7).

II

In the end Socrates does attend the symposium and the party proceeds apace. Philip the Buffoon enters at 1.11 and the guests eat. After dinner, a Syracusan man enters with a dancing girl, a flute girl and boy, who is able to dance and play the cither, to provide entertainment for Callias' guests. As a whole, we shall see that the dinner reveals the shortcomings of Athenian elite society, which is perfectly content to continue as it is. At 3.3 Socrates asks Callias to give the dinner party an exhibition (ἐπιδειξιν) of his profundity. ἐπιδειξις is a word that suggests the rhetorical display made by sophists to display their skills, and Callias had already employed the verb ἐπιδείξω, 'I shall display', in declaring that he would show his knowledge was worth much at 1.6. At 3.4 Callias reveals that the particular skill in which he takes pride is his ability to make men better;

Antisthenes queries whether this is a manual skill or a skill resulting from the nobility of his nature (i.e. καλοκαγαθία). Callias responds that he improves men by καλοκαγαθία, or by nobility of character.

The conversation then quickly moves on to determine what each member of the dinner party takes particular pride in (3.5ff.). Callias' apparent 'skill' at discourse leads Niceratus to next boast, declaring that he can recite the whole of the *Iliad* and the *Odyssey* by heart because his father had forced him to learn the epics (3.5). Niceratus confesses that he has listened to the rhapsodes recite the poems every day. He has paid a great deal of money to these individuals so that nothing worthy has escaped his attention (3.6). As a counterpoint, Antisthenes declares that the rhapsodes are actually a rather stupid tribe (οἶσθά τι οὖν ἔθνος, ἔφη, ἠλιώτερον ῥαψῳδῶν) (3.6). Antisthenes' comment is one that threatens the illusion that the teachers of the καλοὶ κἀγαθοί actually know something. Socrates takes up the lead provided by Antisthenes and proceeds to declare that the rhapsodes do not know the underlying meanings (ὑπονοίας) of the poems. Furthermore, rhapsodic teaching is at least amoral, if not immoral. At 4.45 Niceratus cites Homer to support his insatiable greed for wealth, which shows his study of Homer to be unconcerned with what is right and what is wrong. Sophistic teaching tends towards the amoral and immoral, which is patently evidenced here.

Socrates observes that Niceratus has paid a good deal of money to Stesimbrotus, Anaximander and other Homer critics. The language is strongly reminiscent of that which articulates Callias paying the sophists for his knowledge. In both instances, Xenophon gives us two names in the dative, with numerous others mentioned more vaguely also in the dative. Niceratus has been duped by the rhapsodes, who have no real understanding of the Homeric poems, just as Callias has been cheated in paying huge sums of money to the sophists and the knowledge he has paid for is worthless. Xenophon's suggestion is that Niceratus has paid for specious knowledge just as his host has. Money does not actually validate something as knowledge, and after all, Antisthenes notes that the rhapsodes, who deal with the verse of Homer, are the most stupid of men (3.6). This is because the rhapsodes do not know the underlying meanings (cf. ὑπονοίας) of the epics.

What one sees is a gap in knowledge between what Socrates knows to be the case, namely that sophists and rhapsodes have no real knowledge or wisdom and what his interlocutors, e.g. Callias and Niceratus, believe to be the case, namely that sophists and rhapsodes can teach them something of value. This rift in understanding constitutes the irony of the text. Socrates merely has to be present as the figure who knows amongst the individuals who do not know in order for there to be irony, just as in the trial portrayed in the *Apology*, where charges against the philosopher revealed a failure to understand his piety.

To continue, Critoboulus takes pride in beauty, himself being handsome (3.7); Antisthenes in wealth (3.8); Charmides in his poverty (3.9), while Hermogenes takes pride in his friends (3.14). With the exception of Charmides, each of the dinner guests takes solace from something bodily or material. Socrates, on the other hand, is made to confess that his pride lies in the trade of procurer or pimp, which also (only) initially appears to be concerned with the bodily (3.10). The philosopher celebrates an ability, i.e. procurement, rather than a thing, and he presents his ability in a rather deprecating and ironic manner as a disreputable skill. The conversation moves on to discuss why what each does has real value (4.1). Callias is quick to declare that he gives men money to make them righteous, even though he must say that righteousness resides in the soul in response to Antisthenes (4.2). And the drinking party proceeds with each of the guests lauding his own particular quality that grants him pleasure or advantage. Critobulous speaks of the effects of his good looks, and their capacity to induce others to do as one wishes (4.10–18). Charmides praises poverty because it leaves him without concern for property and belongings (4.29–32). Wealth allows Antisthenes to satisfy all his desires and wants (4.35–44) and Niceratus takes pride in his boy, being able to sleep with him every night and all night (4.52).

The discussion of the *Symposium* suggests other ironies in the banter that has occurred at the drinking party. Callias' pronouncement that he is able to make people better (βελτίους) now appears ridiculous, as does his assertion that people become better because he teaches them nobility of character (καλοκἀγαθία) (3.4). Callias' relationships are physical and bodily so that no virtue or morality is bestowed upon his partners or associates. Furthermore, Callias states he makes men more righteous by putting money in their purses so that they may buy the necessities of life and have less need to take to criminal activity (4.2). Again, Callias is concerned with the physical, rather than the moral or psychical, aspects of life.

In addition, the fact is that all the guests at the drinking party, with the exception of Socrates, who is firmly married, are involved in physical relationships that are non-marital: they are concerned with each other's beauty (as Critias at 4.9), while Critoboulus seems to imply that his beauty is indeed the asset he takes most pride in (3.8). At 4.11 Critoboulus declares that he would not take the kingdom of Persia in exchange for being handsome (4.11) and claims that he would rather gaze upon the beautiful Cleinias rather than upon all the beautiful things in the world (4.12). He is the object of some desire at the drinking party, for the members of the party urge him to receive his kisses after he wins at a contest at 6.1. Finally, the dinner guests come to Socrates and they inquire why he is proud of being a procurer, which in their eyes is without honour (i.e. ἀδόξῳ) (4.56). Socrates begins by commenting that procurement seeks to make one attractive to others (4.57), whether this lies in one's appearance or in one's speech (4.58–9). According to Socrates, Antisthenes has acted not as a procurer but as a go-between in recommending philosophers and poets to his friends (4.63–4).

The concern with the body explains why Socrates leads into a discussion of the procurer or pimp (μαστροπός) (4.56). The pimp is an individual who acquires prostitutes for the enjoyment of his clients, and is therefore concerned with physicality. Indeed, it is the task of the pimp to render the male or female he is procuring pleasing (ἀρέσκοντα) to the persons he or she will be with, and their attractiveness will depend on their hair and clothes (4.57). The procurer will also teach the words that one must speak to make them attractive (4.59). For these services, he ought to receive a high remuneration (4.60). Socrates names Antisthenes the ideal procurer because he has brought Callias together with the sophist Prodicus and Hippias, the teacher of a memory system, the former wanting the philosophy and the latter two money (4.62). Antisthenes is thus the perfect intermediary, the man who makes relations happen.

Socrates is being extremely ironic. The procuration being discussed is far from ideal. Antisthenes, as a 'pimp', has brought the rich Callias together with sophists so that he believes he has gained some knowledge and skills. This is the specious intellectuality that the philosopher takes issue with and seeks to uncover as such. The discussion of the art of the pimp in this section of the work serves to underscore the fact that the concern of Callias and his friends is with the body and its desires rather than with the soul, which Socrates much rather prefers. The philosopher thus offers a radically revised understanding of procurement: this activity is for the sake of bringing people into contact with one another for their benefit rather than just their pleasure. A bodily concern has ironically been transformed into a spiritual matter by Socrates: being a pimp is now ideally concerned with the non-bodily.

III

The dinner party guests are extremely materialistic in that they are concerned with physical things – money, beauty, property (or lack of it as in Charmides' case), food and sex. (Pucci has seen this materialism as the source of irony elsewhere in the *Apology*.⁴) Indeed, the symposium is a scene of materiality and physicality. Indeed, Callias has proposed that perfume be brought in, to which Socrates objects, proposing that the ideal scent for the party is nobility of soul (καλοκαγαθία, 2.4). The guests' complete focus on what can be felt and physically experienced is the larger irony of the dialogue. Callias is entirely concerned with the bodily: he loves his youth, Autylocus, he has so much money that he can pay the sophists for an 'education', and now he seeks to anoint everyone with perfume. His world is the physical world of senses and pleasures. In contrast, Socrates' world is that of the soul, of the immaterial qualities that make an individual. Accordingly, the worlds inhabited by Callias and his associates do not easily meet or mesh with that inhabited by Socrates and his friends, so there is necessarily an ironic distance between them. The dinner guests and their desires represent the city and its desires. The city wants money and glory in stark contrast to Socrates, who is only concerned with wisdom and having other people see this state of affairs.

In chapter 8 of the *Symposium* Socrates introduces a topic that is also central to the *Symposium* of Plato; that is desire or ἔρως (8.1). If one follows the discussion of the whole chapter, which I shall summarize in some detail, it becomes apparent that the philosopher seeks to shift the concern of desire for another from the bodily and the sexual to that of virtue and benefit of others, even if that involves a degree of sacrifice. The ironic gap becomes most pronounced here in the section, which Holger Thesleff suggests might have been written after the first part of the text, which was written around 385 BCE following the author's reading of Plato's *Symposium* and was planned as a revision of the conversation between Socrates and Diotima.⁵ Here Socrates leads the discussion into the topic of Eros, or Desire. The philosopher observes that everyone present, including himself, has experienced desire for another or has been desired by others (8.2). Certainly, Charmides, Critoboulus, Niceratus, Hermognes and even Antisthenes desire others or are desired by them (8.2–4). The philosopher engages in banter, identifying the partners in love and the objects of desire of his interlocutors (8.2–7) until he makes a distinction between a 'heavenly' (οὐρανία) and a 'vulgar' (πάνδημος) desire at 8.9. It is here that a further ironic distance begins to open up between the philosopher and those at the drinking party, for they do not grasp what Socrates is about to tell them. Socrates distinguishes between vulgar desire as one which is physical and carnal while the heavenly desire is concerned with the soul, friendship and good deeds (8.10). This desire Socrates perhaps ironically identifies as that which his host Callias possesses due to the individual he has selected, Autolycus, and due to the fact that Autolycus' father is present at their meetings (8.11). Socrates then launches into his discourse, which distinguishes between a heavenly Aphrodite and a vulgar Aphrodite who correspond to the Ouranian and Pandemian Aphrodite in Plato's supposedly earlier *Symposium* (cf.180e). Each of these goddesses is entirely distinct from the other, with separate altars, temples and rituals (8.9). Each Aphrodite is responsible for a different type of desire; the vulgar one for desire for carnal things and the heavenly one for the desire for the soul, friendship and noble deeds (8.10). Socrates declares Callias' love to originate with the heavenly Aphrodite as he is content to have his own father present, implying that there is no shame involved in his love (8.11). Hermogenes notes that Socrates is actually and surreptitiously educating Callias' desire to conform to the heavenly Aphrodite by praising him for doing such (8.12). Thus, the philosopher operates as the persuasive pimp, or, perhaps more accurately, the effective go-between.

The point that Socrates wants to make is that desire for the soul, the heavenly desire, is superior to the vulgar desire for the body (8.12). Physical attractiveness passes while one's soul becomes more lovable as it progresses towards understanding and becomes more sensible (cf. φρονιμώτερον) (8.14). Furthermore, one can experience a fullness and satiety of the body, whereas one who desires the soul is less likely to feel that he has had enough of his partner as the goddess Aphrodite bestows her graces on the beloved's words and deeds (8.15).

Moreover, Socrates observes that one can feel satiety in desire where physical beauty is concerned just as there is fullness with eating (8.15). In any case, the bloom of youth passes so that love (φιλία) also diminishes; however, with time the soul becomes more intelligent and more desirable (8.14-15). A friendship based on the soul is gentle and less likely to achieve satiety, for the goddess endows one with desirable words and deeds (8.15). So a soul that is free, modest and noble shows leadership amongst its age-mates and is likely to have its love reciprocated by its beloved (8.16). An individual possessing such a soul would not hate his beloved if the latter were thought to be handsome and good by him, and he would see to it that his beloved's honour was of a higher precedence than his own pleasure. He also would not be less loved if his appearance were to be somehow damaged or lessened (8.17).

Nobility of the soul ensures that the partners will feel affection for each other and that desire will be reciprocated (8.16). This mutual affection will determine that the lovers will gaze upon each other, talk to each other, trust and be trusted by the other. They will feel joy at each other's success and distress at each other's misfortunes (8.18). On the other hand, the lover who desires only the flesh would not make a return to his partner, despising him and concealing from his relatives what he has in mind for him (8.19). The youthful partner in the relationship also will not feel affection for his other when the latter is no longer so handsome or even when his older man is feeling desire for him (8.21). Concern for the body rather than the soul characterizes the relationship as a servile one, as desire for the body makes one resemble a beggar, following in the footsteps of his lover and begging for some sign of affection (8.23). Desiring the body only also means that the lover is like someone who rents a farm; he will try to get as much out of the land as possible. In contrast, the lover in friendship will try to enhance his lover's value, as someone who owns a farm seeks to increase its worth (8.25).

Having a relationship solely based on the flesh would not compel the beloved to return his lover's affections. Such a lover might only give to himself what he himself desires and the most contemptible of things to his beloved. Furthermore, he conceals from the beloved's relative what he desires to do with him (8.19). Using persuasion on the beloved corrupts the soul of the one who is persuaded (8.20). A union based on the body is an unfree or ignoble (cf. ἀνελεύθερια) one, unlike one based on the soul (8.23). This lover instructs the beloved in what to do and so is honoured as Cheiron and Phoenix were by Achilles. In contrast, the one ruled by bodily desire would follow his beloved as a beggar, as he is always pleading for another kiss or some form of affection (8.23). The lover who bases his relationship on his beloved's appearance is like the tenant farmer who wants to get as much as he can from his farm rather than increase its value (8.25). In contrast, the individual who wants a friendship (φιλία) is rather like the one who possesses a plot of land and tries to make it more valuable. So he does with his beloved. The beloved of the first lover is more likely to be loose in his behaviour, while the beloved of the second lover will take more thought for cultivating virtue (8.26).

There is also a contrast of behaviour between the lover of the body and the lover of the soul, with the former engaging in unrestrained behaviour and the latter in keeping a noble character and thus, cultivating virtue (8.26). Friendship determines that the lover will habitually practice virtue in attempt to render his partner shameful, continent, self-controlled and reverent, and this is the greatest blessing of his relationship (8.27). Socrates has endeavoured to show Callias that not only mortals but also the gods set a higher value on friendships of the soul rather than bodily relationships (8.28), implying that Callias prefers the latter. And so also with regard to friendship: Zeus loved Ganymede (8.29–30), Achilles loved Patroclus (8.31), and many other demi-gods, such as Orestes, Pylades,

Theseus and Peirithous did good deeds because they admired another lover (8.32). It is the case that those willing to endure hardship and danger are more likely to do good and noble deeds rather than those who are accustomed to pleasure.

At 8.35 Socrates decries physical, carnal attraction by noting that the Spartans view desire for the body as leading someone to no good end. The Spartans are brave even when they are placed in a battle line with foreigners because they worship the goddess Modesty rather than Shamelessness or Impudence. As a consequence, one, even the carnal lover, is inclined to trust someone who has a good and lovely soul (8.36). Socrates then commends Callias for his desire for Autolycus, an individual who has undergone many labours and pains for the pancratium. Autolycus will bring honour to himself and his father and do well for his friends and fatherland; he will furthermore be worthy to be looked at and famous among both Greeks and barbarians (8.38). Yet Autolycus may not be quite as perfect a youth as the philosopher suggests at face value. He was after all the subject of a comic play (423 BCE), a comeback for an attack on the playwright in Aristophanes' *Wasps*,[6] and of a revision of this play by Eupolis (421/420 BCE), and therefore lampoonable. Apparently, the play featured a symposium and the playwright himself as Autolycus' tutor.[7] Socrates goes on to say that Callias must consider what sort of knowledge made Themistocles able to free Greece, and what sort of knowledge enabled Pericles to appear to be the strongest counsellor in Greece, how Solon made the strongest laws for Athens and what practices and customs made the Spartans the strongest leaders (8.39).

Socrates' goal is to show Callias that the gods and heroes value the friendship of the soul more highly than the enjoyment of the body (8.28). The evidence for this is that when Zeus fell in love with mortal women he let them remain mortal, but when he loved individuals for their good souls he made them immortal. Heracles, the Dioscuri and others are examples of individuals made immortal for their souls, while Ganymede was carried to Olympus by Zeus because of his soul rather than his body (8.29–30). Where mortals are concerned, Achilles regarded Patrokles foremost as his friend and so sought to avenge his death (8.31). Likewise, Orestes, Pylades, Theseus and Peirithous did the greatest deeds not because they did not sleep with any other, but because they had admiration for another. Furthermore, the Spartans, who do not think that anyone who feels bodily desire for another will come to a good end, will be brave and will not desert their comrades due to their more noble desire (8.35). Socrates seeks to make the point that one would rather trust another who seeks the loveliness of the spirit rather than one who seeks bodily beauty (8.36). Clifford Hindley thinks that the *Symposium* had to reject the charge that Socrates corrupted the youth. Accordingly, the dialogue inveighs against a physical homosexual love because such love generally resulted in the corruption of the younger partner.[8] Indeed, such a relationship may have brought shame to the youth and, as David Cohen notes,[9] was in theory forbidden by the law of *hubris*, especially if one of the partners were penetrated as if he were a woman.[10] (There is some uncertainty as 'may' suggests because Cohen is adamant that attitudes towards homosexual love were diverse and variant in Athens.[11]) Hindley observes that *if* the *Hiero*, which affirms and condones homosexual love as a physical relationship, were written after the *Symposium*, then Xenophon must be recanting his supposedly earlier rejection of homosexual *eros*.[12] But I suggest this is not necessarily the case. Even if the *Hiero* were the prior text, it suggests that a homosexual relationship is in any case hard for the tyrant, so that such desire is hypothetical.[13] As we shall see, both Hiero and Simonides are severely lacking as figures in the *Hiero* and consequently, what they say need only be taken with a grain of salt.[14]

It is in sections 8.38–9 that, I suggest, Xenophon locates the major irony of this text, whether this is Socratic or his own. Socrates has commended Autolycus for his bodily attributes – after all, athletics involves the body in training and in competition – so that it is implied that Callias sustains a bodily desire for his partner. The philosopher does not mention Autolycus' character or his moral attributes. Yet, the philosopher has just spent the largest part of chapter 8 commending the cultivation of and desire for the soul. This is where true virtue and benefit for the community lie. Socrates is engaged in an ironic commendation of Autolycus' and so, of Callias' desire for him: the relationship of the lovers has an insecure and unfounded basis, namely the body. This is something that the philosopher perceives and realizes, unlike the others, especially the host, at the drinking party. And this is not surprising in light of the characterization of Callias in the text. The earlier part of the *Symposium* has set up Socrates' host Callias as someone unenlightened by his 'education' with the sophists and unable or unwilling to learn the truth. Thus, it is the case that Callias has failed to comprehend Socrates' teaching on the soul and its virtues with regard to his relationship with Autolycus, which the philosopher apparently now celebrates.

And here is an irony particular to the individuals in the *Symposium*. They are clearly the social and monetary elite of Athens; however, they do not display the upper-class virtue of moderation (σοφροσύνη) in the slightest with their excessive eating, drinking and sexual behaviour. Xenophon through Socrates demonstrates that this segment of society does not behave as the aristocratic class of Athens should, and perhaps otherwise does if it is truly aristocratic. And aristocracy ends up suffering for this shortcoming. Although Callias is from one of the most distinguished Athenian families, he wastes all the wealth he has inherited – his family made their money on the silver mines at Laurion – on sophists, flatterers and women. Literary sources suggest that this a well-known fact and would have been evident to Xenophon's audience. Lysias, in *On the Property of Aristophanes* 19.48, informs us that Callias wasted away his inheritance of two hundred talents to less than two talents, and even worse, Athenaeus *Deipnosophistae* 12.52 presents a Callias who died in such poverty as a consequence of his extravagances that he had only one barbarian woman as an attendant and could not even afford to support himself. Socrates thus demonstrates the ephemerality of wealth and his audience would have probably been aware of Callias' final condition, as he lived in the fifth century while the dialogue was probably written in 360 BCE. There is ironically no security in wealth, however great it might be.

Yet pretending to think well of Callias, Socrates suggests that the former would suit public office (8.40). Callias is an aristocrat, is of Erectheus' line and an Alcmaeonid, and performs priestly duties at a festival. Furthermore, he is good-looking and is able to endure hard work and effort (8.40). But Callias and the other guests fail to perceive that the philosopher is playfully making his suggestion. The host does not have the proper qualities to be a civic leader, and at 8.42 Callias and Autolycus engage in the physical behaviour of looking at each other, which suggests that they follow the vulgar Aphrodite rather than the heavenly and chaste Aphrodite. Socrates' proposal that Callias enter Athenian politics is an ironic one that the rest of the party fails to understand as ironic because they are caught up in the world of vulgar Aphrodite with their concerns with money and with beauty.

The final tableau of the dinner party simply affirms the gathering's overall concern with the material and the physical. The Syracusan enters to stage a play: Ariadne comports with Dionysius. Ariadne is dressed as a bride; Dionysius enters and lovingly gives her a kiss (9.4). He then gives his hand to Ariadne and the two kiss and caress (9.5). The onlookers at the party regard Dionysius as handsome as the two lovers pledge themselves to each other (9.6) and they leave for the wedding couch (9.7). This gives the banqueters inspiration for their own actions as the unmarried make a pledge to take wives and those who are married are determined to ride home to their wives on horseback (9.7).[15] The heterosexual relationship, indeed the marriage of the two gods, depicted in the final section of Xenophon's *Symposium*, follows on quite seamlessly from the pronounced homoeroticism which is evident earlier in the work. And it compels the diners to seek out their partners, whether they are of the opposite or the same sex.

This tableau is emblematic of the dinner party as a whole as it highlights the carnality of desire as the banqueters at the symposium understand desire to be. Dionysius and Ariadne display a physical heterosexual relationship to the diners, some of whom may prefer a homosexual relationship. This follows Socrates' discourse on the heavenly Aphrodite, where love and desire are to be above all of the soul rather than the body. This tableau thus suggests a big misunderstanding on the part of Callias and his fellows, even after Socrates has taught them otherwise. There is a complete gap in understanding such that the diners do not comprehend what the philosopher has been trying to tell them about desire, about the body, the soul and virtue. The diners understand on one level, which is uninformed, while Socrates comprehends as a wise man. This constitutes the overall irony of Xenophon's *Symposium*.

IV

Reviewing the discussion of the *Symposium* suggests other ironies in the banter that has occurred at the drinking party. Callias' pronouncement that he is able to make people better (βελτίους) now appears ridiculous, as does his assertion that people become better because he teaches them nobility of character (καλοκἀγαθία) (3.4). Callias' relationships are physical and bodily so that no virtue or morality is bestowed upon his partners or associates. Furthermore, Callias states he makes men more righteous by putting money in their purses so that they may buy the necessities of life and have less need to take to criminal activity (4.2). Again, Callias is concerned with the physical, rather than moral or psychical, aspects of life. In addition, the fact is that all the guests at the drinking party, with the exception of Socrates, are involved in physical relationships: they are concerned with each other's beauty (cf. Critias, 4.9), while Critoboulus seems to imply that his beauty is indeed the asset he takes most pride in (3.8). At 4.11 Critoboulus declares that he would not take the kingdom of Persia in exchange for being handsome (4.11) and claims that he would rather gaze upon the beautiful Cleinias rather than all the beautiful things in the world (members of the party urge him to receive his kisses after he wins a contest at 6.1).

The *Symposium* presents Socratic irony in Xenophon at its most pronounced. Socrates is present in a scene with individuals who live a privileged and largely carefree life in Athens. They are rich, have many friends, have sex whenever they wish and generally enjoy themselves. The philosopher offers them his teaching and while they are pleased to have him there, they do not generally listen to his words or doctrines. They continue to live in their own world, while Socrates is in his although he temporarily has his foot in theirs. Perhaps the greatest irony in the *Symposium* is that Callias, who has paid vast sums of money in an attempt to learn from the sophists, who are specious and ineffective teachers of apparent wisdom, has the philosopher Socrates at his drinking party and even though he converses with him, fails to learn anything from the one who truly knows what is. A gap is evident to the reader who knows what the philosopher and his teaching are about. The reader is thus complicit in the irony of the dialogue.

From other sources, we know that the abundantly rich Callias, who fails to heed the philosopher's teaching, will become a pauper later in life, but irony is also present in the work, as readers of the work will know that one of the apparently genial 'gentlemen' becomes responsible for the death and destruction of others, including those present at the symposium, at Athens. Indeed, Charmides, who valued his poverty so much in his dialogue in the *Symposium*, later becomes the leader of the Thirty,[16] who were responsible for the deaths of so many in the city-state. Socrates' teaching on moderation and desire for the spiritual rather than the carnal has clearly had no effect on this member of the dinner party. It is indeed significant that, as Thomas Pangle has noticed, Socrates does his best to distance himself as much as possible from Charmides' speech, giving the floor to Antisthenes instead of commenting on the former's discourse.

4

The Economies of Pedagogy in the *Oeconomicus*: Xenophon's Wifely Didactics[1]

I

Xenophon's *Oeconomicus* is a work which has prompted a number of widely divergent responses. A predominant reading offers that the work is a testimony to Greek misogyny in the classical period: the husband Ischomachus takes a young, inexperienced wife, who is accordingly and following custom tamed and *instructed* to manage the space within the οἶκος.[2] Another interpretation regards Xenophon and Ischomachus as better-than-average Greek men with respect to women's standing in society, or even as proto-feminists.[3] In this treatment of the dialogue, the fact that the husband allows the wife her *own* space – the home (as distinct from the farm outdoors) – and teaches his companion her *own* activities – housework and the management of the household slaves – demonstrates a considerable degree of respect for the wife and for woman's worth, while Socrates' exclamation that the wife has a 'masculine intellect (ἀνδρικὴν διάνοιαν)' (10.1) is to be taken as proof of the Xenophontic wife's authority.[4] There are further variations which qualify these interpretations: either, the husband is regarded as echoing Socratic sympathy towards women while continuing to insist that the wife be a domestic;[5] or the husband, despite being a misogynist, is seen as granting the wife some degree of autonomy.[6] And then there is Leo Strauss' analysis of the dialogue as 'Xenophon's Socratic *logos* or dialogue par excellence'.

The readings I have briefly rehearsed present us with opposed and/or complementary binary terms, and furthermore, give us a way into seeing the text as an ironic one because not all is as appears, certainly as far as the roles played by the different sexes in the dialogue are concerned. After all, Pomeroy sees Socrates showing irony and humour in this work.[7] One can schematize the dialogue in terms of the following dichotomies: male/female, where the dialogue's chief actors are concerned; wealth/deficiency, where the work's economics is concerned; outdoors/indoors, where the spheres of activity are the issue; and of misogynist text/pro-woman text, where the dialogue's ideology and the reader's reception are in question. Alternatively, the reader might characterize the work as a presentation of complementary pairings: husband and wife, teacher and student, speaker and respondent, author and audience, and so on. Dualism is neat, manageable but constrained, and it fails to admit that Xenophon is a complex author whose texts may lend themselves to readings that could surprise expectations.[8] Straussians have read Xenophon 'between the lines', arguing that his texts sustain a gap between what seems to be said and what is in reality – that is, a Straussian reality – the case. I wish to argue that even without reading an implied text, Xenophon's works themselves contain deliberate discrepancies which suggest that we should read them in ways that stand apart from received tradition. So for instance, the *Cyropaedia*, which has been regarded as presenting an unqualifiably positive portrait of the leader, may also be seen as a work which displays at particular moments and through explicit contradictions the flaws in Cyrus' rise to power.[9] This chapter seeks to argue that the *Oeconomicus* is no less critical of an individual generally regarded as deserving of praise: the husband Ischomachus. Here the figure of Socrates, the work's privileged pedagogical actor, is a presence who unsettles what might otherwise seem to be unproblematic conversations about the domestic scene and in this way conforms to the literary Socrates, who, as produced by Plato, is a questioning and unsettling presence who disturbs conventional categories and assumptions.[10] Socrates is the individual who introduces the ironic dimension into the household: things are not at all as the husband sees them.

II

Despite the work's central concern with the careful management of resources Socrates disrupts the dialogue as a work structured around opposing, or complementary doubles. He appears in an outer, framing dialogue with Critobulus on the question of what it means to be a gentleman (καλὸς κἀγαθός), which in turn stages a reported dialogue between Socrates and Ischomachus on the same topic. This inner dialogue becomes the frame for a third dialogue, the discussion between Ischomachus, the husband and his nameless wife, on how to run a household – for which the *Oeconomicus* is best known and most frequently read. And the embedding does not stop there, for this third, central conversation harbours further dialogues: located within it is the husband and wife's instruction of the housekeeper (ταμία) in chapter 9.

The work's recessive structure proposes that some of its discursive spaces may be privileged over others,[11] although Socrates' presence throughout the different levels of dialogue proposes that the philosopher's discursive authority is accordingly broadly disseminated throughout the work. It is also the case, however, that if no one section of the text can be taken as *the* privileged scene of teaching and learning, then it seems highly questionable whether the portion where the philosopher is conspicuously absent, namely the discourse between husband (Ischomachus) and wife, should be taken to be the paradigmatic discussion of 'economics' despite readers' almost exclusive attention to this portion of the work. Furthermore, there is a sense in which the innermost dialogue is one least accommodated by the work's overall structure, and is, I suggest, far from exemplary as a didactic scene, standing quite apart from the Socratic ideal of a didactic scene. And such a scene, according to Alexander Nehamas, presents the Xenophontic Socrates, quite apart from the Platonic one, as an individual ever ready to correct others, and yet as an individual so innocuous he leaves us wondering why he should have been executed by the Athenians.[12]

In a work on the management of resources and wealth, a wifely didactic has its precedents.[13] Hesiod showed why the teaching of a wife should be a concern, especially if household economy was to be maintained in an orderly fashion. According to the poet, the wife was on the one hand a token in the transaction 'marriage' between father-in-law and son-in-law; she is a token whose value is articulated in terms of the wealth that she might bring to her husband's household.[14] But beyond her symbolic value, the wife is either an economic liability or an asset. This is an assumption which becomes apparent from the work of the archaic poet Hesiod, which needs to be read as a sub-text for the misogyny of Critobulous to be fully uncovered. In the *Works and Days* Hesiod observes that a man can obtain nothing better than a good wife, and nothing worse than a bad one (702–3). In Hesiod's prejudicial system of value the bad wife is a predatory consumer; she is a figure who satisfies her greedy hunger on the household's resources (cf. δειπνολόχης) and then, finally on the husband, who is metaphorically cooked, that is 'roasted', as a meal and given to consuming (cf. ὠμῷ, literally 'raw' or 'savage') old age (703–5). Elsewhere in this work the poet presents the woman (γυνή) as a member of the household who sates her thirst on the grain stores (cf. τεὴν διφῶσα καλιήν), deceiving her husband with wiles and tricks (374–7). In the *Theogony* women are declared suitable companions for a household where excess (cf. κόροιο), rather than destructive poverty (οὐλομένης πενίης), is present (593). The poet compares them to the drones in the hive which simply feed off the labour of the busy worker bees in a reverse simile (594; cf. *WD* 308–9). It is for this reason that the man who hopes for his οἶκος to prosper must wish for a son rather than a wife, albeit that the wife is the one who makes the son possible (*WD* 378–80).[15]

The devouring wife is one aspect of the iconography of woman as 'empty vessel' in Hesiod's poetry, for the narrative of Pandora in the *Works and Days* extends negative equity to all women. At vv. 59ff. of this poem the author recounts how the gods fashioned from earth and water a woman, indeed an archetypal woman, whom Athena teaches to weave (64), Aphrodite adorns (65–6) and in whose breast Hephaestus places the discourse of deception (67–9). The name 'Pandora', literally 'all gifts', which Hermes grants, acknowledges that this woman is well-endowed with gifts from the gods (80–2). Yet it is precisely such a gift – one poignantly named 'all gifts' – which Prometheus warns his brother Epimetheus not to receive from Zeus and which Epimetheus, characteristically named as 'Afterthought', recognizes too late for what it is (85–9). Pandora is the origin of womankind, which is in turn a source of grief to mankind (cf. πῆμ' ἀνδράσιν ἀλφηστῇσιν, 82). Hesiod observes that the tribes of men lived on the earth without trouble, pain and disease until this fabricated female removed the lid from the jar she brought to mankind and scattered with her own hands the pestilences contained therein, leaving only hope in an otherwise empty vessel as a consolation for man (90–8). Pandora takes all life, security and wealth from mankind and offers in their place troubles: she bears and is the producer of griefs.

Hesiod's negative portrait of the wife as economic liability has a legacy. In his famous diatribe against women, Semonides of Amorgos (poem 7, West) portrays – whether straightforwardly or ironically – this figure as one who disrupts production and resource in the household and in the larger community. With the exception of the blameless bee-woman (83–93) who is extolled for her virtue at the end of the poem, the poet emphasizes the identity of the female as an empty vessel, a consumer, and a waste of resources. He provides a taxonomy of unsavoury womankind, which Loraux terms the 'tribes of women':[16] the 'pig-woman', who grows fat while she sits unwashed and filthy on the dunghills (vv. 5–6); the crippled woman, who, knowing nothing good or bad, understands only how to feed herself (vv. 23–4); the donkey woman, who refuses to do any work and simply eats all day and night unless she is making love (vv. 43–9); the weasel woman, who steals (κλέπτουσα, 55) from neighbours and consumes altar sacrifices (vv. 50–6); the mare woman, who grooms herself with expensive perfumes and cosmetics and will be a vast drain on resources for any husband who is not a nobleman or king (vv. 57–7). Women are also consumers in a far more terrible sense. Poem 7 concludes with the observation that women are the 'greatest evil (μέγιστον … κακόν) and cites the case of the wife, namely Helen, who began the Great War, the Trojan War. Alluding to the *Iliad*, Semonides demonstrates that love for a woman, and according to him, therefore woman herself, has destroyed the lives of so many men by leading them to war (vv. 115–18).[17]

The good wife is a consequence of the husband's formation, owing her identity as such to his teaching.[18] As far as Hesiod was concerned, the wife is a mere girl-woman in the fourth or fifth year of her adolescence, that is either thirteen or fourteen, and a virgin (παρθενικήν) (*Works and Days* 698–9). The new bride is to all intents and purposes a *tabula rasa*, an empty slate, to be metaphorically written upon. Thus Hesiod (699–701) declares that the wife is to be instructed (διδάξῃς) in the customs of the husband (ἤθεα κεδνά) lest the latter become a laughing stock to his neighbours. His instruction to the audience of the *Works and Days* concerning a wife emblematizes the poem's concern with 'works' and with 'days'. If the latter issue of seasons and times is addressed by the age at which a man can expect to marry and the girl can expect to be married, then 'works' is addressed by the poet's advice to 'teach' the young wife to accustom her to his habits and lifestyle. The poet passes on his own role as teacher to the audience that he has been instructing as a strategy for ensuring that the wealth of the household is preserved and increased, despite the addition of another member who potentially eats what she does not produce and in this manner threatens to destroy even the individual – the husband – who is responsible for the creation of wealth in the οἶκος.

Thus, the poet locates the representation of the wife within a discourse of commodification which regards her as a threat to the commonality of the οἶκος unless she is properly domesticated, that is, turned into part of the household's wealth and property. Indeed, for woman to be figured and accommodated as a possession appears to be the safest way of introducing her into the household. Hesiod instructs his reader to acquire a household, a woman *or* a wife, an ox, and a plough in order to ensure this individual's material security (405). Line 406 adds the qualification that the woman must be 'owned (κτητήν)' rather than wedded as her role is to follow the oxen (406), and it is uncertain whether the author actually states this or whether an ancient hand interpolated this line in order to follow through to their logical conclusion the implications regarding woman in the *Works and Days*.[19]

III

Where wifely didactics is concerned in the classical period, the Hesiodic paradigm continues to make its influence felt (although, as we shall see, not unquestioningly so). Inasmuch as Xenophon's *Oeconomicus* concerns the issues of production, material wealth and administration in the context of 'estate management', it is in some sense a fourth-century Athenian 'works and days'. In the dialogue (between Socrates and Ischomachus) within the dialogue (between Socrates and Critoboulus) which properly begins at 7.3, Socrates inquires whether the husband has educated (ἐπαίδευσας) his new wife so that she is able to run (cf. διοικεῖν) the household or whether she has come to him already knowledgeable in such matters (7.3–4). The philosopher thus prompts a discourse on wifely didactics, and permits his interlocutor to give an account of his role as 'teacher'.

At Socrates' invitation Ischomachus rehearses the conventions of the wifely didactic and the conventional rhetoric of economy that justifies it. He asks what his wife could possibly know as she comes into his household at the age of fourteen and having lived a very restricted existence in her parents' house, no doubt in keeping with the conventional gendering of the 'indoors' as the female sphere. Accordingly, the new wife's experience and knowledge must be limited as, while a young girl, she sees, hears and speaks as little as possible (7.4–6). The most that Ischomachus says he can expect as a husband is that his wife can spin wool into garments and assign the work of spinning to servants, but this apart, the most important thing that she should have learned is how to control her appetite (τὰ γε ἀμφὶ γαστέρα) (7.6). The husband at first implicitly inscribes his new bride within the misogynistic anxieties about the wife as the consuming, empty vessel in order to displace it with the image of her as the clean slate upon whom he will set down his teachings.

The husband's language simultaneously evokes and rejects the Semonidean taxonomy of beast-women when he declares that he began to instruct her when he perceived her to be sufficiently 'tame and domesticated (cf. ἐπεὶ ἤδη μοι χειροήθης ἦν καὶ ἐτετιθάσευτο)' (7.10). Yet unlike the various caricatures sketched in Semonides, poem 7, the tamed wife is the disciplined, non-consuming woman. Against and in contrast to the background of representations of the female presented by early Greek poetry, the wife is rather a productive member of the estate. If the gods permit, the wife will produce children who will assist the parents in their old age; she will engage in the biological (re)production that Hesiod privileged in the *Works and Days* so that children are now the outcome of, rather than the alternative to, marriage (7.12; also 7.19). The wife is to be 'moderate (cf. σωφρονεῖν, 7.14)' and Ischomachus understands σωφροσύνη to entail that both he and his wife act so that their wealth increases as much as possible through just means (7.15). Husband and wife now constitute a co-operative partnership, which divides responsibility for the greatest benefit of both involved (τὸ ζεῦγος . . . ὅτι ὠφελιμώτατον ᾖ αὐτῷ εἰς τὴν κοινωνίαν, 7.18–19).

Ischomachus' wife is now the protector of what others, and especially her husband, have produced. In a further invocation of archaic poetic image, she is to be the queen bee who resides in the hive to ensure the proper management of the οἶκος (7.17–18). Xenophon establishes the identity of the wife as such when he has the husband declare that he is at liberty to leave the estate as his wife is the trustworthy manager of the οἶκος (cf. αὐτὴ ἡ γυνή ἐστιν ἱκανὴ διοικεῖν, 7.3). The wife is the individual who now conserves, rather than devours, the resources of the estate. Her responsibility is to guard what the husband brings in from outside as the fruits of his ploughing, sowing, planting and herding as the resources of the estate (7.20–1). Ischomachus develops the comparison of the wife to the queen bee at 7.32–4 when he observes that god has made it the lot of the female to exercise herself at indoor matters: she is to ensure that the worker bees are not lazy, to assign tasks to those who must go out, and then to receive and store what is brought in until the time appointed for their use (7.33). Moreover, the queen bee rears her offspring, and when they have grown up, she sees that they start their own colony (7.34). Since the queen bee is paradigmatic for the wife, the latter likewise sends slaves out to work and assigns tasks to those who remain indoors to receive and to ration the household stores (7.35–6).

As a result of Ischomachus' didactic the household is radically reorganized so that the indoors becomes a space of production, or perhaps more precisely, a space which complements production. At 7.40 the husband remarks that if no one were to put away the gathered supplies, it would be as if he were putting water in a leaking jar (7.40). He invokes, in order to displace from his wife, the imagery of the empty vessel, which is central to the rhetoric of misogyny and which elsewhere signifies futility, as in the case of wretched souls such as the husband-murdering Danaids who carry water in leaky pots in the underworld (e.g. Plato *Gorgias* 493b and *Republic* 363de).[20]

Ischomachus puts forward the view that τάξις, that is 'order' or 'structure', is an important aspect of resource in that if poverty (πενία) consists in not being able to use what is requested, then lack (ἐνδεία) is all the more regrettable when one cannot retrieve what is requested (8.2). The ordering and structuring of resources and equipment within the household and on the estate in general are useful (εὔχρηστον) and fine, no less than a well-ordered chorus (8.3), a well-disciplined military campaign (8.4), an army in battle (7.5-7) and a Phoenician merchant ship (8.12-14) are.

τάξις is to a degree what the pedagogy of the κύριος enacts and achieves. This becomes apparent from the account of the training of the housekeeper (ταμίη), who has to learn to be well-disposed to the master and to the mistress (9.11). Indeed, it is the responsibility of the husband and the wife to educate this servant so that she increases the wealth of the household (καὶ τὸ προθυμεῖσθαι δὲ συναύξειν τὸν οἶκον ἐπαιδεύομεν αὐτήν, 9.12) and in this way, they *install* her in her place in the household (καὶ αὐτὴν δὲ ἐν ταύτῃ τῇ χώρᾳ κατετάττομεν, 9.13). The verb κατετάττομεν articulates the training of the housekeeper as a conscious act of 'ordering (τάξις)'. The fact that Ischomachus almost immediately switches back to recounting the education of his wife to Socrates proposes that the instruction of the wife and the housekeeper are in some sense co-extensive even if the wife also participates in the teaching of the former. Similarities exist between housekeeper and wife such that the former's role seems to duplicate and to complement the role of the wife to some degree. The housekeeper, like the wife, is someone who can control her appetites and has the capacity to be taught (cf. ἐδιδάσκομεν) (9.12). But if teaching puts the ταμίη in her proper place, then it presumably also puts the wife in her appropriate station if making her responsible for placing each item in the household in its proper place. And accordingly Sheila Murnaghan has argued that in the course of the dialogue Ischomachus' wife is assimilated to male space rather than granted her autonomy.[21]

Where the estate and its management are concerned, pedagogy is not a process of intellectual development so much as a mode of socialization into a communal role. After all scholars have made us aware that in classical Athens marriage is itself an aspect of and subordinate to civic relations and structures. Ischomachus' invocation of political example reinforces the idea that pedagogy is a mode of regulation and discipline of woman as a figure contained by the household. Cities write fine laws but also appoint νομοφύλακες to praise those who obey and to punish those who transgress. Likewise, as head of the household, the husband appoints the wife to ensure that order is kept, implying his own position as legislator (9.14). Ischomachus will later explain that instruction creates productive slaves by making them aware of the self-interest and personal advantage to them involved in being productive (esp. 13.9), or for that matter the good wife or housekeeper by making themselves likewise realize the benefits which accrue to them if they fulfil their roles properly.

In Ischomachus' world, one teaches and one learns less to gain knowledge and more to seek material gain and to maintain what one already has. Ischomachus concedes that governing is harder than farming but proceeds to draw an analogy between the principles of self-interest involved in both activities. He offers that education is similarly a strategy of political (self-)conservation, insisting upon the value of παιδεία to enable one to rule and to govern subordinates for the good of the commonality, provided that the ruler in training possesses a 'good nature (φύσις ἀγαθή)' and divine qualities (cf. 21.11–12; cf. *Cyropaedia*). The utilitarianism of the education of the wife is echoed by Aristotle, who declares that as the household (οἰκία) is part of the city, one must educate (παιδεύειν) its members, namely children and wives, so that they are respectable (τὸ τοὺς παῖδας εἶναι σπουδαίους καὶ τὰς γυναῖκας σπουδαίας) and so that in turn the city may also be respectable (*Politics* 1.1260b15–18).

Socrates' interlocutor casts himself as the ideal governor of the οἶκος, where this is to be regarded as a political microcosm. The disciplinary aspect of his pseudo-political role is established by his recalling how he once came upon his wife wearing make-up and high-heeled shoes which made her appear taller than she actually was (10.2–3). He tells the philosopher how he chastised her for falsifying her appearance and how he insisted upon his love for her as she really is (10.4–8). We are to perceive the falsifying wife as having her metaphorical counterpart in the deceptive 'mistresses' (cf. ἀπατηλαί τινες δέσποιναι), namely gambling, whoring, drunkenness and other such extravagances, which purport to be pleasures but actually ruin men by leading them to squander their estates (1.18–22). This perhaps is an allusion to the 'other', historical (?) wife of Ischomachus – Chrysilla, who sleeps with her daughter's husband, Callias, the extravagant host of the drinking party portrayed in the *Symposium*,[22] and leads her daughter to attempt suicide (Andocides *Or.* 124–6).[23] But this 'other' wife is perhaps one who should be brought into the foreground. At section 124 of *On the Mysteries* Andocides tells his audience that Callias married a daughter of Ischomachus and within the year made her mother, namely the wife of Ischomachus, his mistress. Furthermore, he lived with them both and kept them both in his house.[24] Strauss may have tried to deny that Andocides' Ischomachus is the same individual as the Ischomachus of Xenophon's *Oeconomicus*;[25] however, he is undermining himself by actually denying the big irony in the work that would have been clear to the Athenians. Certainly, Ischomachus has not taught his wife well and perhaps the wife is after all an unteachable liability, possibly showing the Hesiodic paradigm of woman to be after all accurate. Or it might be the case that Ischomachus' pedagogy has driven Chrysilla to the bed of

Callias. She is anything but the faithful wife; rather a lustful opportunist who runs after her daughter's extremely wealthy (at least at the time) husband.

Xenophon's Ischomachus draws a poignant analogy between his wife's use of cosmetics and his own hypothetical exaggeration of his wealth to make himself more attractive (10.3). What this example suggests is that true wealth is actual wealth, rather than the aura of wealth. In a passage which to some degree parallels the disquisition on appearance and reality between the son Cyrus and the father Cambyses in the *Cyropaedia* (1.6.22-3), the wife asks how she might actually (ἐν ὄντι) be beautiful rather than merely appear to be so and Ischomachus counsels her to be active as befits the mistress of an οἶκος. She is thus to weave, to instruct others in what she knows best, to supervise the baker and the housekeeper as the latter measures provisions and generally to oversee the running of the household. Beyond her supervisory role, the wife is herself to be active and productive. She is to knead bread, to shake, and fold clothes lest others perceive her to be the sort of woman who wears make-up and deceives (10.11-13).

IV

Where the wife is concerned, the husband invokes the pedagogy of archaic poetry, rehearsing the voice of classical Athens' traditional teachers. Yet rather than reaffirming this didactic, the *Oeconomicus* is a case in point of the philosopher attempting to displace the poet (which we shall also see to be the case where the figure of the poet Simonides is concerned in the *Hiero*). There are suggestions that Socrates' invitation to Ischomachus to relate how he instructed his wife is ironically staged. Socrates converses with Ischomachus as himself a successful practitioner of wifely didactic. In another Socratic work, the *Symposium*, the Xenophontic Socrates remarks that neither a child (παῖς) nor a woman is worse than a man, except that both lack knowledge (γνώμη) and strength. The philosopher counsels those at the drinking party who have a wife to take courage and to instruct (cf. διδασκέτω) her to do with knowledge whatever he wishes her to (Xen. *Symposium* 2.9-10). Antisthenes responds to the advice by noting that Socrates has not bothered to educate his own wife Xanthippe (οὐ καὶ σὺ παιδεύεις Ξανθίππην), the most difficult of all wives who have been and who will be. The philosopher responds that just as an owner of horses chooses a high-spirited animal rather than a docile one because he believes he can handle it, so he has a difficult wife because he thinks he can handle her. Thus Socrates' prompting of the account of wifely didactics in the embedded dialogue, 'tell me what you first began to teach her' (τί πρῶτον διδάσκειν ἤρχου αὐτήν, διηγοῦ μοι, 7.9) is to be regarded as scene-setting for the philosopher's own larger pedagogy in the *Oeconomicus*, namely that one does not need to train and subdue other people, especially one's wife. The irony here is that Socrates' teaching rejects the need for pedagogy.

Even regardless of Socrates' implicit identity as practitioner of wifely didactic *par excellence*, there is a sense in which Ischomachus' teaching is superfluous as far as the economy of didactic discourse is concerned – and this is whether we believe the Andocidean portrait of the wife as the abominable Chrysilla or we hold to Ischomachus' depiction of his wife. Gini argues for an independent intelligence for the latter,[26] and closer inspection suggests that the wife is anything but an empty vessel to be filled with her husband's teachings or with the resources of the οἶκος. Indeed, the husband's teaching actually palimpsests prior teachings, retracing, for instance, his mother-in-law's earlier instruction to her daughter to be moderate (cf. 7.14–15). At 9.1 the husband recalls that his wife promised to pay heed to all his instructions, discovering some 'abundance out of an unmanageable situation' (ἐξ ἀμηψανίας εὐπορίαν τινὰ ηὑρηκυῖα) and that she then proceeded to ask him to arrange affairs as he had described as quickly as possible (ὡς τάχιστα ἧπερ ἔλεγον διατάξαι). But Xenophon opens the husband's role in the relationship to qualification, for the wife's comments may also be read as an attempt to make her husband a more effective, that is, less pedantic, teacher as she implicitly turns his own teaching back onto himself.[27] When she directs him to order (διατάξαι) – the τάξις-compound is conspicuous – that is to discipline, the household as rapidly as possible in accordance with his own understanding of order, she proposes that the non-negotiability of the household (cf. ἐξ ἀμηχανίας) might lie above all in the husband's wordiness. It is possible to read the wife as troubling the fixity of the role of teacher upon which Ischomachus insists for himself through the discussion with the wife and even with the philosopher Socrates (cf. 17.6).

After all, the husband's pedagogical discourse on order in the household unconsciously overwrites itself through a rhetoric of excess and ἀταξία, although the scholarly attention given to this section of the *Oeconomicus* has meant that it has become a paradigm for a husband's discourse in classical antiquity. Ischomachus' account of the conservation of material resources is a discourse of plenitude and excess in marked contrast to the light and deft style which ancient and modern scholars ascribe to Xenophontic dialogue.[28] In his *Characters* (3) Theophrastus describes idle chatter (ἀδολεσχία) as a narrative of long and undirected discourse (διήγησις λόγων μακρῶν καὶ ἀπροβουλεύτων, 3.1), as when a man tells someone he does not know how fine his wife is, what he dreamt the previous night, what he had for dinner, how cheap wheat is in the marketplace, that there are many foreigners in town and so on (3.2–3). The interchange between Socrates and Ischomachus fits Theophrastus' characterization of idle chatter. Two barely acquainted individuals (cf. 6.17) converse, with one of the interlocutors lauding at great length the wife he believes he has trained well in order to praise himself indirectly and to get himself praised by another (but to no avail with Socrates). The conversation is indeed a case of λογοὶ μακροί, for the husband's account of his training of his wife is far from restrained. Ischomachus' account of what constitutes household order is overindulgent: it proliferates discourse with gratuitous enumeration and analogy. The individual components of an army on campaign exemplify the ordered οἶκος despite their irrelevance to the domestic sphere: ὄνος ὁμου, ὁπλίτης, σκευοφόρος, ψιλός, ἱππεύς, ἅμαξα (8.4). But the inappropriateness of the examples is further extended at 8.6:

τίς μὲν γὰρ οὐκ ἂν φίλος ἡδέως θεάσαιτο ὁπλίτας πολλοὺς ἐν τάξει πορευομένους. τίς δ᾽ οὐκ ἂν θαυμάσειεν ἱππέας κατὰ τάξεις ἐλαύνοντας, τίς δὲ οὐκ ἂν πολέμιος φοβοθείη ἰδὼν διηυκρινημένον, ὁπλίτας, ἱππέας, πελταστάς, τοξότας, σφενδονήτας, καὶ τοῖς ἄρχοθσι τεταγμένως ἑπομένους;

Which friend would not gladly view many hoplites marching in formation? who would not marvel at cavalry men charging in order? what enemy would not fear, seeing hoplites, cavalry men, shield-bearers, bowmen, and sling-bearers in divisions and following their leaders in an orderly manner?

Then, this is followed in turn by Ischomachus' pedantic description of the orderly trireme:

Καὶ τριήρης δέ τοι ἡ σεασαγμένη ἀνθρώπων διὰ τί ἄλλο φοβερόν ἐστι πολεμίοις ἢ φίλοις ἀξιοθέατον ἢ ὅτι ταχὺ πλεῖ; Διὰ τί δὲ ἄλλο ἄλυποι ἀλλήλοις εἰσιν οἱ ἐμπλέοντες ἢ διότι ἐν τάξει μὲν κάθηνται, ἐν τάξει δὲ προνεύουσιν, ἐν τάξει δ᾽ ἀναπίπτουσιν, ἐν τάξει δ᾽ ἐμβαίνουσι καὶ ἐκβαίνουσιν; ἡ δ᾽ ἀταξία ὅμοιόν τί μοι δοκεῖ εἶναι οἷονπερ εἰ γεωργὸς ὁμοῦ ἐμβάλοι κριθὰς καὶ πυροὺς καὶ ὄσπρια, κἄπειτα, ὁπότε δέοι ἢ μάζης ἢ ἄρτου ἢ ὄψου, διαλέγειν δέοι, αὐτῷ ἀντὶ τοῦ λαβόντα διηυκρινηένοις χρῆσθαι (8.8–9)

Isn't a trireme laden with men frightening to the enemy and wondrous to regard as far as friends are concerned for no other reason than that it sails quickly? For what other reason do sailors not get in each other's way than that they sit in order, lean forward in order, lead back in order, embark and disembark in order?

> I think that disorder resembles a farmer throwing together barley, wheat, and pulse, and then, when there is need for a barley-cake, bread, or prepared food, having to pick out instead of taking for use the discriminated [grains].

Anaphora or parallelism (ἐν τάξει . . . ἐν τάξει . . . ἐν τάξε . . . ἐν τάξει . . .) on the one hand appears to discipline and structure the husband's language, but on the other hand it also highlights his verbosity. Furthermore, embedded within this analogy of order is a further analogy of disorder, the image of grains indiscriminately mixed together in a large bin by a farmer. Within this inset image of chaos the husband enumerates the various grains which have been mingled, κριθὰς καὶ πυροὺς καὶ ὄσπρια, and the foods that they might be used to make, δέοι ἢ μάζης ἢ ἄρτου ἢ ὄψου. If Sappho 16 shows that military images might be invoked to elaborate insights into the life of women, the husband, however, directs the similes at 8.6 and 8.8–9 through and to the viewpoint of his fellow men: cf. τίς . . . φίλος . . . τίς . . . τίς . . . πολέμιος (8.6), φοβερόν ἐστι πολεμίοις ἢ φίλοις ἀξιοθέατον (8.8), and εἰ γεωργὸς ὁμοῦ ἐμβάλοι (8.9). While Ischomachus is now speaking to Socrates, the pedagogy itself is explicitly gendered male, rendered extraneous to the wife's own position.

Furthermore, Ischomachus' instructions concerning the ordering and disciplining of goods *within* the οἶκος are far from succinct. The husband states the general principle that household equipment should be easy to find and that everything should be suitable and after this goes away: footwear, cloaks, bedding, bronze wear, various vessels for eating and drinking (8.19). In the following the account of the gendered division of the οἶκος into male and female quarters provides the husband with the opportunity to multiply further the classification of household equipment, for he proceeds to distinguish between male clothing for festive occasions and for war, bedding for the male and female quarters, likewise different types of shoes (9.4–5). Beyond this, he declares to the wife the various types (φυλάς) of weaponry, basketry, kitchenware, tableware, toilet equipment, kneading troughs and tableware.

I suggest that the outer discussion with Socrates reinforces the superfluity of the husband's pedagogy in order to erode the latter's discursive authority. Socrates in effect tells Ischomachus to shut up at 11.1 when he declares that he has now heard enough (ἱκανῶς) about the wife's labours in the household, and following 11.1 the philosopher takes control of the discussion, implicitly placing under scrutiny, or at least qualifying, Ischomachus' account and evaluation of his relationship with his wife. He entices his interlocutor to turn from his account of wifely didactics to a justification of his reputation as a gentleman (καλὸς καγαθός), indeed to the very issue which prompted the reporting of the inner dialogue (11.1; cf. 6.17 and 7.2–3). It is also here that Socrates invokes εἰρωνεία, deliberate self-debasement, as the lure to draw his interlocutor into further discussion. He declares his readiness to learn in full (cf. καθαμάθων, 11.2) and insists upon his own reputation as a chatterer (ἀδολεσχεῖν τε δοκῶ εἶναι), as a fool (cf. ἀνοητότατον δοκοῦν) and as a poor man (cf. πένης) (11.3). Yet this account of how others perceive him is a strategy for the reader to distinguish between appearance/seeming and reality. Socrates may *seem* to prattle, to be foolish and to be resourceless, but the grammatical construction δοκῶ plus the infinitive suggests that appearance may not be reality.[29] He proceeds to insist upon the discrepancy between what *seems* to be the case and what *is*. He invokes the example of a horse, which cannot own anything material as an animal but which can be good by virtue of its soul (ψυχή), to make a distinction between *having* and *being* (11.5). He elaborates the point made earlier in the *Oeconomicus* to Critobulus that *using*, rather than merely *having*, an object constitutes wealth (χρῆμα) (1.8ff.). Sheer materialism, which is after all Ischomachus' main concern, is being called into question as a goal of human life.

Socrates' self-depreciation is the preface to his devaluation of his interlocutor as καλὸς καγαθός, a phrase which Pomeroy glosses as '[a] decent gentleman' and observes of it that Xenophon generally uses it as a term of commendation.[30] My reading of the *Oeconomicus* suggests that 'gentleman' is a far more negotiable and ambivalent term here. After all, when Ischomachus uses καλὸς καγαθός as a description for his faithful slaves at 14.9–10, he allows for two distinct interpretations: either that he respects the humanity of slaves, or that he inadvertently permits the term 'gentleman' to be debased.[31] The staging of the discourse with Socrates as a critical and subversive presence favours the second option, so that by extending the term 'gentleman' to non-citizens he not only blatantly disregards the connotations of elite social class, which are the *sine qua non* of καλὸς καγαθός, and he also interrogates the principle of political τάξις, which underlies his wifely didactics. In some sense Ischomachus is the very figure who destabilizes the meaning of καλὸς κἀγαθός. Socrates' interlocutor admits that, while the philosopher may think he is called a καλὸς κἀγαθός by many people and while he implies that this is a sign of his good fortune, he is nonetheless the subject of numerous litigations which are to be expected for someone with his considerable wealth and luxurious lifestyle.[32]

Certainly, the framing discussion with Critobulus at 2.5–6 has shown that material wealth has its liabilities: the rich are summoned to court by envious sycophants, are responsible for undertaking numerous taxes, i.e. liturgies, for the benefit of the community, and have to maintain political allies by staging lavish entertainments.[33] Material wealth consumes itself within the context of the democratic city and Ischomachus' pedagogy exacerbates the predicament by recreating the actual structure of the πόλις within the οἶκος, even as it seeks to reproduce the ideal city. Taken to its logical conclusion this line of argument proposes the pointlessness of wealth creation through household economy. And after all, Ischomachus paints a picture of social class both victimized by and responsible for the relentless legal proceedings that fall under the category of behaviour known as πολυπραγμοσύνη, that is political meddling, to conservative authors of fifth and fourth century Athens (11.21–5).[34] He admits that even within his own household he has paid out numerous fines at the hands of his wife, whom he has, as Pomeroy observes, appointed as the νομοφύλαξ, the disciplinarian, of the house (11.25).[35] Moreover, there is evidence external to the work which suggests that a/the historical Ischomachus was part of classical Athens' litigious culture. The speaker of Lysias 19 observes that the aura of wealth may be deceptive, and that after they have died, many individuals are found to have been poorer than anticipated. An Ischomachus is named along with Stephanus, Nicias, Miceratus, Callias, Cleophon, Diotimus and Alcibiades as individuals who ended their lives in such circumstances (19.45–52). Moreover, Pierre Chantraine cites Athenaeus 12.537 as a text which informs us that a certain 'Ischomachus' was ruined by parasites.[36] Ischomachus as καλὸς καγαθός is thus an individual whose own identity as such renders him vulnerable to the envy and to the destructive activity of his jealous rivals and enemies. It would appear that neither husband nor wife (given the suggestions of who the historical wife actually was) are quite who they initially appear to be to the audience of the *Oeconomicus*, nor do they quite lead the life to which they lay claim.

Robert Wellman seeks to prove that the *Oeconomicus* is truly Socratic by discovering anamneutic discourse on the part of the philosopher within the dialogue, but I argue that it is not necessary to discover this to see the Socratic quality of the dialogue.[37] Beyond dismantling the 'economy' of Ischomachus' discourse, Socrates also questions the husband's identity as teacher. The latter lapses into *Works and Days*-mode at 17.3–4, identifying the seasons suitable for particular sorts of agricultural activity, but his assumption of this poetic pedagogy is inappropriate. The husband misappropriates a text originally directed to a recalcitrant student, Perses, in speaking to Socrates and the wife, who are hardly problem pupils. Socrates responds by observing that the farmer should remove the weeds from the garden just as one might remove the inactive drones from the hive, and he goes on to note that Ischomachus' (Hesiodic) metaphors (αἱ εἰκόνες) generally have the effect of stirring up anger against the elements that impede the creation of wealth (17.15). The husband uses Hesiodic analogies, which equate women with the male drones and men with the female worker bees to insist upon the resourcelessness of the female, but the preceding dialogue with Socrates shows him to be seriously mistaken. After all, it is the earth, conspicuously gendered as female, which provides all resources (20.13–14), while the wife belies her assumed unknowingness with her patient and humouring responses to her husband's didactic.

Earlier on in the dialogue at 3.14 Socrates had suggested that he would introduce Aspasia to Ischomachus so that she can explain how good wives have trained themselves to be such; he does not do so, perhaps in recognition of his interlocutor's inability to learn. Aspasia is a significant and poignant figure in the *Oeconomicus*. She was an immigrant to classical Athens from Turkey and became the lover and partner of the general Pericles. Apparently, Aspasia's house became a centre of intellect at Athens, attracting to it writers and thinkers including Socrates himself, and Aspasia herself was known for being a person who engaged in discussions and who dispensed advice.[38] This woman thus demonstrates the possibility of an alternative role for the female sex in Athenian society: she was clever and connected to political power at Athens through her relationship with Pericles. She was influential in and well-integrated into her new community despite being an outsider. Aspasia might have provided a model for a more insightful Ischomachus: she is a symbol for the wife as someone who enters a new community, i.e. his household, and brings to it her skills and abilities. Aspasia is thus a figure who shows up the irony of the husband and his view of women in the *Oeconomicus*.

I find myself agreeing with Stevens and Strauss in seeing Ischomachus as the superfluous teacher who merely socializes his pupils into a productivity which does not necessarily result in real wealth.[39] He is the husband-farmer who does not recognize the value of the resources he already has – his wife – nor does he know where to put his discursive energies and resources. What particularly disclose this lack of awareness are the roles he assigns both to himself and to the philosopher within the dialogue. The husband may name Socrates as his pupil in the matter of estate management (17.6); however, the philosopher disturbs this identity when he queries whether asking questions is a method of teaching that elicits previously unrecognized answers and knowledge from the respondent (19.15). Socrates' question serves several functions. Where Ischomachus is concerned, it constitutes a concession that the former has elicited from his interlocutor knowledge about agriculture which he did not realize he had until being questioned (cf. 18.9). But it also makes the point that, despite the husband's insistence on their roles, Socrates cannot simply be the 'student' in this discussion for he too poses questions, in particular this question about pedagogical method, which points to the Platonic theory of knowledge as a 'recollection' of the already-known and to the status of the 'teacher' as a catalyst for learning.[40]

The observation about the role of questions in didactic discourse, however, is not so much addressed to the issue of 'recollection' as to whether Ischomachus' pedagogy is necessary. Socrates uses the question he poses at 19.15 as the pretext for observing that his gentleman-interlocutor has persuaded (ἀναπείθεις/ ἀνέπεισας) him of his ability to farm despite the fact that no one has taught (ἐδίδαξέ) him this activity (19.15–16). The philosopher succeeds in getting Ischomachus to declare that farming is an activity which itself teaches (διδάσκει) through trial and error (19.18–19) and later, to concede that what makes a good farmer – and for that matter anyone – good at what they do is not the amount of knowledge they possess but rather experience (ἐπιμελεῖται) (20.4). According to the husband, it is after all the earth *herself* (ἡ γῆ) – Ischomachus personifies the earth as female – which will teach what the farmer should plant and accordingly, provides the truest test of whether the farmer is diligent or lazy (20.13–14). As John Stevens has persuasively argued, the philosopher's interlocutor is the crude materialist who pursued a chrematistic policy without any regard for virtue or moral consideration, which is the Socratic imperative.[41] Socrates' non-materialistic outlook perhaps can only be the consequence of the wealthy elite member of society who realizes that he actually has everything he needs.

Socrates shows up the husband to be the babbling fool whose own discourse defeats its purpose in ensuring the wealth of the estate, and who, in addition to enacting ἀδολεσχία, perhaps also prefigures Theophrastus' loquacious man (ὁ λάλων), who insists that he knows better than anyone else and who goes into schools and gymnasia to chatter at the teachers and trainers such that children are prevented from learning (*Characters* 7.2 and 5).

V

Eve Cantarella reads the Xenophontic Socrates as one who is well-disposed to women because he interrogates women's biological difference as the basis for her supposed inferiority with respect to men (again cf. *Symposium* 2.8–9).[42] Similarly, Murnaghan understands Socrates' exclamation that the wife must have a 'masculine intellect (ἀνδρικήν . . . τὴν διάνοιαν)' (10.1) to efface gender difference, but in such a way that the husband-Xenophon subordinates the wife to his masculine concerns.[43] It is of course tempting to hypostasize Socratic discourse in the dialogue, particularly as the philosopher in other representations has been shown as learning from a woman, who taught him about the resources of feminine deficiency (i.e. Diotima in Plato's *Symposium*).[44]

My interpretation leads me rather to sever the links between the bad teacher and the author so that the text is less misogynist.[45] So wrapped up in this world of appearances is he that the interlocutor cannot be taught or learn from the philosopher. In this text, Ischomachus purports control over his household whereas in reality he does not have as much authority as he thinks and is misguided in its management. Socrates attempts to make Ischomachus aware of his shortcomings but to no avail. Once Ischomachus' voice is distinguished from Xenophon's, the author together with the philosopher re-authors the traditional, misogynistic wifely didactic and its unnegotiable essentialisms, which resolutely gender productivity as male and unproductivity as female. I want to insist upon the status of *Oeconomicus* as *Socratic dialogue*, one in which Xenophon assumes the role of philosopher's spokesperson in order to co-produce a Socratic refutation (ἔλεγχος) of what the psychoanalyst Alice Miller might have termed a 'poisonous pedagogy'.[46] If the *Oeconomicus* cannot be simplistically a misogynist's text or a pro-woman/proto-feminist text, it is, nonetheless, a dialogue where the issue of household resource is ironically (because of the gap of knowledge between Socrates and the husband) articulated in terms of pedagogical resource.

Part Two

Xenophon on Athens

5

The Critique of the Sophists in *On Hunting*

I

The authorship of *On Hunting* has been in some doubt. Vivienne Gray observes that while its authorship was accepted as Xenophon's in antiquity, it was cast into doubt in the nineteenth century.[1] To illustrate the controversy, we have Arrian, an author who flourished in the 2nd century CE and who also wrote a work on hunting, regarding it as genuine (*Cynegeticus* 1.1–3),[2] while Radermacher (1867–1952) rejected Xenophon's authorship and regarded it as a composition of the third century[3] and Norden (1868–1941) located it as a work of the second century.[4] More recently, R. Nickel denied that *On Hunting* was a work written by Xenophon,[5] against Werner Jaeger, who had treated the work as authentic.[6]

This chapter sees *On Hunting* as a work by Xenophon, which is wholly unified and which plays a game with its audience that is entirely characteristic of the author. It is one of four works including *Hipparchicus* (*The Skilled Cavalry Commander*), *Peri Hippikês* (*On Horsemanship*) and the *Oeconomicus* (*On Household Management*), which concern themselves with the arts that are associated with the wealthy householder of classical Athens. This text ostensibly and in particular extols the art of hunting, and hunting is indeed an art, as this work seeks to demonstrate to the reader. The work lays out what is entailed in hunting in a very matter of fact manner but this is not to suggest that it is a boring or dull text. *On Hunting* is offset by a beginning and ending, which quite radically qualify the material in the central body of the work. The title of my chapter suggests that the ending of the work, which contains the critique of the sophists, constitutes the author's social criticism of his fourth-century environment.

II

Let me begin with something of a paraphrase of the work. *On Hunting* begins with a mythical excursus which seeks to locate the origins of hunting in the age of gods and heroes. Hunting is presented as an invention of the gods Apollo and Artemis, who then give it to Cheiron to use (1.1). Cheiron is a centaur, a creature that is half horse half man, and so, a being who mediates between the animal and human world. Cheiron is a figure who therefore has a foot in both the world of the hunter and the hunted. He is a teacher and becomes the instructor and tutor of some notable Greek youths. He teaches hunting to Cephalus, Asclepius, Meilanion, Nestor, Amphiaraus, Peleus, Telamon, Meleager, Theseus, Hippolytus, Palamedes, Odysseus, Menestheus, Diomedes, Castor, Polydeuces, Machaon, Podaleirius, Antilochus, Aeneas and Achilles, and his instruction is commendable. We are told that the gods honoured each of these heroes in turn, implying that Cheiron had a role in their greatness (1.2).

The introduction moves away from directly addressing hunting after this impressive list of Cheiron's pupils into a vaguer mythological narrative. Xenophon then goes on to state that Zeus and Cheiron were brothers, born of the same father, namely Cronos (1.4). The author then returns to stating the achievements of each of Cheiron's pupils, which are directly or more indirectly due to hunting. Among those less clearly influenced by the teaching in hunting are Cephalus, who was carried away by a goddess (1.5), Asclepius, who achieved fame as a healer and became a god amongst men, and Meilanion, who won the hand of Atalanta (1.7), and Amphiarus, who excelled in battle at Thebes to such a degree that Peleus wanted to give him Thetis in marriage and to celebrate their wedding in Cheiron's home (1.8). Next Xenophon celebrates Telamon, who married Periboeia and received gifts from Heracles after the capture of Troy (1.9). Meleager won many honours and Theseus slew many enemies of Greece with the result that he continues to be admired (1.10). Hippolytus was honoured by Artemis and considered blessed in his life while Palamedes was known for his wisdom (1.11). Menestheus paid attention to hunting, worked hard and was considered superior in the art of war, and he was acknowledged by his contemporaries (1.1.2). Odysseus and Diomedes are celebrated for their role in capturing Troy, while Castor and Polydeuces, the twins, are immortal through the attention they paid to hunting, the skill which they learned from Cheiron (1.13). Machaon and Podaleirus, also trained to hunt, proved themselves good men in crafts, reasoning and war. Antilochus gave his life for his father (1.14). Aeneas is renowned for saving the gods of his parents' family and became known for piety (1.15). Finally, Achilles, who was also instructed in hunting, is known amongst later generations (1.16).

Xenophon has taken the qualities and achievements for which these heroes are best known and made it appear that they are due to the education in hunting that they received from Cheiron. Yet perhaps it is the case that, in fact, the author has simply juxtaposed facts which make them appear to owe their skills to the art of hunting. Cause and effect are actually tenuous in this first chapter of *On Hunting*; they are rather a product of narrative structure. Xenophon gives his reader a list of all the great heroes of Athenian antiquity and somewhat tenuously credits their achievements and fame to the art of hunting. This skill, which these heroes learned from Cheiron, made them who they were. Hunting has made Greece the great nation it is today (1.17) and thus, Xenophon urges the young not to neglect this aspect of their education or for that matter, any part of their education. The writer advises his readers to pursue a traditional and aristocratic model of education – personalized instruction from a master in his subject to the person instructed – even though they may be living in a city where hunting is less practical and much less needed, as would have been the case in fourth-century Athens.

The first chapter of *On Hunting* is written in a mythical style. It is concerned with the age of gods and heroes. It evokes an old-fashioned educational structure: the training of youths by an elder known for his knowledge and/or skill, here Cheiron. But the whole topic of hunting as a subject for study for modern elite Athenian youth is strange and at best, anachronistic. Hunting wild animals for food is a skill for the estate holder. The Athens of the fourth century is rather a world where rhetoric and speechmaking would seem to be much more central to the success – his wealth and political standing–of an individual in society.

III

The next section of *On Hunting* begins the long middle section on how the young man should go about learning the skill of hunting. It is clearly written in Xenophon's voice and one might ask if the author has assumed the role of Cheiron for fourth-century youth? I suggest that Xenophon indeed becomes a latter-day Cheiron inasmuch as the role of teacher was key to what he was doing as a writer: one of the roles of fourth-century prose was to instruct the audience. Cheiron did not teach everyone but only those youths of some distinction due to their ancestry and family wealth, and likewise, Xenophon is somewhat aristocratic in his focus. He intends for youths – specifically those who belong to the elite class – to take up hunting when they are out of boyhood and then, if they have further means, to pursue other branches of education. The money that the youth has for his education is to be spent as benefits him most and if money is lacking, then the youth must supply the enthusiasm for what he needs to learn (2.1). In this respect Xenophon seems rather less elitist than Isocrates, who advocates learning philosophy, i.e. rhetoric, only for those who have means and sufficient leisure (ἱκανὸν κεκτημένους καὶ σχολὴν ἄγειν, *Antidosis* 304) – means are necessary for the second condition. The implication is that banausic skills are to be learned by those who are poorer or without means. Isocrates' elitism is also expressed at 7.43–4, which assigns the sons of the less affluent to various different occupations which keep them in less prominent roles to ensure that they do not turn to mischief.

That hunting is an activity which requires some wealth is made apparent in the second chapter of the work. It requires equipment and other personnel. Xenophon declares that he will outline the necessary outfit for the hunter at 2.2 and proceeds to describe some of the other things required for this pursuit (2.3). He also details what is required for the net-keeper – he should be interested in hunting, speak Greek, be about twenty, and be strong and agile – so that hunting is an activity that requires other personnel (2.3). Hunting is not as expensive as horsemanship, which requires one to have even more substantial wealth (cf. οἱ τοῖς χρήμάσι τε ἱκανώτατοι καὶ τῆς πόλεως οὐκ ἐλάχιστον μετέχοντες) so that he can keep the horse and a groom (*On the Art of Horsemanship* 2.1), but it suggests that Xenophon has a bias towards the training of the wealthier sectors of his society. The remainder of the chapter concerns itself with the nets required by the hunter. They should be made of Phasian, i.e. Colchian or Carthaginian flax and should have a certain number of threads depending on their exact function in the hunt, be it purse, net or road net. Everything – including nets, equipment for the journey and bill-hooks – is to be placed in a calf-skin bag (2.9).

Chapter 3 concerns itself with the type of dogs needed for the hunt. They should be Castorian or Vulpine (3.1), as the majority of other dogs are inferior and not physically up to the rigours of the hunt or else they are unsightly. Xenophon notes that dogs vary in behaviour amongst themselves even if they are of the same breed and will pursue their prey either more or less diligently. Chapter 4 continues with the matter of the dogs on the hunt. The author is concerned with the physical form of the hounds and with their diligence in tracking the game. Xenophon seems to think that the hunt is for the sake of catching hares (4.5). One should take one's hounds to the mountains often as it is easier to track hare in mountainous regions than on cultivated lands (4.10). It seems that the person learning to hunt does indeed have wealth if he is to keep hounds, for although they are by no means as expensive as horses, it still costs money to feed them and it is necessary to have property on which to keep them.

Chapter 5 is focused on the hare itself. Xenophon comments on when its scent is detectable to the hounds and how it is detectable (5.1–7). The author continues to describe the behaviour of the hare, noting that she will find a resting place under objects (5.8) and observing that she will reproduce very readily (5.13). The hare runs at different speeds on different terrain, fastest in the mountains and less speedily on the plains and in the marshes (5.17). There are two types of hare, one large and dark brown, the other chestnut and to be found in the islands (5.22–26). The hare does not see very well (5.27); she runs well and is very agile (5.28–31); and in his search for her the hunter is to avoid growing crops, pools and streams (5.35).

The following chapter, 6, returns to discussion of the hounds. Xenophon talks about the collars, leashes and body straps, ensuring that they should not be abrasive for the dog (6.1). Hounds should not hunt when taken off their feed (6.2) and they should not be allowed to track foxes (6.3). The author then turns to the net-keeper, who must wear light clothing when hunting and who must put purse-nets where the hare is most likely to hide (6.5). The huntsman is also to wear light clothing and to track his hare with a cudgel in his hand. He will bring hounds close to where he thinks the hare is and catch the animal, shouting encouragement and congratulations to his dogs (6.11–18). There may be a chase involved but the hare is envisaged as being caught by the hunter on the hunt or in nets (6.26).

Chapter 7 is devoted to the breeding of the hounds with attention given the time periods required for gestation and their feeding on milk (7.1–5). Xenophon lists a series of ideal names for the hounds; short names so that they can be called easily (7.6). The young hounds are to be trained at chasing hares (7.7–11). The next chapter, chapter 8, advocates hunting hare on a snow-covered ground, but not when it is snowing too heavily (8.1). The cold also can freeze the noses of hounds (8.2).

Chapter 9 moves on to deal with hunting animals other than hare, namely fawn and deer. One is to use a larger hound – the Indian hound – for such prey. Xenophon advises hunting the deer in the spring when they are newly born (9.1–2). Slightly larger deer trample on the hounds when they are chased by them (9.8–10). He next discusses caltrops, which are traps to be set for deer in the mountains (9.11ff.). The next chapter deals with the hunting of boars, an enterprise which might use Indian, Cretan, Locrian and Laconian hounds, boar nets, javelins, spears and caltrops (10.1). Xenophon describes the boar nets (10.2) and the javelins (10.3). He gives an account of what an encounter with a boar might be like, with the creature possibly running into nets and spears and javelins being thrown at it (10.9–16). Boars are strong animals and the huntsman must not find himself under one (10.18). Catching boars is actually not so different from catching deer with spears (10.23).

Chapter 11 is a brief excursus on other creatures which are hunted, namely lions, leopards, lynxes, panthers, bears and other animals. These creatures may be poisoned with aconite (11.2) or they may be trapped in pits which have been dug for this purpose (11.4).

Chapter 12 is a summary of the benefits of hunting to the young man who undertakes and studies it. This section of the work seems to provide an all-important raison-d'être for hunting. It acknowledges that hunting keeps one healthy and is a good preparation for war, as we shall learn it is in the *Cyropaedia* (12.1). It accustoms one to travelling long distances while bearing arms and it gets one used to sleeping on hard beds (12.2). As it is an important aspect of the hunt to follow orders while pursuing an animal, hunting also enables one to follow orders more readily on campaign. Thus, when those who have hunted go on campaign, they will be able to attack the enemy more readily (12.3). It would seem that hunting is envisaged as a rehearsal for warfare. Furthermore, as a consequence of hunting, the men will be able to make advances over rough terrain even though their allies have been routed (12.5).

Later in this chapter Xenophon feels compelled to answer those individuals who criticize hunting. Some say that those involved in sports of this nature neglect affairs of the city and of the home (12.10). The author declares that these people are envious and that by their words and actions they bring diseases, loss and death upon their loved ones (12.13). After his criticism of the envious, Xenophon extols a good education, which the reader is to understand as including hunting. A good education enables men to observe the laws and talk and hear of righteousness (12.14). He goes on to say that those who undertake toil and labour for the sake of a good education will seek the safety of the city, while those who do their best to avoid it and live by pleasure are evil (12.15). He returns to praise the companions of Cheiron, who learned hunting among other things at 12.18. The final part of the chapter is an encomium of virtue and an exhortation to follow her (12.19–21).

IV

On Hunting appears to be a how-to text. Xenophon instructs his audience on how to hunt hares, deer and boars, and tells them to bear in mind that the care of dogs is paramount. He offers a justification for these activities. Hunting is part of a good education, and a good education sustains the Greek city-state. For Steven Johnstone, hunting takes away the elite competitiveness between aristocrats and redirects it towards animals, permitting the youths to get on better with one another.[7] Johnstone sees the aristocratic youth thereby becoming nobler.[8] The introductory section to the work, chapter 1, appears to uphold this view of the work by demonstrating that it was an activity undertaken by the Greek heroes under the instruction of the famous teacher Cheiron. The work might have ended with the final mention of Cheiron at 12.18 because this would have provided a neat ring composition, but there is one more chapter which unsettles the work somewhat.

So far so good as far as a pedagogical pamphlet is concerned, but chapter 13 is very different in tone and purpose. And its distinctiveness is very characteristic of Xenophontic irony, as opposed to the author's depiction of Socratic irony, which is usually consistently present in the text. A sudden, if not startling, change in the text marks the irony and the social criticism that irony effects here. So, chapter 13 is a somewhat unexpected tirade against the sophists and sophistic education. It is as it were an 'Against the Sophists', after the polemic of Isocrates against these individuals, which is planted at the conclusion of an otherwise unremarkable work on hunting and which takes the reader quite by surprise. The sophists, when criticized, are always a nameless group, as they are here, and the education they provide requires some financial means on the part of the student and his family, with little return and certainly no guarantee of a return. One has to pay a great deal for a sophistic education.[9] But a sophistic education differs fundamentally from the more traditional education that the author outlines in the foregoing portion of his work. What Xenophon is most concerned about is the result of sophistic education. Instead of making the student better, it makes them far worse. Rather than leading young people to virtue, it leads them to its opposite, vice (13.1). The sophists may write lots of books but they write on trivialities which have no virtue. Antiphon might have written *On Truth* but he also writes on the relativity of truth in the *Dissoi Logoi*. There were also works on non-existence (Gorgias), an encomium of Heracles (Prodicus), an encomium of death (Antisthenes),[10] praises of bumble bees and salt (cf. Isocrates *Helen* 12), a speech on financial deposits (Isocrates *Panegyricus* 188), and so on. They do not instruct in anything good or useful but only teach what is irrelevant or bad (13.2). The language of the sophists which is found in their books is strange and far-fetched (13.3). For Xenophon the imperative is to teach what is good by one's nature (13.4) and maxims, not just words, are essential for this purpose (13.5). The author is insistent here that he does not write as the sophists do and therefore is not interested in playing with words as they do (13.4). They do not in any case recognize good writing as such, arbitrarily determining what is well and methodically written and what is not (13.6). If they are teaching rhetoric this should call their abilities to do so into serious question.

The sophists seek to deceive their pupils and Xenophon makes a distinction between sophists and philosophers and between the sophists and himself. He aims to make other men wise and good unlike the sophists, who have no such concern (13.7). Furthermore, sophists seek only the rich and young from whom they can benefit in a predatory manner, while philosophers are available to all, not caring about the acquisition of wealth (13.9). Money is not the concern of the philosopher. Xenophon is implicitly distancing himself from the sophists in order to identify himself as a philosopher here. His teaching on hunting is available to all who read it without prejudice and he does not insist on wealth as a prerequisite for learning this art.

Xenophon turns to moral instruction at this point in his work. He tells the reader not to envy those seeking their own advantage in private or public life (13.10). Those who rob others – namely the sophists – do not help the state or the common safety, while huntsmen offer their property and lives for the common good (13.11). The huntsmen become better and wiser people through their efforts because they must expend energy and labour to be successful at what they do (13.14–15). The conclusion of the work extols hunting as being an activity directed against a common enemy for the state and as being something that the gods like. All hunters are good men and even some women have hunted too, and so, it is assumed, are also good (13.18).

V

I have been paraphrasing *On Hunting* but I have done so to demonstrate that there is a twist to the work, which suggests that it is not all it seems. Gray sees the unity of work as lying in exhortation or *paraneisis*, which is signalled by the appearance of παραινέω in the work at 1.18, 12.14, 13.9 and 13.17.[11] Because *On Hunting* is a work of *parainesis*, she argues that it is legitimate as a text of Xenophon, one that may work as a preparation for war.[12] Together with Gray, I observe that exhortation interestingly is thematized at the beginning and ending of the text and clearly declare the integrity of at least these portions of the work with one another, but I seek a larger unity of the work – one that is more fundamental to the text and one that argues more persuasively for it as an integral whole.

Indeed, the work appears to be one that is concerned foremost with the art of hunting and it is: it deals with the individuals who hunt (the beginning and ending) and how to hunt (the middle). It is also appended with a critique of the sophists so that *On Hunting* seems to be a text dedicated to a good (Xenophon's) and a bad (the sophist's) form of education. Yet the addition of this critique is not the interesting twist in itself. *On Hunting* might be read differently if one realizes that the sophists are also hunters after a fashion so that the work is concerned with hunting throughout and is concerned with contrasting good and bad hunting. Hunting is not just an aspect of education; it is education itself. That is a very good reason why the authenticity of this final chapter cannot be doubted, as it has been.[13] At 13.10 Xenophon states that the sophists do not hunt hare, deer and boars, but they hunt the rich and the young (οἱ μὲν γὰρ σοφισταὶ πλουσίους καὶ νέους θηρῶνται). The verb θηρῶνται draws the link between Xenophon's topic and the activity of the sophists, one which Jonathan Hesk has also identified in his review of A. A. Philips and M. Willock's book *Xenophon and Arrian, On Hunting*.[14] Much earlier, A. E. Taylor had observed that the sophist is a hunter of 'civilized living beings'.[15] The analogy of rich young men and animals, with which the former are equated, is quite a horrible one.

Xenophon turns away from an account of how one is to learn to hunt to an account of another kind of hunter (the sophist) and his human prey. The sophist seeks out young men for money, a presentation which David Blank has demonstrated to be such a commonplace of the sophistic iconography,[16] whereas in the first chapter there is no inkling that the true teacher, Cheiron, had to sell his skill at teaching. Students willingly came to him without any signs of coercion or inducement. This realization is what essentially differentiates the conclusion of *On Hunting* from the first chapter of the work. Interestingly, Xenophon's mythical excursus involving Cheiron and the heroes whom he educated mimics sophistic writing. The sophists also used myth and mythical discourse in their writings and teachings, as Kathryn Morgan has well demonstrated in her book *Myth and Philosophy from the Pre-Socratics to Plato*.[17] Morgan observes that myth denoted truth because it came from the realm of poets, sage kings and seers of the archaic age.[18] If the sophists thus falsely appropriated the truthfulness of this age and its discourse, Xenophon wrestles it back through his own text. By evoking the mythical figure of Cheiron, he writes an alternative mythical discourse to that produced by the sophists and thus restores myth to the realm of truth.

In depicting the sophists as hunters of young men Xenophon is drawing on a commonplace of fourth-century writing.[19] He is not the only fourth-century author to refer to sophistic fee-taking as hunting. In Plato's *Sophist* the sophist is depicted as someone who must be hunted down by the interlocutors of the dialogue (cf. δυσθήρευτον, 218d) but he is also in turn depicted as a hunter of young men. Hunting is of live and dead creatures, the latter being a topic which the interlocutors ignore, and it is of land and water creatures (220a). The pursuit of water creatures is called angling, while the pursuit of land creatures is hunting (221c–e). Of the creatures of the land the hunter may seek a wild creature or a tame animal, and that tame animal is man (cf. εἴτε ἥμερον μὲν λέγεις αὖ τὸν ἄνθρωπον, 222b). In the hunting of man one can be engaged in piracy, tyranny or kidnapping or one can be involved in rhetoric (222c). If the latter, then the hunter is a sophist (223a). At *Sophist* 223b the Stranger states to Theaetetus that sophistry is an art which seeks out men privately and for pay and that the sophist is a hunter after rich and promising youths. He observes that this art must be called sophistry (cf. νέων πλουσίων καὶ ἐνδόξων γιγνομένη θήρα προσρητέον ... σοφιστική; cf. also 231d). Sophistry is actually an acquisitive enterprise rather than a legitimate form of pedagogy, seeking money for its practitioner (cf. 224c) and using 'knowledge' as its commodity.[20]

It is interesting that sophistry turns the relationship of the human and animal world upside down. Humans, not animals, are now prey, and perhaps the implication is that the ideal teacher is Cheiron, who is part animal, namely horse, and part human. As such and unlike the sophists, he does not, and cannot, cannibalize humanity. Cheiron is thus Xenophon's ideal role model, a teacher who does not turn young men into victims of his greed and acquisitiveness.

It is the fee paid to the sophist which is the focus point for criticism of this figure. In Isocrates, *Against the Sophists*, these individuals appear as the greedy persons that they are identified as being and what makes them worse is that they exaggerate, making far greater promises than they can fulfil, cf. καὶ μὴ μείζους ποιεῖσθαι τὰς ὑποσχέσεις ὧν ἔμελλον ἐπιτελεῖν (1). They purport to teach wisdom and happiness to young men, charging some three or four minae for the privilege (4) even though they say they do not want money (4). They do not care about truth and they are, moreover, so stupid that even speeches improvized by the average Athenian citizen are better (10). They have neglected what is necessary and in consequence become teachers of meddling (πολυπραγμοσύνη) and greed (πλεονεξία) (18).

Xenophon himself expands upon the faults of the sophist in the first book of the *Memorabilia*. At 1.2.6 the reader is informed that Socrates regarded the student who paid a fee to the professional teacher as someone who had sold himself into bondage to the former, τούτου τούτου δ' ἀπεχόμενος ἐνόμιζεν ἐλευθερίας ἐπιμελεῖσθαι· τοὺς δὲ λαμβάνοντας τῆς ὁμιλίας μισθὸν ἀνδραποδιστὰς ἑαυτῶν ἀπεκάλει διὰ τὸ ἀναγκαῖον αὐτοῖς εἶναι διαλέγεσθαι παρ' ὧν ἂν λάβοιεν τὸν μισθόν: The host of the drinking party, Callias, is someone who has mistakenly paid out enormous sums of money to the likes of Prodicus, Protagoras and Gorgias in order to learn (1.5). Later in the same book Socrates declares that just as it is prostitution to offer beauty to all who come with money for someone's beauty, it is likewise prostitution to offer wisdom to individuals who come for it with payment. The sophist thus becomes one 'who prostitutes wisdom' (πωλοῦντας σοφιστὰς [ὥσπερ πόρνους] ἀποκαλοῦσιν). Socrates regards the one who instead makes friendship the basis of such a relationship to be an individual who fulfils the duty of a citizen and gentleman (1.6.13). In the *Memorabilia* Socrates consorts with the young of Athens without any payment. At 1.2.48 we read that Criton, Chaerophon, Chaerecrates, Hermogenes, Simmias, Cebes, and Phaedonas amongst others were those who spent time with Socrates not to become good orators but rather to do their duties both in the private and public sphere.

Overall, *On Hunting* takes the topic of hunting and places it within a larger framework. It is in the larger sense a work concerned with pedagogy, about how to teach young men a particular topic, namely hunting. What is being taught in this work may seem somewhat anachronistic, old-fashioned and certainly out of place as being sited to a more agrarian setting, but it is what allows Xenophon to engage in his critique of the sophists. Sophists do not teach hunting and this topic leaves him able to not discuss them until the end of the work. But there is also a thematic link for this choice of topic: namely, men used to hunt animals but now men hunt other men. And this latter sort of hunting is not at all good or acceptable where the author is concerned, for it results in damage to the hunted, the students. The sophists hunt others and do not teach them anything. That is the irony of what the sophists do. They are by no means teachers. They only purport to teach, something that Cheiron and Xenophon rather actually do. Therefore, Xenophon offers as his critique in the largest context a damning criticism of education in fourth-century Athens through individuals who purport to teach but actually offer no knowledge of anything useful.

VI

There are unities in *On Hunting* which characterize it as a carefully authored work, and there is a very evident (at least to me) ironic twist in the work which characterizes it very much as a work written by Xenophon. It is, as its title suggests, about hunting, first the hunting of animals and then, later and more importantly, the hunting of rich, young men. The former is approved of and advocated for the young Athenian, while the latter is not, for it destroys the young Athenian, turning him into prey for the greedy sophist, who may not in any case be an Athenian. Hence Xenophon goes to great length to explain how the first is done but tells us nothing about the hunting of young men. After all, sophistry is most definitely not his thing.

6

Xenophon on Equine Culture

Two works in the Xenophontic corpus are concerned with horses and the equine culture: *On Horsemanship* and *On the Cavalry Commander*. Both texts are thought to have been written around the same time (350 BCE), and the author suggests that they should be considered together given the cross-reference to *On the Cavalry Commander* – which discusses what is necessary for the cavalry commander to know – in the conclusion of *On Horsemanship*, which treats the buying and care of horses (cf. 12.14). For this reason, I shall read the works together to suggest that Xenophon undermines equine culture in fourth-century Athens.

I

Let me begin first with *On Horsemanship*, which patently presents itself as a didactic text, invoking a privileged discourse in the fourth century BCE (see Introduction). In this work, there is a whole vocabulary of pedagogy, of teaching and learning. For instance, διδάσκειν, μανθανεῖν and their various cognates are particularly evident and notable throughout the text and this is because Athenians regard it as necessary to instruct the horse in its duties and one must teach the horse-breaker how to tame the horse as if one were giving a child to an apprenticeship in a particular skill (cf. ἐπὶ τέχην, 2.2). As the wielder of this vocabulary, the author casts himself as the teacher of horsemanship and he provides notes (ὑπομνήματα), as it were, that serve as reminders so that the horse-tamer or -breaker gets his money's worth from the purchase of the horse (2.2). And the horse-breaker is not the horse owner, for in chapter 1 of the work he observes that those who ride, and therefore probably also own, horses are the wealthiest citizens and are most involved in the city's politics. Certainly, in the *Agesilaos* Xenophon observes that by encouraging his sister Kynkiska to breed chariot horses *Agesilaos* demonstrates that the creature is a mark of wealth (cf. πλούτου) rather than of manly virtue (*Agesilaos* 9.6) – which will indeed become evident from the two works I am examining in this chapter. Equine culture is a culture of the Athenian moneyed elite, amongst whom Xenophon can count himself but may not wish to identify with (as will become apparent in *On the Cavalry Commander*). It is after all only moneyed classes who have resources to maintain horses, whether one or many.

According to this text, a person's relationship with horses ideally depends upon one's time of life. Xenophon notes that it is better for a young man to concern himself with his own condition but once he has learned horsemanship, he is to practice it rather than undertake the activity of taming horses, while it is best for the older man to spend his time on his household, his friends, political matters and affairs of war rather than in breaking horses (2.1). Accordingly, the groom (ἱπποκόμον) must be the horse-breaker; he is the individual who must be most concerned with the taming of the horse. Thus, it is the groom who must be educated (cf. πεπαιδευκέναι) in what he must do concerning the horse (5.1). And the instruction of the groom is quite detailed. For instance, he is to know where to put the knot in the halter (5.1) and he must learn the importance of clearing out dung and litter from the stable (5.2). It also involves the groom knowing how and when the muzzle should go on the horse's head (5.3), where and how to rub down the horse (5.5), how to wash the creature (5.6–7), and how not to over clean the horse's belly (5.9).

Education is one the major themes of this work, and elsewhere, it is perhaps only in the *Constitution of Sparta* that Xenophon concerns himself with the topic so explicitly, when he discusses the education of the young Spartans (*Constitution of Sparta* 2ff.). In *On Horsemanship* there is also a set of pedagogies which involve the rider of the horse and the horse itself. The young man needs rather only to be concerned with riding the horse and maneuvering it in battle. Indeed, at 7.3 Xenophon declares that he must learn (μαθεῖν) to lead his horse and to hold his spear with both his right and left hands so that his horsemanship is effectively ambidextrous. The horseman is in his turn required to teach (διδάσκειν) the horse to be still when he mounts it until the horseman has taken up what he needs to, evened out the reins, and taken up his spear as is most convenient for him (7.8). Xenophon then proceeds to describe the exercises which the rider must undertake with his horse; namely, taking the creature through his various exercises but also ensuring that the horse has his rest at the conclusion of the exertions (7.19).

In the following chapter, the author outlines the pedagogy for the horse. In the end, it is perhaps the horse that is above all on the receiving end of the teaching laid on in *On Horsemanship*. Xenophon declares at 8.2–3 that it is necessary to teach (διδάσκειν) the horse, and that he will write how one must instruct the creature. The rider must first teach (διδάσκειν) the horse to be calm (7.8). Because the horse must at times run downhill, uphill and on a slope and perform various jumps, he must learn (διδάσκειν) and practise these moves. If the horse does these things, it will be able to help others and will seem to be generally useful (8.1). Xenophon counters any accusations that he is repeating himself and goes on to say that it is necessary to teach (διδάσκειν) the horse and furthermore, that he will now write in what manner it is necessary to teach (διδάσκειν). He observes at 8.13 that the gods have given the power to man to teach (διδάσκειν) by word of mouth; however, horses cannot learn from verbal commands or instructions and therefore must be taught by a system of rewards and punishments so that they learn to do their duty.

Then, more generally, the horse learns its lesson (cf. δίδαγμα) through non-verbal sounds, such as chirps and clicks (9.10) and is taught (cf. διδάξῃ) to hold up its neck by movements of the bridle (10.3). The horse is educated (cf. παιδευθῇ) by hard and smooth bits so that it too is acculturated in what it must do as well as the groom (10.6).

Moreover, if one teaches (διδάξῃ) the horse to go forward with a slack bridle and to hold its neck up and to arch it from its head, one enables the horse to do what it delights and what it rejoices in (10.3). At 10.6 Xenophon discusses the relative merits of smooth and rough harnesses: the rough one will cause the horse to drop the bit, while he will much prefer the smooth one and do its bidding because of the contrast with the rough bit. The author notes that the horse had been educated (cf. παιδευθῇ) by the rough bit. The rider can also cause his horse to learn by performing certain actions. He can pull it up short with the bit and he can signal the horse to go forward but this is after the horse has learned (μεμαθηκότος) to proceed more quickly after turning (10.15). Non-verbal sounds, the textures of the harnessing equipment and particular movements by the rider provide the education for the creature that needs to be domesticated for use in war by his owner. Non-verbal sounds and physical gestures apart, it is the case that training by physical means is of the greatest efficacy in training the horse. Rest and relaxation amidst exertion prove to be the most effective teaching (cf. διδασκαλιῶν) for the horse (11.5). Xenophon refers to this training of the horse as a δίδαγμα, a teaching, and furthermore, he describes the animal as learning (cf. μάθοι) from it. In addition, some people choose to teach (cf. διδάσκουσιν) their horses by hitting the balls of the creature's ankles with a stick, or else they order someone running alongside the horse to hit it with a staff on its thighs (11.4) and certainly, at 8.4 he advocates hitting a horse as hard as is possible with a stick to make it leap over a ditch, but the greatest lesson of all (cf. τὸ κράτιστον τῶν διδασκαλίων) is to allow the horse to rest once it has done something which is in accordance with the rider's wishes (11.5). This less violent mode of teaching is preferable because it will render the horse more graceful and brilliant in appearance (11.6). Note that Xenophon also decries violence done to the horse as a means of forcing the horse to approach what it is scared of at 6.15: blows only increase the horse's terror at what it is already anxious of, and make it think that the pain is caused by the object of its anxiety.

The final chapter of the work *On Horsemanship* reiterates the notion that the author's discourse is a form of teaching about the topic and implicitly, that Xenophon is the overall instructor on equine matters. In the very last paragraph the author states that the work has been notes (cf. ὑπομνήματα), lessons (μαθήματα) and practice exercises (μελετήματα) composed for the layman (12.14). *On Horsemanship* is a manual for the upper-class citizen – for it is the upper-classes who could afford to maintain a horse – on buying, training and maintaining a horse. Another work, namely *On the Cavalry Commander*, deals with the concerns of the cavalry commander.

II

So far so good, but the question that remains is: what was the horse to be maintained for? Indications in *On Horsemanship* are that the work seeks to give advice about equestrian matters with regard to the cavalry (cf. ἱππεύειν), which is a body of mounted men supposedly trained and kept available for war. These men are the same individuals known as the 'knights' in Aristophanes' comedy of the same name, although the comic knights are of a somewhat more conservative outlook and disposition as they are of an older generation and they seem to dislike orators like Cleon (cf. *Knights* 974–80 and 1111). Accordingly, at 3.7 Xenophon states that the horse is to be bought as a creature of war (cf .πολεμιστήριον,. 1.2) and so, must be taught to jump over ditches, mount walls, rush up banks and run down them. This explains why it is the horses that must above all be educated, for it is lack of experience which leaves them wanting rather than their lack of natural abilities. Thus, they must learn (cf. μαθόντες), become accustomed to (ἐθισθέντες) and practise (μελετήσαντες) so that they may do everything a warhorse should, and they need to be healthy and not be lacking (3.8). At 7.3 and elsewhere, Xenophon speaks of the individual knight, who rides the horse in question leading the creature with his left hand and holding a spear in his right hand, and of the need for the individual to be able to do the same with the opposite hands. The horse rider is clearly and ideally to be a cavalryman equipped for war.

But Xenophon's narrative is not quite as it seems, as it generally is not, in any of his works. I suggest that the didascalic text which *On Horsemanship* appears to be may after all be a ridiculous parody of teaching as far as the equestrian arts are concerned. In the ancient world, pedagogy was generally to be regarded as a process of socialization,[1] that is, as the means by which the educated individual learned his position in society, whether and most commonly, to rule or to be ruled. Education was something that individuals, usually of the upper classes, undertook in ancient Athens, particularly because it required considerable fees unless one was being trained by Socrates, who took no fees and therefore, contrary to the charges against him in the trial, did not corrupt young men.

In *On Horsemanship* pedagogy goes awry and is questionable because teaching involves almost everyone *except* the young owner of the horse, the individual who should most of all be taught. The work begins with Xenophon giving instructions to an assumedly wealthy individual on how to buy a horse so that he is not cheated. The buyer must inspect the feet of the horse since good feet are necessary for the warhorse (cf. ἵππου πολεμιστηρίου), just as good foundations are important for a house (1.2), while the bones above the hoof are not to be too straight (1.4). Xenophon continues to elaborate the best features of a horse up to its head in the rest of this chapter (so 1.2–1.7). The author then states that the young man who owns the horse must not be concerned with breaking his animal (2.1) and that the horse given to the care of horse-tamer must in any case be gentle, easy to manage and inclined to like people (cf. φιλάνθρωπος) (2.3). The groom must teach (διδάσκειν) the horse by calming it down so that it has no fear (2.5). Significantly, Xenophon does not in these directions seek to educate the young man who owns the horse except on the matter of buying the animal, but rather aims to teach the groom how to manage the creature and to instruct the horse itself on its behaviour around humans. The individual, who is generally the object of pedagogy in the Ancient Greek world, is largely ignored and his underling, who is someone much less important in society, and the animal become the objects of instruction.

Indeed, at 5.1 Xenophon observes that a good horseman must ensure that his groom is educated (πεπαιδευκέναι) in what he must do in the care of a horse. The groom, rather than and above all, the young man, must be acculturated into equine care and culture. Although it is the case that the author instructs that the rider must teach both himself and his horse to gallop up and down and along hills and to leap in and out and over (8.1). Yet there is one bit of teaching for the groom that raises some questions. It is perhaps rather odd that Xenophon should have the groom help his master mount his horse in the Persian fashion with a lift (6.12). Persian ways are not at all Greek or Athenian ways, and it would appear that by advocating an eastern custom Xenophon perhaps suggests that his advice is not to be taken seriously after all.

That didacticism stands as the focus and purpose of *On Horsemanship* is made most apparent at 8.13 as Xenophon comments that the gods have granted to mankind the ability to teach one another by speech, but have not enabled them to instruct horses in the same manner. Man is rather to use rewards and punishments to urge him towards or deter him from certain actions, ἀνθρώποις μὲν οὖν ἄνθρωπον ἔδοσαν οἱ θεοὶ λόγῳ διδάσκειν ἃ δεῖ ποιεῖν, ἵππον δὲ δῆλοςὅτι λόγῳ μὲν οὐδὲν ἂν διδάξαις. As a gift from the gods, teaching is the art that Xenophon invokes in this work to instruct the young man, the groom and above all, the horse in the equestrian arts. Yet the instruction that occurs is somewhat disproportionate, for the young man is taught only how to buy a horse and to ride with a spear in his hand. The groom is instructed in the care and nurture of the horse, but it is the horse that receives the bulk of the teaching in the text.

Accordingly, if teaching is aimed at reinforcing and reconstituting the structure of society, it would appear that the equine arts do not really assist in the make-up of Athenian society. The ruling classes, formed by the rich young men who own the horses, are largely unformed, while the lower class grooms but it is the animals who receive the majority of the training.

Xenophon does point out at the very beginning of the *Poroi* that such as the leaders of the state are, so is the constitution, ὁποῖοί τινες ἂν οἱ προστάται ὦσι, ταιαύτας καὶ τὰς πολιτείας γίγνεσθαι (*Poroi* 1.1). Rearing horses for the cavalry as *On Horsemanship* lays it out implies a largely uneducated and unsocialized class of young men who own and run the city, and in turn, become its rulers. The youth of Athens are essentially uneducated and improperly socialized into the art of ruling because, according to *On Hunting*, they are pursued and are taught specious skills and arts, such as the art of persuasion, by the sophists for vast sums of money (cf. *On Hunting* 13.10). These young men as its future leaders consequently determine the nature of the city Athens as a rather undisciplined and ignorant political entity. Certainly, the cavalry, which is largely unformed by a misdirected pedagogy, suggests a city which does not behave well on the political stage. The irony of *On Horsemanship* is that it is a didactic text which renders the elite young of Athens without an education but supplies the state with ably trained steeds. Society teaches horses rather than people to engage in an activity – warfare – that Xenophon does not seem to approve of.

As an aside, one notes that the problem of an improperly prepared cavalry is not limited to Athens but is also rife at Sparta. At *Hellenica* 6.4.10 the narrator Xenophon observes that the city state's body of horsemen was extremely poor at its art at the time, unlike the cavalry of the Thebans, who were well-trained as a consequence of the war with the Orchomenians and the Thespians … τοῖς δὲ Λακεδαιμονίοις κατ' ἐκεῖνον τὸν χρόνον πονηρότατον ἦν τὸ ἱππικόν.[2] The sentence that follows this statement makes clear the target of the criticism. Xenophon states that this is due to the fact that the richest men in the city state of Sparta raised the horses, ἔτρεφον μὲν γὰρ τοὺς ἵππους οἱ πλουσιώτατοι (6.4.11). As far as the author is concerned, wealth and warfare do not necessarily mix and in fact, more often than not, are a combination that leads to an improper training for war.

I suggest that if Xenophon is offering *On Horsemanship* as a didactic text, then he is ironically teaching his audience that society misunderstands the targets of pedagogy. He is parodying the teachings offered at Athens, for instruction should ideally be of the leading young men of the state and not the grooms and horses who have no role in political leadership.

III

On the Cavalry Commander is the second work of Xenophon's which directly deals with equine culture in the context of Athens' military might: it concerns the individual, the leader of the cavalry, who just directs the men and the horses in war manoeuvres. Yet *if* it is the case that the author is something of an elite quietist and that he is opposed to a militaristic Athens (whether because such a state makes financial demands of its wealthiest members, or because war is so ideologically opposed to ἀπραγμοσύνη), then the reader can expect to find the work ironically undermining itself and the figure of the cavalry commander, and I shall suggest that it certainly does so. As we shall see, *On the Cavalry Commander* calls into question the merits of the Athenian cavalry when compared to foreign cavalries. Yet it may also be the case that Xenophon is discrediting a segment of elite society that puts too much value in its own wealth and the appearance of wealth.

But first let me discuss the way in which *On the Cavalry Commander* appears to be a serious text dealing with important issues as far as war is concerned.

Xenophon begins the work by observing that it is of utmost importance that the commander sacrifices and prays to the gods so that his command is most pleasing to the gods and so that he brings to himself, his friends and the city affection, glory and advantage (1.1). The cavalry commander must be a religiously observant individual and Xenophon reiterates the importance of piety throughout the work. At 3.2 the author advocates a gala spectacle in the marketplace where the cavalry begins and ends at the Herms, and rides around and salutes the gods at their shrines and statues. Such a procession would please the gods and the spectators, even though it is the case that the riders are not accustomed to such movements (3.5). At 5.14 Xenophon observes that the commander may have various means and contrivances to work against the foe, but it is most important for him to work with the gods so that fortune may favour him and his forces. In chapter 7 the author impresses upon his reader the importance of the gods' help. And for this reason, he again reiterates that the cavalry commander must take care to observe his duties towards the gods, τῷ τοὺς θεοὺς θεραπεύειν, 7.1). At 7.3 he notes that the cavalrymen will be better, with the gods' help (σὺν θεῷ), if they are well taken care of, presumably by their leader. Furthermore, if the cavalry is to be expected to guard the city outside the walls and to stand alone against all its enemies, then it must do so with the gods, who are strong allies for the city (θεῶν μὲν οἶμαι πρῶτον συμμάχων ἰσχυρῶν, 7.4). With god's help (σὺν θεῷ) the commander must enter enemy territory stealthily after learning where the latter has positioned his outposts and lookouts (7.14). In fact, in the last chapter of the work, Xenophon observes that whether one is involved in farming, in sailing or in ruling, one must bear in mind that he is likely to accomplish this with the help of the gods (σὺν θεοῖς): divine assistance is necessary for human accomplishment. Xenophon was himself pious and observed the gods' will carefully, but here I suggest that he seeks the reliance of the gods as far as the success of the cavalry is concerned because this body of fighting men is not so efficient or effective as far as their performance in war is concerned. The appeal to religious observance is here a case of the plea to the gods for help made in desperation. Piety and worship of the gods are advocated to conceal the inadequacies of Athens' commanders and fighting men: the divinities are to compensate for the shortcomings of the cavalry and their leader. Indeed, *On Horsemanship* indicates that this is the case because the individuals who ride the horse, that is, the cavalrymen, are not properly trained, since the παιδεία where horsemanship is concerned is focussed rather on the groom and the horse.

One hint of this comes at the beginning of the work, where the author states that it is necessary for the commander to recruit a sufficient number of men according to the law so that the cavalry is not diminished. He notes that some will necessarily give up serving due to old age, while others will leave for other reasons (ἄλλως, 1.2). The word ἄλλως raises more questions than it answers: what are the other reasons that younger men might drop out of the cavalry? Are they not fit? Are they not able to carry out their duties? Are they improperly suited for the task? Or perhaps, are they more inclined to be involved in the unsavoury politics of the day? And so on. The suggestion is that the men who drop out have no strong proclivity or inclination to equestrian activity, or to the defense of the Attic state. Being in the cavalry is an activity that one might take up without any strong commitment to it or to the state, a condition which being in the cavalry should assume.

Later in this first chapter Xenophon discusses further the recruitment of the cavalry in such a way as to reveal some of its problems. The author proposes that the cavalry commander (the phylarch) should have to assist him and in turn should have suitable orators. These orators are available to put fear in the men in the Council, since fear will make them better cavalrymen, cf. Φοβῶσι τε τοὺς ἱππέας (βελτίονες γὰρ ἂν εἶεν φοβούμενοι) (1.8). The men who are to serve in the cavalry are perhaps somewhat reluctant to do so. At 1.10 Xenophon speaks of men who might bribe the cavalry commander not to bring court judgements grounds against them for not serving, while the men who are smaller will have excuses for escaping service. Young men try to escape service in the cavalry. Furthermore, the guardians of the young men are also inclined to object to their charges undertaking military service unless the commander tells them that they will be forced by someone, if not the commander himself, to maintain horses due to their wealth (1.11). In addition to the reluctance of the men and their parents, the commander must deal with the fact that some owners only buy expensive horses for the sake of having them as an indication of their wealth and status (1.12), or they do not feed or take proper care of their horses (1.13) or their horses are too vicious (1.14).

The rich young men who form the cavalry are extremely materialistic and status conscious. The state gives forty talents a year for the cavalry so that it does not have to rely on mercenaries (1.19), and this is spent in part on equipping the horsemen. At 1.22, however, Xenophon notes that the arming of the men will be properly achieved only if the phylarchs can convince those under them that the brilliance of the regiment is far greater than that of their own στολή. The word στολή can mean 'equipment' or 'armament' as well as 'garb' and 'accoutrements'. One suspects that it has the latter meaning as far as the wealthy young men are concerned. The author states that the men must be obedient (εὐπειθεῖς) and furthermore, he impresses upon the cavalry leaders a need to teach obedience (πειθαρχεῖν) to the men (1.24; also 8.22). Perhaps the implication of this observation is that by their natures and inclinations, the men are otherwise rather disobedient and insubordinate. The picture he paints of the cavalry is far from flattering; it is of rich, reluctant, showy and less than amenable young men. The horseman becomes in effect a centaur, as Cyrus suggests at *Cyropaedia* 4.3.22–3, and D. Johnson notes that the centaur was deemed to be an unstable figure.[3] They are only introduced by Cyrus and become a mark of what we shall see to be his rule of excess and self-indulgence.

Furthermore, on the whole, the cavalrymen do not appear to have any physical stamina. At 4.1 the commander is urged to give rest to the backs of the horses, having the men alternately walk and ride a moderate amount (cf. μέτριον). Xenophon observes that one cannot make a mistake in judging what is moderate as each person has his own sense of the moderate and would not fail to notice if he were overextending himself, τοῦ δὲ μετρίου ἐννοῶν οὐκ ἂν ἁμαρτάνοις· αὐτὸς γὰρ μέτρον ἕκαστος τοῦ μὴ λαθεῖν ὑπερπονοῦντας. (4.1). It would seem that the cavalrymen are not used to stretching or exerting themselves and prefer to take things at a rather more leisurely pace. And the author goes on to mention that the cavalry commander must give his men rest (cf. ἀναπαύειν) in shifts in case they encounter the enemy and all of them happen to be dismounted (4.2). Yet there is a problem because then the cavalry as a whole will be separated into smaller groups as one part of it takes its rest and the other proceeds and is, therefore, less powerful and effective in war. Later in the work, the author observes that those who undergo gymnastic training have much more trouble and find it more difficult than those who practise the equine arts (8.5; on the benefits of horsemanship, see *Cyropaedia* 4.3.15–16). The reason is that gymnastic activity requires much sweat and labour while horsemanship is productive of the greatest pleasure (8.6). It would appear that serving in the cavalry is an activity which the participants enjoy because it does not require too much exertion. And this is bearing in mind that war brings more glory (cf. ἐνδοξότερον) than, say, a boxing match (8.7).

The problem is that both these activities, gymnastics and equine training, are precursors and a form of practice for war, with the result that they should be equally strenuous and taxing for the participants (cf. *Agesilaos* 1.25). Nonetheless, it appears that dealing with horses, as an activity for the wealthy of Athens, is a somewhat lax affair.

That Xenophon is ultimately denigrating and mocking the whole Athenian enterprise of horsemanship as far as the cavalry – and also implicitly, war – is concerned becomes most apparent in the final chapter, 9, when he declares that it would be much easier for the city-state to raise its complement of one thousand cavalrymen by establishing a force of two hundred *foreign* horsemen (9.3). It is ironic that Xenophon has just spent most of his work detailing how the cavalry at Athens is to be trained and now at the last moment surrenders his project – it is, after all, a futile one – to suggest that the city get its cavalry from elsewhere. The author envisages these non-Athenian horsemen as improving discipline and spurring competitiveness with regard to bravery (cf. ἀνδραγαθία), suggesting that where the Athenian cavalry is concerned, discipline is wanting and that the men are not so courageous, which we have seen to be the case. Xenophon notes that foreign contingents have been well-respected in Sparta and also in other states (9.4). They are a mercenary force and the author envisages money for the foreign troops coming from those who strongly object to military service in the cavalry (9.5). Even those who are currently in the Athenian cavalry are willing to pay to escape service, ὅτι καί οἷς καθίστησι τὸ ἱππικὸν ἐθελόυσι τελεῖν ἀργύριον ὡς μὴ ἱππεύειν (9.5). Others who will pay what is essentially a bribe are the rich who do not have the physical ability to be equestrians, or are orphans with large estates. The author goes on to suggest that metics would be proud to serve in the cavalry, for they often willingly do the honourable tasks assigned to them (9.6).

Thus, Xenophon's Athenian cavalry is far from fully Athenian and is comprised in part of foreigners who will spur the Athenian contingent to greater military prowess. The city-state cannot on its own sustain this body of men and horses who appear to be there to fight, and it is thus not surprising that the author should again stress the importance of divine favour in military endeavour at the very end of the text. The cavalry must act with god (cf. τὸ σὺν θεῷ πράττειν), knowing that it often faces danger (9.8) and the gods alone give men counsel, giving warnings and advice to men in sacrifices, in bird signs, in voices and in dreams (9.9). And it is important that men not only ask what they must when they need something, but also worship the gods as much as they can, even when things are going well for them (9.9).

IV

Xenophon gives a picture of a rather flawed equine culture in fourth-century Athens. The major, unspoken problem is that horsemanship supports an ostentatious Athenian war effort, the expense of which the author strongly opposes. Horse ownership in classical Athens is largely concerned with wealth and the display of wealth, an ironic affair because horse maintenance brings about the diminution of wealth. Hence, in *On Horsemanship* the author offers a didactic text in which the groom and the horse are instructed in equine culture rather than the young horse owner, who is only told what to look for when buying the creature, but who is nonetheless the individual who needs to understand in a larger sense the role of the horse in Athenian society, while *On the Cavalry Commander* reveals the individual who leads the cavalry dealing with this uneducated and unenlightened group of privileged youth who are reluctant and unmotivated to serve the state on their horses, are unfit to do so and/or offer bribes of money to evade this service. In the end, the commander is advised by Xenophon to look to a foreign contingent to bolster his ineffectual cavalry and to rely on the gods to help his work here.

Xenophon is differentiating himself as an economically privileged individual from other wealthy Athenians in his writings on horses. Horses are indeed the concern of the wealthy, for only they could purchase and maintain them; and they are an aspect of the showy trappings of military culture. But the individuals who buy horses are cast as profligate, spending their money on ostentatious things, and undisciplined. They are unlike the author, who implicitly casts himself as conservative with regard to spending money and as uninvolved in the public, supposedly military culture of the state. Equine culture in classical Athens is thus an extraneous concern as far as Xenophon is concerned, one which is the concern of the wealthy upper class conservatives, who are either unable to function adequately, or are very reluctant participants in it.

7

Xenophon's *Poroi* or 'Ways and Means'?

The *Poroi* is the last work of Xenophon's and it was written after Athens' defeat in the Social War (357–5 BCE), probably in 354 BCE.[1] The ostensible aim of 'Ways and Means', as it is generally translated from the Greek, was to seek ways of increasing public revenues for the city-state after what had been a disastrous war as Athens lost control of the Second Athenian Confederation.[2] It is thus an apparently economic text, one that at first glance treats matters of how a nation is to deal with its financial outgoings and incomings. Scholars have thus tended to deal with distinct portions of the work, dealing particularly with such issues as the city's support of the citizens, and also the cost and value of slaves.

But in my reading of the *Poroi* I intend to expand the context for considering the work. 'Economics', a word which is derived from the Greek οἶκος, has a larger sense than just the monetary, for it may concern the management of the household in both its small context, i.e. the individual home (as it does in the *Oeconomicus*) and in its larger context, the state. And so, it is with this largest frame of economics in mind, namely as far as concerns the state of Athens – and Xenophon speaks as an Athenian in this work – that I seek to approach the *Poroi*. I propose that is necessary to consider that the work's focus upon the outgoings from and incomings of wealth to the state of Athens exist within a great ideological framework, to which, I shall observe, Xenophon directs attention at the beginning and end of his text. The text is, I suggest, a work which ironically articulates what became after the experiences of the *Anabasis* at the end of Xenophon's life the position and views of someone disinclined to war, if not actually a quietist (cf. 5.11–12) (see chapter 11).[3] The city-state had suffered a loss in its latest war and I suggest, in agreement with John Dillery and Karl Polanyi,[4] that the author now takes a stance against imperialism and the assumption that it might make a thriving Athenian economy.[5] And here I suggest lies the discrepancy between what Xenophon ostensibly says and what he means.

I

Xenophon draws attention to the city-state as the context for his discussion of economics. He begins the *Poroi* with the observation that the constitution of a state reflects the character of its leading statesman (1.1). He signals that the state's leadership determines the way in which the state behaves, both in itself and in its relationship with other states. Xenophon observes that those who lead Athens have stated that they know what justice (τὸ δίκαιον) is but due to the poverty of the masses they have been forced to be somewhat unjust (cf. ἀδικώτεροι) towards other cities (1.1). Athens, as the head of an empire, had thus been forced to exploit other states to feed its own people, but the means of benefitting its own people is less apparent. This statement is the impetus for Gauthier's article focussing largely on the payout of three obols, which is quite distinct from jury pay, to each citizen, which he deems insufficient to support the family of a poor individual.[6] The state had imperial revenues which resulted from an annual tribute by the 440s and rather than helping the poor directly, this actually went towards Athens' war effort and military infrastructure, enabling the state to hire lower-class citizens as soldiers and to equip warships.[7] Soldiering, as Pritchard notes, enabled the poor to be useful to society and to enact virtues, such as courage, self-control, and loyalty, which had otherwise been the domain of the wealthy.[8] The focus on wealth is thus external to the state proper.

In this model, wealth does not derive from, and is also not circulated within the city, and this is a problem. Income from the empire flows into Athens from her subject states, and this income aids the poor of Athens by paying them to be the state's soldiers and sailors. These soldiers and sailors are in turn part of the Athenian war machinery, one that creates other vassal states and one that can be understood as enriching the state and as producing an even greater military force, which in turn needs to be ever increased. Imperialism has its injustices and the economy forces the state to turn outwards and to be concerned for external matters, behaving, as is most likely, in an oppressive fashion. Yet at the end of the *Poroi* Xenophon postulates that a state cannot have full revenue from all its sources unless it has peace (5.1). Furthermore, it is in peace that Athens is as likely to gain ascendency, because after the Persian Wars Athens became leaders of the fleet and treasurers of the league fund (5.5). He sets out a point of view which one is inclined to associate with the rich citizens in the city, namely, that Athens is best off without war, and he undermines his initial economic perspective.

The quietist or ἀπράγμων tended to be a wealthy and privileged Athenian of a conservative outlook. Such an individual stood in opposition to the meddling busy-body πολυπράγμων, who came from a lower class and used oratory to further his influence and wealth in the state.[9] The meddlers brought people to court in lawsuits over contracts, for instance, as did the fictional Lysimachus with Isocrates in the *Antidosis*, and they often demonstrated a desire for military expansionism. Chattering loudly and incessantly on the orator's platform, their aggressive ambition (πλεονεξία) is responsible in the first place for creation of Athens' hegemony and empire. So in Thucydides the Spartan king Archidamus articulates a position of quietism that stands in opposition to the ambitious striving of the Athenians (1.80ff).[10] At Isocrates *Archidamus* 6 and 15 the figure of Archidamus demonstrates an awareness that speaking publicly constitutes political activity and states his own hesitations with regard to it in order to present himself as a moderate figure. To be a moderate (σώφρων (e.g. Solon 13.7–8, 71–3; 24.7–10 West; Isocrates *Helen* 31; *On the Peace* 104), suggests a satisfaction with what one already possesses – which is probably already a lot because moderates were wealthy citizens – and a contentedness with the way things are – because that maintains the status quo, a position of comfort for the wealthy moderate.

Xenophon was of the class of the authors I have mentioned, and I suggest that he was certainly a moderate, and possibly also something of a quietist. He proposes that military expansion leads to a rather distorted view of state and economy in which the power of the state and its economy have to keep increasing to sustain themselves, and he thus quickly moves to consider if the Athenians could rather be nourished from the state itself, which he regards as the most just (cf. δικαιότατον) option, one that would remedy its poverty and would allay the suspicion with which other Greeks view the state (1.1). The author turns towards a consideration of the land's fertility for growing vegetation, namely cereals, grapes and olives, in the state, declaring that its seasons are the most temperate (πραοτάτας) so that it can produce crops which will not grow in other places (1.3). Yet Xenophon may be pulling the wool over his readers' eyes, for it was the case that Attica was poor for growing cereals and unpredictable weather made crops uncertain.[11] Citizens were peasants who held small plots which were sufficient for their own subsistence/existence, and no more than this. The author states, furthermore, that the sea around Attica is very productive and overall, the gods have seen to it that what goes out later elsewhere comes to fruition earlier in the Athenian state (1.3). According to John Dillery, Xenophon is offering a portrait of Athens as a fertile place such as that also found in *Airs, Waters, Places* 12 and Isocrates *Panegyricus* 42.[12] But the fact of the matter is that Athens was a difficult land to farm as good soil and areas for growing crops were rare so that only twenty per cent of the land was available for growing.

Apart from things that grow, as the author states, the state also has good things that are eternal (ἀίδια), such as an endless amount of stone that goes into the construction of the most beautiful temples and altars and statues of the gods, which one assumes to be so long-lasting as to be eternal (1.4). Xenophon goes on to observe that there is land which does bear fruit, but excavated land supports many more individuals than land which produces grain. Both Greeks and barbarians have need of stone, a substance that is dug out of the earth. This leads Xenophon to proclaim that Athens is at the centre of the earth with a surrounding sea that permits the bringing in of what she needs and the sending out of her exports (1.7).

And beyond stone, Athens also has another excavated substance, silver, which the pious author observes is there by the will of the gods (1.5). The mention of silver here anticipates the concern of the longest chapter in the work, chapter 4, and the major topic of the *Poroi*, which is a discussion of the silver mines which were based in Laurion in the eastern part of Attica, their economics and their workforce.

In chapter 2 Xenophon considers the importance of metics, or resident aliens, to the Athenian economy. They support themselves and in addition, they seem to benefit the city by paying a tax to it (2.1). The author advocates for increased rights for these individuals so that they become of greater assistance and benefit to the state. These rights include a relief from the obligation of serving in the infantry and the possibility of serving with Athenian citizens rather than with other foreigners (2.2–3), the right to serve in the cavalry (2.5), and the right to erect houses on vacant sites within the city walls (2.6). The metics would be more loyal and increase Athens' revenues (2.8). But reliance on metics entails that Attica is not so self-reliant, since metics are not home-grown Athenians and must be used in warfare (2.4).

In chapter 3 Xenophon discusses the merits of Athens as a shipping centre. Athens has a good harbour and does not require her merchants to convey a cargo in return for its usage (3.2). In fact, the city might offer privileges to merchants who bring goods of high quality to her by reserving seats in the theatre and offering them hospitality (cf. ἐπὶ ξένια), since they benefit the city. This in turn leads a greater number of visitors to Athens, who will increase its revenue, at no increased cost to Athens (3.6). Xenophon then inserts in his text a criticism of the Athenian war machine as he observes that the state contributed large sums of money when Lysistratus was general and troops were sent to Arcadia (3.8). He recalls the events of 366 BCE. The same thing happened in the time of Hagesilaos, that is 362 BCE, which concerned the battle of Mantinea. He goes on to note that money is also given to fund warships even though no one knows if the outcome will be good or bad. No one can be certain of getting a return on what they have paid into the war effort, whereas payments into the capital fund, probably the Theoric Fund that funded sacrifices, processions, theatre, gymnastic contests and games, might yield at least – and most often more than – one hundred per cent of what is paid in each year (3.9–10). In fact, the capital fund would be so profitable for the investors that foreigners, including kings, despots and oriental governors, would want to pay into it if they were recorded in a roll of benefactors (3.10). The Theoric Fund had helped to establish the cultural infrastructure of the city. Mention of this fund is very timely for Xenophon as it was re-established after the Social War around 350 BCE by the statesman Eubulus to help poorer citizens buy tickets to the annual religious festivals and theatre productions.

Xenophon is most interested in the harbour flourishing in a situation of trade rather than war. Increased income should lead to the building of more houses for ship-owners near the harbour and of hotels for merchants and visitors (3.12). Houses and shops in the Piraeus meant more income for the city (3.13) and rather than building a fleet of warships, the author proposes constructing a fleet of merchant ships to increase trade and therefore wealth for Athens (3.14). Xenophon is most concerned with the peace-time activities of commerce, which makes income better for the Athenian state.

Chapter four, by far the longest one in the *Poroi*, addresses silver mining, certainly including that conducted at Laurion in Attica. Silver was an important source of wealth for Athens, and indeed, Asechylus had spoken of the silver mines as θησαυρὸς χθόνος, 'the treasure of the earth', at *Persians* 238.[13] Xenophon regards the silver mines as being able to supply Athens with a huge revenue despite the fact that they have been in existence for a long time and their potential has not yet been realized. In fact, the mines are much smaller than the size of the mineral deposits (4.2). He observes, however, that mines require many workers, and the more workers there are, the greater the profits to be had (4.3–6). Silver is a hugely valuable ore, more so than even gold (4.10), and the desire to acquire more never ceases (4.7). Money can also be made not only from the silver itself, but from hiring out one's workers. Xenophon notes that Nikias, son of Nikeratus, once hired out a thousand workers who were slaves to Sosias, for a mina in total per day. Philomenides earned half the amount for three hundred slaves (4.14–15). Ideally in Xenophon's view there would be three public slaves for every citizen to work the mines for public revenues (4.17).

Slaves are to be bought up by the state from private owners (4.18), and while they may be few in number at first, their capacity to provide revenue means that there will be an increasing number of them and an increasing amount of revenue from them (4.24).

Interestingly, in the passage Xenophon shifts from discussing the profitability of silver ore to the secondary topic of the labour force required to mine the ore. Silver makes money not of itself but from the larger economic structure that it engenders with citizens operating as slave holders who hire out their labour force for considerable cash. Furthermore, the author also sees apart from the income earned from the rent of slaves, such that there is the creation of wealth in the market economy that grows up around the mines. There will be a large population surrounding the mines and income will be derived from the local market, from the state-owned homes near the mines, from the furnaces that turn the ore into ingots and from other sources (4.49). Xenophon envisages a densely populated city in the area of the mines, and real estate worth as much as that in the city of Athens itself (4.50).

But this secondary wealth creation has some problems. It is to be realized and certainly, it was apparent to Xenophon's reading audience that the life of a slave in the silver mine was one of squalor, starvation and extreme, hard labour. Slaves were often beaten and seldom saw the sunlight. Their life-span was expectedly short. Accordingly, Paul Cartledge sees the mining slave as the lowest level to which a man could sink.[14] While Xenophon would probably have been unconcerned with the quality of the slave's life and the slave was an expendable resource as far as his owner and the mines were concerned, their numbers would have been required to be large. Labour was thus an inevitable cost to the Attic state if the mines were publicly owned.

Significantly, in this long chapter on the silver mines there are references to war, actual and potential, which would have been anathema to the wealthy and conservative Xenophon. The author typically makes a statement only to qualify it with other details and facts in order to produce an irony. These references break into the idealistic discourse on the economy provided through mining to perhaps suggest that the silver mines are not after all as lucrative a prospect as they might initially have appeared to be. At 4.40 Xenophon alludes to a late war, the War of the Allies, occurring in 357–5 BCE, when Athens' allies revolted from her. The author observes that people might think that they have no money to contribute to the mines because they have already given to the expenses of the war, but they can contribute if they keep down the administrative costs and invest the amounts that will be generated in peace and from the increase in imports and exports together with the increase of the market from the harbour (4.40). He also advocates a decent care for the metics and traders. Overall, the notion is that war is extremely taxing and costly to the state, while peace can only increase Attica's revenues.

Xenophon goes on to observe at 4.41–2 that war requires manpower to serve as the crews in the warships and to serve as infantrymen. Even so and in light of the discussion of slaves, it would appear that Athens need not abandon her mines in a state of war. In any case, there are two fortresses in the mining district, at Anaphlystus to the north and Thoricus to the south, and if a third fortress were built at Besa, which is between them, the mines would be linked up by fortresses and each man would only have to go a short distance to find himself safe (4.44). Yet the fact is that in war corn, wine or cattle are of great value to the invading party, whereas silver is as much use as a pile of stones (4.45). It would appear that the necessities of life are the real wealth of any community. The enemy is thus not likely to march to silver mines as the distance to them is far (4.46), and if the enemy were to come to Athens, he will probably be destroyed by her cavalry and patrols if he has a small force (4.47). If there is a large invading force, then they would have problems with finding supplies (4.48).

Xenophon deals with war waged on Athens by others rather than addressing that condition of Athens going to war against other states. Yet it is the case that the production of silver did support the Athenian war effort. At Herodotus 7.144 one reads of Themistocles building ships against Aegeniticus with a large sum of money gained from the product of the mines at Laurion.[15] There had been a proposal to give each person in the state of Attica ten drachmas and thus to increase their personal wealth from the silver mines, but Themistocles persuaded them to put the funds towards the construction of two hundred ships in the war against Aegina. Herodotus notes that this move made Athens a naval power and had the result of saving Greece. Herodotus observes that these ships were not actually used for war but became part of the city's fleet, one which enabled Athens to meet any invader at sea with force together with any other ally that wished to join them. In the *Memorabilia* we find a Glaucon who is sorely lacking in the military strength and the resources of Athens as he is not even aware of the resource provided by the silver mines (3.6.12).

It is the case that silver historically underpinned Athens as a military and militaristic state, although it is the case that the mines could provide Athens with a sufficient maintenance for all its citizens. And this latter option of security for all, indeed, will have notable benefits for the citizenry. Those who are undertaking gymnastic training will take more trouble in the gymnasium, which is regarded by the Greeks as preparation for war, than even when they are under training for the torch races, while those on military duty in the fortresses or serving as targeters or on patrol in the countryside will show greater devotion and speed in their tasks (4.52). All this will ensure that Athens becomes better disciplined, more obedient and more efficient in war (4.51).

II

On the basis of the foregoing discussion, I propose that there is a perverse logic in Xenophon's account of the silver mines in chapter 4. According to it, silver creates wealth for the city, which it had previously used for war, an activity that in turn impoverishes the state. Wealth funds an activity which leaves the state poorer and thus, wealth leads to poverty. Alternatively, and in actuality, silver is not to be simply equated with wealth because silver and wealth have enormous liabilities, namely the diminution of the workforce that mines the silver, itself a notable source of wealth creation, as a consequence of the conditions of slavery and the support for the activities of war. In short, wealth has its costs.

These are the work's central ironies, which Athens can only avoid by subtracting war from the equation. If Xenophon now at the end of his life casts himself as someone who does not seek war or trouble, silver is the ore which should be characteristically associated with his antithetical 'other', the political meddler. One cannot have enough of it, as he notes at 4.7, just as the πολυπράγμων or political meddler cannot have enough power, influence and wealth whether within the city or outside of it. Silver is an acquisitive substance, making its owner want to amass more and more, while the political meddler has the same acquisitive relationship towards control and ascendancy at Athens and in Greece, seeking to ever increase his influence through his oratorical skills. As in the works concerned with equestrian matters, Xenophon again engages in criticism of the wealthy class at Athens, which is above all obsessed with having more and showing the rest of society that it has more. In the *Poroi*, he is concerned with a civic activity that demonstrates the city-state's overall acquisitiveness. Yet both political meddling and silver mining are not as they seem to be: the former does not create real, but only illusory, power for the πολυπράγμων, while the latter's wealth is diminished by the other activities, primarily war, which it sponsors and encourages.

It is in chapter 5 that, I suggest, Xenophon comes out fully as a pacifist at the end of his life. He observes that the state cannot have a full revenue unless there is peace (5.1) and for this to occur, the state must appoint 'peacekeepers' (εἰρηνοφύλακας). Polanyi had realized this when he commented that 'wealth, power and security are the produce of peace rather than war'.[16] A city at peace becomes more beloved and more of a home to all men (5.1). Some may think that the city at peace is less powerful, less well-regarded and less renowned, but the contrary is actually the case (5.2). Peaceful cities exist for the longest time in the most blessed state (cf. εὐδαιμονέσταται) and of all states Athens is most likely to increase (cf. αὔξεσθαι) (5.3). What this means is greater wealth, more culture, and more trade and indeed, Xenophon proceeds to enumerate the benefits in a peaceful Athens in sections 5.3 and 5.4. There will be ship owners and merchants; there will be men rich in corn, wine, oil and cattle, and beyond this, there will be investors and intelligent people. There will be craftsmen, sophists, philosophers, poets and those who use their materials and works and generally appreciate culture. In a peaceful Athens there will also be a freer market that will enable people to buy and sell as they wish (5.4).

Xenophon then goes on to insist that peace can guarantee Athens' ascendancy among the Greek states. He notes that in the Persian wars, the city provided leaders of the fleet and treasurers of the league funds by rendering service rather than by forcing the other Greeks to do as she wished (5.5). Ceasing from injustice and empire also resulted in Athens regaining the presidency of the fleet (5.6), while Thebes placed herself under Athens' authority when the latter enacted services and behaved well, and while Sparta allowed Athens to rule as she wished because the latter treated the former generously (5.7). Athens thus has the capacity to win back the Greeks to her side without labour, danger or expense and she will do this by behaving benevolently towards the other states (5.8). Indeed, Athens might accomplish making the Delphic oracle independent again not by war but by sending embassies throughout Greece, where she would discover that all the Greeks would seek to take back the oracle were the Phocians to abandon it (5.9). If Athens were to seek peace in every land and sea, she would find that every Greek would be praying for the safety of the city (5.10). In the following two sections of this chapter Xenophon emphatically states that peace is better for the economic situation of the city-state. In past days much money was paid into the treasury during peacetime, but war resulted in it being completely spent. Revenues cease in war, but they increase upon the cessation of war with the result that the citizens can do as they please (5.12). The only situation in which war is justified is if the city has been wronged, otherwise the state's economy suffers (5.13).

The final chapter of the work continues to articulate the need for peace for the good of the city of Athens, but in particular for the wealthier citizens such as Xenophon himself. Living in peace means that the Athenians will be looked upon with greater affection by the other Greeks, that they will live in greater security (cf. ἀσφαλέστερον), and that they will be more glorious (cf. εὐκλεέστεροι). The Athenian people will have more food and the rich will no longer have to pay for the expense of war (6.1). The absence of war also means that the Athenians can provide for the festivals, repair walls and harbours, and give their privileges back to the priests, the council, the magistrates and the knights. Xenophon's ideal Athens, as John Dillery has also observed, is to become the peaceful, rather than being the meddling, acquisitive state so that it becomes a thriving cultural centre.[17] The author promotes an anti-imperial vision, which (as we shall see) is much the same as that proposed in the *Hellenica*, which was a virtually contemporary work.[18]

In a world without war, the people of Athens will see their city prospering securely (6.1). It is with these comments that Xenophon reveals the class bias of his view of wealth and prosperity. His wealth is the wealth of the leisured and privileged few, rather than of the working poor citizens who subsist in Athens. Avoiding war enriches in large parts and on the personal level because it saves the rich from having to pay vast sums for the support of hostilities. The wealth that Xenophon is ultimately concerned with is the inherited, old money that comes with class, rather than that earned in trade or in the mines – hence, the ironic discussion of the silver mines in chapter 4. His concern is the preservation of pre-existing monies, both private and public.

Xenophon concludes this final chapter and the work with what is for him a typical gesture at piety. He asks Athens to consult the gods at Dodona and Delphi regarding whether it is better for the city to be at peace (6.2). And if the gods agree that peace is in the best interests for Athens, then the embassy is to enquire which gods must be propitiated to this end. When it has received good omens, the state must begin the work of peace, for working together with the gods it would reasonably proceed in a better fashion for the city (6.3).

III

The *Poroi* is a strongly class-inflected work. The text *appears* to advocate and indeed, to celebrate wealth creation through silver mining in particular while in actual fact raising some serious questions about this activity. The mines may create a large income for the individuals who own them and for the state as a whole, both in terms of the hiring and renting out of its massive workforce of slaves and in terms of its acquisition of silver ore, but there are notable costs to be taken into account which qualify the wealth that is gathered. First, there is the immense cost in human life where slaves are concerned due to the horrific work conditions in the mines. Then and more importantly where Xenophon is concerned, silver creates a never-ending hunger for itself and it has historically been what funds the Athenian war effort, enabling the building and upkeep of its warships. Wealth creation is a self-defeating prospect in the *Poroi*. But it is necessary to remember that Xenophon is a member of the wealthy set and as such, he is not so much concerned with wealth creation as wealth maintenance. Accordingly, because war consumes private funds, especially those of the wealthy class who are obliged to fund the triremes, and public funds, the author is strongly opposed to it and to Athens' hegemonic aspirations. As a member of this class, he seeks the status quo, which is best preserved through the quiet life.

The *Poroi* begins with the observation that states are like their leaders, Ἐγὼ μὲν τοῦτο ἀεί νομίζω, ὁποῖοί τινες ἂν οἱ προστάται ὦσι, τοιαύτας καὶ τὰς πολιτείας γίγνεσθαι (1.1). Indeed. S. Schorn seems to regard the *Poroi* as a work concerned with leadership,[19] while John Dillery takes this as referring to the fact that the poverty of some of the Athenian citizens has caused the state to behave more unjustly towards other states.[20] This statement might appear to be an observation casually dropped into text. Or else, one might see no attempt to address this statement anywhere in the work, as it is not ostensibly a text about political leadership or political rule. But the beginnings and the ends of texts are significant points, and this statement does thematize the work, especially if one reads the work ironically; that is as not saying what it really means, as I do. Indeed, the leaders of fourth-century Athens are the demagogues and rabble rousers who mount the speaker's platform to incite the citizens to war and to acquire more and more. They are the busy-bodies or πολυπράμονες who reveal themselves as greedy and who thus make the state greedy for more land, power and revenues. The economy of Athens is thus a dysfunctional one, for it wastes any wealth reserves it might have on pursuing war among the Greek states. Peace, according to Xenophon, is the most effective means of achieving and preserving 'means'; it is best for wealth acquisition in promoting tourism and trade between the states, and it is ideal for wealth preservation in not requiring the 'means' acquired to be spent on a war effort. Wealth is thus the consequence of a state of mind and being.

Part Three

The Rest of Greece

8

Why Xenophon's *Hiero* Is not a Socratic Dialogue

I

The *Hiero*, one of the shorter works in the Xenophontic corpus, is dated by G. P. D. Alders to *c.* 360 BCE,[1] and it is a text that seems to have both historical and philosophical concerns. Its historico-political concern is the conversation that the tyrant has with the poet Simonides about what it means to rule and the problems associated with ruling – Simonides offers Hiero his wisdom and thoughts on these topics. But with the wise teaching of Simonides to the less enlightened tyrant it would seem to be a quasi-Socratic, and so a philosophical dialogue. The only thing lacking is the presence of the philosopher Socrates and this is of course due to two things: the early dramatic date, about 474 BCE, of the dialogue and the fact that the participants in the dialogue are in Syracuse rather than Athens. The Socratic model is, nonetheless, one upheld by scholars. Most famously, Leo Strauss treated the work by discussing the role of philosophy and politics in his *On Tyranny*.[2] Vivienne Gray in quite a different mode sees the influence of the philosopher on this dialogue, as the poet Simonides is, in her view, Socratic.[3]

Even though Hiero and Simonides are conventionally featured in stories concerning the meeting of a supposedly wise man and the tyrant (cf. Plato *Second Letter* 311a–b[4]), the fact is that the *Hiero* cannot be a Socratic dialogue – despite what V. Gray posits[5] – because Simonides is not Socrates or even Socratic in any way. Dorota Tymura thinks that Socrates is absent to avoid the possible charge of being a teacher of tyrants.[6] Simonides is a poet, albeit one of some distinction, rather than a philosopher. And neither is the work history beyond the fact that it depicts an actual moment at which tyrant and poet met, thus reworking the motif of a meeting between wise man and ruler, as Gray suggests.[7] But the attention need not go only to the tyrant and his role in society in this work, as Strauss has given it in *On Tyranny*. This is a far too limited and misdirected perspective on the dialogue. I suggest that what is at stake in the work as much as the position of the tyrant is the authority of Simonides as a poet. Xenophon is working in a time when prose has achieved a prominence in the Greek-speaking world with himself, Plato, Isocrates and Demosthenes composing their respective works, and, I suggest, he writes as a prose writer to erode both the authority of the poet in the fourth-century Greek world and the authority of tyranny, which the poet helps to support.

II

The ostensible dialogue initially lulls the reader into accepting the authority of the poet. Hiero and Simonides meet to discuss the happiness of the tyrant relative to that of the private individual.[8] And in this conversation Simonides would seem to be a figure to be granted some credibility because he is an author and his wisdom is well-regarded in the early classical period but not so much in the world that Xenophon inhabits. The dialogue begins with the author noting that both Simonides and Hiero are at leisure, cf. σχολῆς δὲ γενομένης ἀμφοῖν (1.1), with the result that the poet takes the opportunity to ask the tyrant what the latter knows better, namely how the ordinary person's life and the tyrant's life differ. After all, Hiero has himself been an ordinary person, an ἰδιώτης (1.2). Clearly, Hiero is at rest from the business governing his state, but the question that immediately looms is: what is Simonides at rest from? Is he taking a break from his job as a poet, which Xenophon named him to be in the third word of the dialogue? Or is his role of ἰδιώτης, or layperson, which Hiero has identified him as (ἐπεὶ νῦν γε ἔτι ἰδιώτης εἶ 'since you are now a layperson'1.3), one of leisure since it is not concerned with activity of public life? Simonides is, undoubtedly, and as Xenophon says, the poet and as such, he has a definite role in society, which he can never step aside from. This identity makes it doubtful that Simonides could ever be a Socratic or a Socrates-substitute as Gray has proposed,[9] because Socrates does not identify himself with poetry at all and actually criticizes it robustly in the *Republic*.

It should be observed that Hiero uses the word ἰδιώτης for his citizens and for the poet Simonides to distinguish himself in his status as a tyrant from them: the thought is that all others in the state are ordinary laypeople because they are not rulers. This seems to be the way in which he uses the word at 4.6, noting that he has more possessions than the ordinary man, and in any case, needs this greater wealth because he cannot cut down on his expenses, unlike the layman. But it is to be noted that Hiero's view of Simonides as a mere ἰδιώτης is mistaken; this becomes clear from an understanding of what was the case in the earlier Greek world. Gregory Nagy writes in his essay, 'Early Views on Poets and Poetry', articulating clearly a general and widely-accepted view in antiquity: 'The ποιητής was a professional; he was a master of τεχνή, the work of an artisan.'[10] Poetic knowledge is something that distinguishes the individual who bears it from ordinary people. More recently, Kevin Robb points to the way in which the poet and those associated with him, the singer and the rhapsode, were regarded as special or highly honoured by society; the singer inspired awe in his world.[11] In the world of the *Theogony* (cf. 75ff.) the poet stands at the right hand of the king and functions as an extension of his authority, which derives from the god Zeus.[12] Later in classical Athens, in the *Ion* the rhapsode is one in the class of craftsmen, although Socrates makes a point of demonstrating that the rhapsode is actually ignorant of what he claims to know.[13] The arts associated with letters have a particular and special status in society, and so its practitioner is no ordinary man.

That the poet should be someone with a particular knowledge is demonstrated by *Protagoras* 312b. Here the term ἰδιώτης receives attention from Socrates. The philosopher observes to Hippocrates that he did not learn from Protagoras to write, to play the lyre, or to train young men in gymnastics as if the latter were a craftsman (δημιουργός) but rather as befits an ἰδιώτης, and at 327c of the same dialogue, Protagoras states that often bad flute players are produced from good ones and good ones from bad ones, but in any case all flute players are good enough when compared with non-flute players, who are denoted by the noun ἰδιώτης, and those who know nothing of flute-playing. Being an ἰδιώτης entails that one does not have ability in any of the crafts or arts practiced in the culture of Ancient Greece. Indeed, as far as the audience of the *Hiero* is concerned, although somewhat curiously not Hiero himself in light of what the poet can do for him, the poet is engaged in public life.

Simonides was one of several poets – Pindar and Bacchylides were others – who wrote for the tyrant and thereby supported his rule. The poet was above all an encomiast of the games, concerned to praise the ruler as patron, and his wealth and his reign as responsible for the victory in the games, while he acknowledged the athlete and, if applicable, the horse(s) as only instruments of the victory.

The dialogue commences with a prompting from the tyrant Hiero, asking the poet to refresh his memory as to the nature of ordinary human life so that the tyrant in turn can draw attention to the differences between this and the tyrant's life (1.3). After all, the tyrant has conceded that the poet, even though he is an ἰδιώτης, is a wise man (σοῦ οὕτως ὄντος σοφοῦ ἀνδρός, 1.1). Simonides obliges, stating that the ordinary person can experience pleasure through sight, hearing, smell and taste. He continues that pleasures and pains can be conveyed through the soul, or through the body and soul together (1.4–6). It is interesting to note that the conversation is curiously skewed because the paradigmatic ἰδιώτης in this dialogue, namely Simonides, is, as we have seen, not quite the ordinary layperson. Hiero responds that the ordinary person's life is different from the tyrant's life (1.7), to which Simonides retorts that the tyrant has many more pleasures (πολλαπλάσια . . . εὐφραίνεται) and far less pain (πολὺ δὲ μείω τά λύπη ἔχει, 1.8).

Hiero argues that the tyrant, who is nearly always the impersonal third person as far as the speaker is concerned,[14] is more limited in his enjoyment of pleasures where sight is concerned than the ordinary man. He cannot go where he wishes to see the sights, whether to cities or to panegyrics, due to fear for his position, and must remain at home (1.12–13). As for hearing pleasurable things, Hiero observes that the praises which men utter are the product of flattery (1.15–16). As for tastes, ordinary people go to feasts more readily than tyrants and this is because the tyrant gets fed up with all the wonderful flavours and tastes presented to him all the time (1.18–26).[15] When Hiero turns to a consideration of personal relationships, he notes that the tyrant is poorly off because he must marry beneath himself unless he weds a foreign bride (1.28). But even where the love of men, such as the tyrant's lover Dailochus is concerned, Hiero is deprived of true love because, unlike the ἰδιώτης, plots are hatched against tyrants by those who pretend to love them (1.37–8). In effect, this tyrant offers a self-centered view of the world in which his wishes and desires take priority over anyone else's.

Simonides goads Hiero into deeper self-loathing by drawing attention to his monetary advantage: the tyrant is so far superior in his wealth such that he can harm his enemies and help his friends (2.2). Hiero answers that if peace is the greatest boon for mankind, then the tyrant is wretched because he never has peace. When he suspects someone in the state is plotting against him, he kills him, a joyless task, and has as a consequence fewer subjects to rule over (2.17–18). The tyrant is daily beset by such a war (2.18). At 3.8–9, the argument is that a tyrant's personal relations are difficult even where friendship, the most important thing for humans (3.3), is concerned. Hiero notes that tyrants have murdered their own children and have been murdered by them and have murdered members of their families. As Gray notes, a quadruple anaphora, πολλοὺς μὲν παῖδας . . . πολλοὺς δ' ὑπὸ παίδων . . . πολλοὺς δὲ ἀδελφοὺς . . . πολλοὺς δὲ καὶ ὑπὸ γυναικῶν, emphasizes the number of murders which trouble the tyrant and his circle (3.8).[16] According to him, the tyrant, furthermore, has no faith (πίστις) in anyone, so he must have people taste his food before he eats it to check for poison (4.2). Cities, moreover, tend to honour tyrannicides, suggesting their hostility towards the tyrant. The tyrant is, according to Hiero's selfish perspective, an isolated and lonely being.

The tyrant is not actually richer than the ordinary man, continues Hiero. While the ordinary man wants to own a household or a field or a servant, it is the case that the tyrant has far greater desires. He wants to have cities, great places, harbours or strong acropolises (4.7), but what the tyrant desires brings him great troubles. The tyrant's position compromises him in another way: while the ordinary man can cut down on his expenses as he wishes, the tyrant has large expenditures connected with keeping himself alive (4.9). But this is also akin to the argument which Socrates employs in the *Oeconomicus* to demonstrate that the wealthy Critobulus is not after all as wealthy as he thinks he is (*Oeconomicus* 2.5–6): the rich man uses up his money in lawsuits as he is summoned to the lawcourt by envious sycophants.[17] Wealth requires further wealth for its upkeep. Unprompted, Hiero goes on to say that the tyrant is so paranoid due to his fear that he may kill those he perceives to be just, wise and courageous (5.1–2). Hiero cannot stop enumerating the long litany of woes suffered by the tyrant and continues by saying that he is deprived of the pleasures the ordinary man enjoys (6.1), having slaves instead of friends (6.3). Fear for his life makes him trust foreigners rather than his own citizens (6.5). Rather than being given honour as someone who can provide benefit, the tyrant is rather condemned to death in the opinion of all men (7.10).

It is after this lengthy litany of apparent woes and misfortunes that the poet asks the tyrant why he does not stop being a tyrant since it is the most wretched of fates (7.12). Hiero elaborates his plight, adding that since he cannot repay all the money he has taken, since he cannot make up for all the chains with which he has imprisoned others and since he cannot repay all he lives he has taken, he thinks it best for him to hang himself. The tyrant's lot is a product of his misperceptions of his own condition. It is at this point that Simonides seems to take/takes control of the conversation and insists that the tyrant's life is after all better than the ordinary man's but not in ways that are conventionally thought so (8.1). He implies therefore that even if Hiero has been speaking ironically about his fate as that of the tyrant, Hiero is quite ignorant of his own status in the world.

Hiero's major complaint has been that the tyrant is hated by his subjects. He draws far greater attention to relationships rather than material disadvantage, but Simonides contends that it is the case that being a ruler does not prevent one from being loved (8.1). When a man with a higher position in the world acts or performs some gesture, such as uttering a greeting, or uttering a panegyric, his action will have more positive impact than if it had been performed by an ordinary person. Likewise, a gift from a tyrant will elicit great gratitude from the recipient(s) (8.7). The man of power is thus the man of greater and more positive influence. Hiero then takes up the argument by observing that the tyrant is obliged to do far more and go to great lengths – the verb used is πραγματεύεσθαι – unlike the ordinary man and so must make more money and have spear-bearers to guard his wealth (8.8–10). The verb πραγματεύεσθαι has, among other connotations, the sense of 'to take trouble' and its proximity to πλεονεξίας (8.10), which connotes 'greediness', 'grasping' and 'arrogance', suggests a negative connotation for the verb, proposing a link with πρᾶγμα, which can, among other things, have the sense of public lawsuit. The negative connotations of the verb here imply that Hiero still does not quite understand what Simonides is trying to tell him. The tyrant thinks that he has to go beyond acceptable behaviour to act as his station requires.

III

So far so good. The *Hiero* conforms nicely to a Socratic dialogue with a seemingly wise interlocutor – Simonides as the Socrates-figure – conversing with a less enlightened member of society, the tyrant Hiero. Ideally, the wise man will help his conversation partner to come to an important realization about his life and the world. Vivienne Gray sees the interview between Solon and Croesus and between Croesus and Bias of Pirene in Herodotus Book 1 to be models for the current dialogue.[18] In the Herodotean narrative the Lydian leader Croesus comes to an understanding of his status in the world as he awaits execution while standing on the funeral pyre.

But seeing an analogy between the *Histories* and Xenophon's work must not blind us to what is actually happening in the *Hiero*, and in fact, drawing attention to this apparent analogy prevents us from reading the dialogue closely enough to see where Xenophon has located the irony he intends. It is important to realize that Hiero does not until the final section of the work, if at all, see what Simonides is trying to tell him when the poet engages in what I argue to be a radical redefinition of tyranny. Teaching and learning are after all not effective in the *Hiero*. Hiero's outlook on his own life is clearly faulty but Simonides only does so much and not enough to alter it. He is a poet and he inevitably calls on his experience and knowledge as a poet; he has no wider horizon, which is necessary in political life. In section 9 he teaches Hiero about the importance of delegating the meting out of punishments to others within the state so that the tyrant does not lose the favour of his subjects by drawing an analogy with the assembling and training of a choir (9.5). Following the analogy of political life with poetry he suggests offering prizes to those who achieve in agriculture or in commerce within the state just as the poetic competitor receives awards for his successes (9.6ff.).

Simonides is not the wise man that Gray sees him to be,[19] and his limitation is notably made apparent with the most important teaching in the dialogue, which I will now outline. The poet argues at the beginning of section 11 that it is better for the despotic leader to spend his own money on the state rather than on himself, καὶ γὰρ ἔμοιγε τὰ εἰς τὴν πόλιν ἀναλούμενα μᾶλλον εἰς τὸ δέον τελεῖσθαι ἢ τὰ εἰς τὸ ἴδιον ἀνδρὶ τυράννῳ, 'for it seems to me that what is spent on the city goes to necessity rather than what is spent on private ends for the tyrannical man' (11.1). The tyrant will have greater pride with the whole city arrayed with walls, temples, colonnades, marketplaces and harbours and with the city well-fortified than with himself set out with armour. Likewise, it is far better for the whole city to have more horses to send into competition than for the tyrant to have many chariots of his own, and for the city as a whole to be blessed (cf. πολεώς ... εὐδαιμονίᾳ) rather than for the tyrant to be celebrated for the virtue of a chariot (ἅρματος ἀρετῇ) (11.5). (Self-interest is perhaps involved here for this would create more opportunities for the praise poet to be commissioned to write encomia for the tyrant.)

Having a city which is most blessed and happy (εὐδαιμονεστάτην τὴν πόλιν) will make the tyrant a victor in the finest and most splendid contest among men and will ensure that he is loved by his subjects (11.7–8). Strauss has argued that the tyrant can be the happiest by being beneficent to his people.[20] In effect, Simonides sees the state as a giant horse race, for which he would write the victory song. The poet is furthermore proposing a communitarian model of society, where wealth and happiness are shared between everyone rather than held by the tyrant alone, as is the case in conventional tyranny. The wealth of the subjects becomes the tyrant's wealth and Simonides ventures 'πλούτιζε μὲν τοὺς φίλους. Σαυτὸν γὰρ πλουτιεῖς', ('enrich your friends. You will enrich yourself.' 11.13). The poet is here redefining the material aspect of despotic rule, and in the process refigures the tyrant's relationalities – he will be loved rather than hated if wealth is more widely distributed. In stating this, the poet has assumed an even more radical redefinition of the tyrant's life in proposing that the latter's wealth is dependent on those around him. Simonides names those whose welfare must be kept in mind as τοὺς φίλους – 'friends' or 'dear ones'. But the transformation of Hiero's world becomes manifestly apparent in the final two sections of the work as Simonides tells his interlocutor to consider his nation as a household (οἶκος), the citizens as friends (ἑταίροι), his friends as children (τέκνα) and finally, his children as his own soul (11.14). The tyrant is to treat his citizens, that is, his friends, well and as a consequence to possess the finest and most blessed possession of all, namely not to be envied for his situation (11.15).

What has happened is that Simonides has dehierarchized the relations in conventional tyranny: the tyrant is no longer a superior but is now among equals. What one sees here is an anticipation of the cosmopolitan fantasy, where everyone becomes one's intimate to a greater or a lesser extent. The third century Stoic Hierocles will say (in Stobaeus 4.671, 7.673, 11) that the city begins with the individual; the individual is surrounded by numerous circles of other individuals, with the closest circle containing his own body and what the body requires; the next ring containing his immediate family, the next one his extended family of uncles, aunts, grandparents, nephews, nieces, cousins; the next, other relatives; the next, neighbours; and then, those living in nearby towns, one's countrymen, and so on in extending circles so that the whole of the human race is contained in a set of concentric rings. Hierocles goes on to observe that one's goal should be to reduce the distance between these relational circles with the result that everyone becomes a 'brother', 'sister', 'mother' and 'father' to oneself and in keeping with the logic of the analogy, mankind becomes a family.[21]

But the question that remains to be asked here is: has Simonides been the ideal adviser to Hiero in this dialogue and so an ideal mediator between the people and the tyrant, as R. Sevieri, in an attempt to view Hiero as starting as an imperfect hero but ending up as a perfect hero, suggests?[22] Let me put it another way: Simonides seems to speak for Hiero in support of his tyranny, although Gray proposes that the poet is ironically championing the view of appearances with which the tyrant surrounds himself.[23] In distinction from this view, I suggest that it is rather possible to regard Simonides' presence as at the very best conflicted. Is the poet there simply to support the tyranny, or is he present to modify and criticize Hiero's view of what a tyrant is? It would appear that by getting the citizens to adore their tyrant as a path to security and good government his advice is well-presented. Yet if the point of an ideal tyranny is not the adoration of the leader, neither is it to be the adoration of one's subjects and it should not be this because it is no less egocentric than Hiero's initial view of himself as someone deprived of true love. Adoration of one's subjects is merely the flipside of adoration of the ruler. It would appear that in proposing the adulation of Hiero, Simonides is engaged in no small measure of sycophancy with regard to the tyrant. In implicitly suggesting this, Xenophon may be here engaging in an implicit critique of Simonides as an effective political agent. The poet does not, and cannot, have autonomy because he is dependent on the ruler's patronage. He writes as the leader wants him to because he is paid by the leader. And ancient sources suggest that Simonides was notoriously greedy as he initiated the commodification of poetry.[24] Certainly, he also had Scopas, tyrant of Thessaly, as his patron and he wrote victory hymns for him.

Furthermore, Simonides' apparent wisdom may only be that, apparent wisdom. Well-regarded and admired in the fifth century and earlier times, as I demonstrated earlier in this chapter, Simonides comes under fire from fourth-century authors. Simonides after all is being retrospectively depicted as a poet in an age of prose, where the prose writer takes precedence and the poet is represented by the rhapsode, who is merely an unthinking mouthpiece in Plato's critique in the *Ion* (cf. *Ion* 542 a, cf. *Apology* 22a–b). The rhapsode and the poet he cites are inspired but certainly not wise. For instance, Simonides' definition of justice, which is originally to be found at 433e, is faulted by Socrates in the *Republic*. In this text Cephalus proposes a view of justice, which is taken up by Polemarchus only to be demolished by the philosopher Socrates (*Republic*, I, 331dff.). In the first book of the *Republic*, Cephalus cites the Simonidean view of justice, that such is to render each his due (331e). But this view of justice is quickly qualified to mean that one can only render back what is good for the person who has given it, provided that he is good and is in his right mind (332b). Socrates inevitably demolishes Simonides' view of what justice is by noting that in the latter's view justice is to do good to friends and to do harm to enemies (336a).

Accordingly, Xenophon provides us with an adviser and an interlocutor who are far from ideal. Their understanding of what rule is and should be remains sorely lacking despite the conversation they have had. But what is the option if one does not accept the adoration of the ruler by his subjects, even if he goes to lengths to make them happy? Greg Anderson has shown that at the beginning Greek tyrants took on responsibilities and engaged in displays of great generosity for their communities, and they also were active in the administration of cults and festivals, activities that would have contributed to the well-being of the community because they pleased the gods, according to Greek notions of civic piety. They gave more with a view to nurturing the people because they had much more.[25] The idea that tyranny could be, and perhaps ought to be, something that benefits those who are its subjects was present in its foundation and furthermore, makes a re-appearance also in one of Xenophon's contemporaries, Isocrates. In the *To Nicocles*, a work where Isocrates writes to the Cypriot tyrant to advise him on what an ideal rule should consist in, demonstrates that Simonides' emphasis on the adoration of the subjects is misplaced. Isocrates writes at *To Nicocles* 15:

> Ἄρχεσθαι μὲν οὖν ἐντευθεν χρὴ τοὺς μέλλοντάς τι τῶν δεόντων ποιήσειν, πρὸς δὲ τούτοις φιλάνθρωπον εἶναι δεῖ καὶ φιλόπολιν· οὔτε γὰρ ἵππων οὔτε κυνῶν οὔτ' ἄλλου πράγματος οὐδενὸς οἷόν τε καλῶς ἄρχειν, ἂν μή τις χαίρῃ τούτοις ὧν αὐτὸν δεῖ ποιεῖσθαι τὴν ἐπιμέλειαν
>
> It is necessary for those who are about to do what is necessary to begin from here; and in addition it is necessary to be a lover of men and a lover of the city, for it is not possible to rule horses, dogs, men or anything well if one does not delight in these things which he must concern himself with.

Isocrates proposes a radical shift in attention from the leader to the subjects and their community as the object of love in a tyrannical rule. What the fourth-century rhetorician says is that a good ruler must be a lover of men and of his city first and foremost. Those ruled must be cared for and nurtured. In *Epistle* 5, the *Letter to Alexander*, Isocrates commends his addressee for being a 'lover of men, a lover of Athens and a lover of wisdom' (ὡς φιλάνθρωπος εἶ καὶ φιλαθήναιος καὶ φιλόσοφος, 2). There is no concern here, or in any of the other letters addressed to rulers, of the people's love for their leaders. Rather one imagines that the love of the subject for his ruler will follow the ruler's own affection for his people and so ensure a state at peace and in good order. The important point here is that the tyrant's feeling for his community will initiate a good rule, not the community's feeling for its ruler, as Simonides and Hiero both mistakenly think.

Isocrates offers further insight into the reading of the *Hiero*. The rhetorician comments that those who come to rulers with gifts are engaged not in an act of giving but in bargaining for something, because they often give what the ruler already has in abundance. They are giving to get back something in return, for example, the ruler's good favour (*To Nicocles* 1). Isocrates observes later in *To Nicocles* that rulers tend to experience most pleasure with those who agree with them rather than with those who admonish them. He goes on interestingly to criticize poets. People have thought that poets – and the emphasis is on thinking in the past – are the best counsellors for tyrants, but the fact is that audiences now prefer the cheapest comedies to their advice (43-4). Isocrates suggests that poetry is no longer of much use to society as far as the teaching of leaders is concerned. He implies that prose is the better medium for the instruction of leaders and indeed the present speech is to be regarded as far better for the purpose of helping Nicocles' state and kingdom (2). And so likewise with the *Hiero* it is the case that the poet, whose voice as a poet is never in any case heard in the dialogue, speaks to pander favour; thus, he yields to Xenophon the prose writer as the teacher of tyrants.

But it is significant that Isocrates is not the only voice in the fourth century advocating a shift away from concern with the ruler. The attention to the love and care of those who are ruled is not at all alien to other prose of the fifth and fourth century. Earlier in the fifth century Thucydides had taken a similar view to Isocrates in his *History*. Here his ideal leader Pericles offers the view that he knows and discerns what is necessary (γνῶναί τε τὰ δέοντα καὶ ἑρμηνεῦσαι ταῦτα, φιλόπολις) in government, and furthermore and most importantly for the discussion here, he declares himself a 'lover of the city (φιλόπολις)' and not liable to bribery (2.60.5). Pericles is a lover of the democratic citizenry. Whether one is dealing with a democracy or an absolutist rule, concern for one's subjects is paramount. To neglect those in the community and the community itself leads to unrest and potential destabilization of the state if dissatisfaction grows and mounts. Conventional tyrannical leadership consumes its subjects but it also becomes for the leader a self-consuming condition, which leads to his despair and great distress.

IV

Xenophon's *Hiero* is a brief but rather complex work. The poet Simonides has a conversation with the tyrant Hiero and endeavours to correct the latter where he thinks his life is miserable and wretched. Simonides seems to embody wisdom, as his position in society suggests he does, and Hiero reveals his ignorance and self-centeredness, as his role in the dialogue strongly proposes. Leo Strauss has seen the *Hiero* to be primarily a critique of tyranny and that is because his mode of 'analysis' is paraphrase. In his view, tyranny has its faults but these faults can be mitigated by a wise man, namely Simonides.[26] But I suggest rather that Xenophon is not specifically concerned with autocratic rule although such rule is found lacking in the case of Hiero. I argue that beneath the narrative of the conversation between Simonides and Hiero is another discourse about the role of the teacher as pertains to the role of poetry and the poet in society. The scene that the author depicts is indeed a fifth-century one, but – and this is of utmost importance – he writes in the fourth century.

The dialogue is an anachronism, misplaced in time and so is the function of poetry and the poet in society. Here lies the irony, which requires that its viewer has a perspective which grants him or her some superior knowledge. Looking back on the past leaves the reader with an enhanced perspective on what was the case. The fourth century is the era when prose comes into a position of prominence and distinction, expressing knowledge in a superior manner. In this context Simonides is a seriously compromised individual. In any case, he is a poet whose ties to the tyrant as his patron do not enable him to speak fully critically of Hiero. Simonides has conflicting interests, namely, the earning of money and the role of giving advice. Indeed, he yields far too easily to Hiero's description of him as an ἰδιώτης. And he does not see the major flaw of Hiero's argument in arguing that the tyrant simply needs to make his subjects happy by beautifying their city. Fourth-century prose writers are the ones who demonstrate that the role of the tyrant is not to be appeased by the subjects but to be lovers and cultivators of their subjects. This is how they maintain the state. The fact is that, even though V. Gray regards the *Hiero* as a Socratic dialogue, albeit that Socrates or any Socrates-like figure does not appear in the dialogue, this work cannot be a Socratic or Socratic-like dialogue in any sense of the word Socratic.

9

Spartan Disappointments

Xenophon, cast as the enemy of Athenian democracy with its rabble-rousing oratory and militancy in the fourth century, was an individual – so the account of his life goes – who was allied with oligarchy and also with Sparta, which was not democratic in any sense. The author was supposedly such a laconophile indeed that he fought under the Spartan king Agesilaus II, who is the subject of the *Agesilaus*, against the Athenians in the battle of Chaeronea in 394 BCE.[1] For this action he was exiled from Athens and the Spartans took him in, giving him a property at Scillus, near Olympia in Elis. Athens may have eventually revoked the exile, and Xenophon moved either back to Athens or to Corinth after the Battle of Leuctra (371 BCE) and following the collapse of Spartan hegemony in the Greek world.

These events in the author's life would appear to make his position towards Sparta apparent. The temptation is to cast Xenophon as straightforwardly and single-mindedly pro-Spartan and anti-Athenian, but there have been different opinions on his Laconic stance. Paul Christensen observes that three positions on Xenophon's stance on Sparta currently exist. First, the author was consistently pro-Spartan and worked to make the city-state appear the best it could in his writings; second, his views on Sparta changed over time, from a unilaterally pro-Spartan stance to growing disillusionment as the city-state gained power in the Greek world, and finally, from a Straussian perspective, Xenophon produced a well-disguised satire of the Spartan state.[2] I want to suggest in this chapter that the actual situation is somewhat more complicated than the dichotomy of either pro- or anti-Spartan stance suggests. The two works that deal with Sparta – the *Constitution of Sparta*, which celebrates the legislation of Lycurgus that was responsible for the Spartan state, and the *Agesilaus*, which is an encomium of the leader who Xenophon marched with against the Athenians – seem at first glance to applaud wholeheartedly the Spartan achievement. Yet I suggest that there are in these two works moments of disappointment with Sparta and her accomplishments, which suggest that if Athens was less than ideal for Xenophon,

Sparta was after all not and never had been the ideal state that the author might have wanted the less accomplished members of his audience to think it to be.

I

The *Consitution of Sparta* is a work that celebrates the city-state founded through the laws of Lycurgus, who flourished in the distant past and, according to the *Constitution of Sparta* 10.8, at the time of the Heracleidae in the age of the heroes. Accordingly, the text rehearses the legendary and somewhat mythical account of the state as one that trained its citizens for military engagement, for virtue and to lead a life of austerity. The author provides a three hundred-year retrospective on Sparta in order, it would appear, to idealize the state. Xenophon declares at the opening of the *Constitution* that he has perceived Sparta to be the most powerful state in Greece even though it has the fewest people, and this is due to the leader who established its law (1.1). The author admires Lycurgus, who demonstrated to his citizens the blessedness they could have if they obeyed his constitution, which did not imitate those of other city-states but rather stood contrary to them (1.2). He goes on to detail the life of the Spartan citizen from procreation to youth to adulthood and to old age in the work in order to demonstrate the distinctiveness and the excellence of Lycurgus' legislation.

As far as procreation is concerned, Xenophon observes that other states nurture those who are to produce children by feeding them the most modest food and delicacies are given in the tiniest portions – they abstain from wine or if they take it, have it watered down. These girls are sedentary (ἑδραῖοι) and they tend to engage in wool work (1.3). In contrast, Lycurgus regards it as sufficient for slave girls to make clothing and rather has the free women exercise their bodies no less than the men, establishing contests of speed and strength for the reason that the children they bear will be stronger (1.4). Courting rituals furthermore ensure that conception occurs at the point most opportune for producing strong children. Sex is limited so that the man gains satisfaction from it and the offspring is again stronger and the man marries his wife at the peak of his manhood to ensure good offspring (1.5–6). Older husbands are required to introduce younger men, whose soul and body they admire, to procreate with their wives (1.7). Again, the goal of this legislation is well-born (cf. εὔτεκνον) and noble (γενναίαν) offspring (1.8).

Lycurgus also took concern for the education and training (cf. παιδείαν) of the young Spartan. Where in other states the youths were given over to a παιδαγωγός to learn letters, music and wrestling and dressed in shoes and cloaks, the Spartan children were sent to a παιδονόμος, who had the authority to gather the children together and to punish them severely if they misbehaved (2.2). The Spartan ruler also assigned whip bearers, who would punish the youths to ensure that modesty and obedience went hand in hand at Sparta (2.3). The male children walked without shoes so that they could climb and descend, and jump and run more easily (2.4); they wore one garment all year round to accustom them to heat and cold; and they were never allowed to feel full from food on the understanding that this made them healthier (2.5). The youths were permitted to steal to satisfy their hunger and this had the aim of making them more resourceful and more warlike (cf. πολμικωτέρους) (2.7). Those who were caught stealing were punished with stripes (2.8), indicating that prowess at theft was to be commended. Lycurgus ensured that the boys were never without someone to rule them, enabling any adult to oversee and punish the young men (2.10) – cf. ὥστε οὐδέποτε ἐκεῖ οἱ παῖδες ἔρημοι ἄρχοντός εἰσι, at 2.11.

Pederastic love was a concern for the lawmaker and while other Greek states permitted men and boys to cohabitate, again Lycurgus did quite the opposite (ὁ Λυκοῦργος ἐναντία καὶ τούτοις πᾶσι γνούς, 2.12). One was permitted to love another if one loved the partner's soul as this led to the finest παιδεία, but if there was desire for the other's body, then this was regarded as most shameful (2.13).

Youth saw the Spartan male strongly acculturated to modesty throughout his lifetime whereas all other Greeks left their tutors and became autonomous (3.1). Typically, Lycurgus planned the opposite of this, cf. ὁ Λυκούργος καὶ τούτων τἀντία ἔγνω (3.1). Knowing that violence and strong desires were inclined to be experienced by the citizens at this age, the legislator gave them great labours and did not allow them any leisure time (3.2). The youths were required to have the outward marks of modesty, walking with their hands within their cloaks, proceeding in silence and looking nowhere but the road before their feet so that the males seemed to be more modest than even the females (3.4).

Lycurgus was most concerned with the men in the prime of their lives, knowing that they could do the most good for the city-state if they were so inclined (4.1). He set up contests so that they could exhibit the greatest valour (cf. ἀνδραγαθίας) with the ephors picking three men, commanders of the knights, who in turn would select a hundred of the best men. The process of selection became a contest which the Spartan men sought to win, remaining fit so that they were able to go to war (4.6). It is at the peak of their lives that the Spartan men held political office, and where other Greeks continued in the military forces, Lycurgus made the hunt their concern (4.7). Xenophon again emphasizes the distinction between those in Sparta and the rest of Greece as far as their lifestyle is concerned.

With the end of section 4 the author concludes his account of Spartan education and acculturation, one that continues well into adulthood, and begins discussion of distinctive Lacedaemonian institutions and customs. At 5.2 we learn that Lycurgus established the messes, communal meals, in the open air at which the Spartans would eat neither too sparingly or too great an amount of food. Extra delicacies were supplied from the hunt (5.3). Again, Xenophon draws a contrast between the Spartans and other Greeks, whom he notes dine at home and as a consequence of this engage in misconduct (5.2). The reader also discovers that Lycurgus abandoned compulsory drinking, which led to the undoing of individuals' minds and bodies (5.4). Meals were conducted in mixed age groups so that the elders, through their experience, might educate (παιδεύεσθαι) the younger and reduce the occurrence of bad behaviour and unseemly talk (5.6–7). Lycurgus also ensured that the Spartans did sufficient exercises in the gymnasium to warrant the amount of the food they were getting so that they would remain healthy and fit (5.8–9).

Lycurgus' Sparta has a communitarian basis. Fathers are parents of all children (6.1–3), slaves and horses are used in common so that they are effectively owned as such (6.4), and food is shared with those who may not otherwise have enough (6.5). In this city-state personal wealth is not to be a concern. Whereas in other Greek states – Xenophon again plays up the distinctiveness of Sparta, ἐναντία γε μὴν καὶ τάδε τοῖς ἄλλοις Ἕλλησι κατέστησεν ὁ Λυκοῦργος ἐν τῇ Σπάρτῃ νόμιμα – citizens have individual professions, as a ship-owner, merchant, or craftsman, that make them money (7.1), the Spartans are forbidden to concern themselves with business (7.2). Sparta regards money as an anathema. They are only to be engaged in things that promote civic freedom. After all, the communitarian basis of society where food is available for all makes money irrelevant, while clothing is rendered inconsequential because it implies an emphasis on one's body (7.3). The Spartan also should not seek to spend wealth on his messmates as it is more honourable to offer the work of one's body rather than an outlay of money (7.4). Sparta's legislator has furthermore prevented the making of money through unjust means and devised a fine for anyone who possesses the gold and silver so that he might discover that it is more troublesome to possess wealth than not to possess it (7.5–6). (We shall see that Xenophon revisits this topic of wealth production in a surprising fashion at the very end of the work.)

Chapter 8 concerns Spartan obedience to the magistrates and law, with Lycurgus visiting Delphi to ask the god if the people of his state should obey the laws, which he himself had framed (8.5). In the next chapter one reads of how the legislator brought it about that the citizens should prefer a good death to a shameful life (9.1). Lycurgus contrived that the brave should have blessedness (εὐδαιμονία) and the cowardly should in contrast have misfortune (κακοδαιμονία). In other city-states the coward is merely named as such but at Sparta he is shunned in the mess and in the gymnasium (9.4). He is also shunned in public spaces and will not be able to find a wife (9.5). Accordingly, Xenophon proposes that death is preferable to a life of dishonour and ignominy (9.6).

Lycurgus ensured that the Spartans practised a life of virtue even into old age and required that virtue be demonstrated in public life as the virtuous were not otherwise able to affect the state positively (10.1 and 10.4). If other city-states punished those who did an injustice to another, Sparta was distinctive in punishing those who did not live as good a life as they possibly could (10.5). It was the case that for the Spartan legislator the wicked and cowardly harmed the whole state and for that reason, needed to be punished most severely (10.6). Lycurgus obliged the Spartans to practice political excellence or virtue (cf. πολιτικὴν ἀρετήν), and ensured that those who did were fully enfranchised, while excluding those who did not adhere to the state's laws (10.7). The author put the legislator's law on the virtue in historical context when he observed that these laws were extremely ancient (παλαιότατοι), originating in the time of the Heraclidae, and being most foreign (καινότατοι) to others, they had no one who wished to imitate them (10.8).

Chapters 11 to 12 discuss the Spartan military, drawing attention to the unmistakable fact that this is a state dedicated to war. In fact, military life and normal, civilian life do not greatly differ in that the former is as well-supplied with food and goods as the latter (11.2). The remainder of the chapter concerns the organization of the army into cavalry and infantry and their battle formations (11.4ff.). The following chapter describes the Spartan method of encampment with acknowledgement that the military forces engage in gymnastic exercises and observation on their meal times (12.5–6). Chapter 13 discusses the authority and role of the king in the battle; his role seems to be to offer sacrifices to the gods as he does at 13.2 at home to Zeus and his fellow gods.

II

All that has been said up to this point in the *Constitution of Sparta* concerns the historical state. Lycurgus was the great legislator of the past who made Sparta what it was, and my use of 'was' is quite deliberate here because the contemporary state that Xenophon knew has turned into a different entity from the city-state of three hundred years ago. He has presented an image of the Laconic state that the majority of the Athenian population perceive to be the case. Yet (as we shall presently see) this is not what contemporary Sparta has become. The author conjectures that if anyone were to ask him if the laws of Lycurgus remained unchanged (that is, literally 'unmoved', ἀκτίνητοι), he would not be able to affirm it with any confidence, that is, courageously (cf. θρασέως, 14.1). The Spartan state founded by Lycurgus and which the author might have idealized does not seem to have been sustained at the present time. And it is in this chapter of the work that Paul Christensen notes Leo Strauss saw an overt criticism of the state that Xenophon had been gently critical of in the rest of the text.[3] Strauss indeed goes so far as to see the text as a satire of Sparta.[4] I, however, do not find 'satire' an apt description of the criticism that the author engages in.

Xenophon rather drops into his text observations that are scathing of the Laconic city-state, and these observations, which readers may refuse to acknowledge, are the basis for seeing the *Constitution of Sparta* as an ironic text. He cites examples of current Spartan behaviour departing from that originally formed through the Lycurgan laws. Xenophon engages in a contrast of 'then' and 'now'. The author states that he knows the Spartans were previously (πρότερον) content to live modestly with one another rather than to be corrupted (cf. διαφθείρεσθαι), while being flattered in other city-states (14.2). If previously (cf. πρόσθεν) the Spartans were not permitted to live abroad so that they would not be corrupted by outside influences, they now (cf. νῦν δ' ἔστιν) are eager to suit their lifestyles to a foreign land (14.4). It would appear that Sparta now has imperialistic designs on Greece, engaging in meddling and overly ambitious activities like Athens. Furthermore, it was the case that in the past (cf. πρόσθεν) the Spartans appeared to fear having gold, although Cawkwell has observed that love of money was an ancient Spartan affliction (cf. Plutarch *Moralia* 239f.; Aristotle frag. 501).[5] Now, however, it is the case (cf. νῦν δ' ἔστιν) that they pride themselves in owning wealth (14.3). This is despite the legislation that Lycurgus enacted which encouraged a communitarian understanding of possessions in chapter 6 and forbidding engagement in wealth-producing professions rather than in care of the state in chapter 7. The contrast between the past and the present state of the Spartan character and actions continues. If previously they endeavoured to be worthy of leading others, now as things stand (cf. νῦν δ' ἔστιν,) they simply engineer ruling (cf. ὅπως ἄρχουξιν) rather than being thought to be deserving of it (14.5). In addition, it was the case that other Greeks would come to Sparta to lead them against those they thought were wronging them, but at present (cf. νῦν δὲ) these same Greeks call on one another to prevent the Spartans ruling them (14.6). It is clear, according to Xenophon, that the Spartans obey neither the god nor the laws of Lycurgus, which were approved by the god (cf. 8.5).

The author has given a portrait, essentially an encomium, of an ideal Sparta framed by Lycurgus' laws from the time of the Heraclidae, over three hundred years ago, from his perspective in chapters 1–13 of the *Constitution of Sparta*. Nonetheless, the current state is not the Sparta of the seventh century, but has been transformed into a city-state rather resembling present day Athens, with its citizens wanting to make and accumulate wealth and with the state seeking to acquire other Greek territories for its own hegemony. Chapter 14 of the work shows up the flaws that the author sees in the Spartan system.[6] Xenophon does not account for the degeneration and decline of the Spartan state in this work but he observes that their laws (νόμοι), even though they are 'old' (παλαιοί), are most revolutionary (cf. καινότατοι, literally 'newest') where other states are concerned, offering an ironic contrast between 'new' and 'old' in this sentence and also a somewhat ironic suggestion that the 'old' can after all be – to invoke all the senses of the adjective καινότατος – the 'newest' or 'most revolutionary' and 'upsetting'. The author goes on to note that while all people praise them as being the most wondrous, no city, however, wishes to imitate them (10.8). It may be that while the laws produce an ideal, noble state, they are difficult and unpleasant to observe and maintain.

One may speculate whether Sparta was doomed to failure as far as Lycurgus' reforms went, because all states are doomed to fail if the cultivation and performance of virtue is their high-minded ideal. Lycurgus' laws could not maintain the virtue and nobility of the soul which the legislator had envisaged, and indeed, Xenophon observes that where the cultivation and practice of virtue are voluntary, those devoted to it are not sufficient to increase their city-states and this is why Lycurgus forced his citizens to practise virtue in public (δημοσίᾳ) (10.4). Virtue is elusive because the state's citizens, and perhaps people generally, are not by nature inclined to it. This may certainly be the case to explain the eventual failure of Lycurgus' legislation but there may be an additional unspoken reason for the decline of the Spartan city-state from its ideal in the eighth century BCE. Lycurgus' legislation consisted of reforms to constitute a militaristic state, which the laws succeeded in forming and maintaining into the fifth century although failing in other respects. Certainly, the first chapter to the *Aegsilaus*, Xenophon's apparent encomium of the Spartan king of his time, presents Sparta as a war machine. Gymnastic exercises in the city-state see the members of the military forces honing their skills for war. The king Agesilaus offers prizes for the cavalry members who are the most accomplished riders, for the company of heavy infantry that demonstrate the highest fitness, and also for archers who are best at what they do. Sport becomes a military training ground with infantrymen exercising, cavalrymen riding in the racecourse and javelin-throwers and archers aiming for their mark (1.25). Furthermore, the market has on sale arms and horses, while craftsmen, coppersmiths, carpenters, ironsmiths and painters were making weapons of war (1.26). As a consequence, the author proposes that one might think Sparta a 'factory of war' (πολέμου ἐργαστήριοιν, 1.26).

Sparta is the city-state which ensures that its progeny is suited for war, trains them to be its warriors and then engages them in a lifelong concern with the military and military virtue. Yet, even though he marched with the ten thousand under Sparta, Xenophon seems to have been opposed to war and the system which supported this activity – so, for instance, he rejected equine culture with its implicit support of the cavalry, an important part of the military, at Athens in two of his works, *On Horsemanship* and *On the Cavalry Commander*, and he opposed the economic system of Athens as presented in the *Poroi* because it would have funded the triremes, which were used in war. So, it would appear that chapter 14 is the author's critique of Sparta as the military state which Lycurgus founded.

But Xenophon backtracks somewhat in the very last chapter, 15, of the *Constitution of Sparta*. The city-state has not after all changed, but remained as Lycurgus established it in the beginning, as far as its king is concerned (15.1). He continues to make sacrifices for the state, to dine in public, and he dies with the status of a hero or demi-god (cf. ἥρωας). Yet one might object that the king is a superficial and ceremonial aspect of the state: the citizens constitute its true character and if they do not cultivate virtue, then Sparta ceases to be such an ideal city-state.

The big question that now remains is to consider whether, or rather in what sense, the *Constitution of Sparta* is an ironic text. Certainly, it undermines itself as an encomium of the city-state with its account of the failings of its citizens at the present time in chapter 14. The *Constitution* thus disappoints in showing that a supposedly ideal city ends up being no different from any other city-state and in fact resembles the rather dysfunctional Athens of the fifth century BCE. Showing that the ostensible text is actually saying other than it appeared to be saying is indeed characteristic of Xenophontic irony as I have understood it to be, e.g. the illogical costs surrounding silver mining, which detract from any advantages it might appear to bring as far as the financial ways and means of Athens are concerned in the *Poroi*, the failures of the poet Simonides as political adviser to Hiero in the work of the same name, and the shortcoming of the equestrian forces in *On Horsemanship* and *On the Cavalry Commander*, which all throw the surface message of the texts into question. But it is also characteristic of Xenophon's irony that the author should appear to conceal his undermining, although in a way that still leaves the irony obvious to those inclined to see it, and this he does in the final chapter of the *Constitution of Sparta*.

Chapter 14 articulates the shortcomings of the city-state and its citizens as they lust after wealth, seek power abroad and lose respect as a just nation in the Greek world, but chapter 15 insists that nothing has actually changed where the Spartan monarch is concerned. The stark contrast between 'then' and 'now' is disregarded with the focus on this one aspect of Spartan life, and the unaware reader will take the overall narrative at face value and regard Lycurgus' legislation as having a lasting influence. It is precisely characteristic of irony to ignore what is jarring and inconsistent in order that the few will acutely gather the criticism at the expense of the 'out' crowd. Chapter 15 covers the tracks of the openly ironic Xenophon in chapter 14.

One can only conclude that the Sparta which Xenophon has come to know and serve under is after all far from ideal. It displays the same problems of greed and militaristic meddling that are found in other states, most obviously Athens.

III

The *Agesilaus* takes the reader to the Sparta, which is contemporary with Xenophon, and thus to the fallen and corrupt Sparta in which the citizens desire wealth, in which they seek simply to rule abroad rather than to be thought worthy of ruling, and in which they are no longer regarded as just and able to deal with conflict between other states. But Xenophon does not mention any of this backdrop in his account of the Spartan king, which J. B. Bury notes is the earliest biography together with the *Evagoras* of Isocrates.[7] In *The Development of Greek Biography* Arnaldo Momigliano points out that Xenophon took Isocrates' *Evagoras* as his model for the current work.[8] The *Agesilaus* is intended to be, or rather, to *appear* to be an encomium, which praises the Spartan leader under whom Xenophon marched in the expedition of the Ten Thousand against the Persians.

But if the *Agesilaus* is a prototype for biography, it is the case that this form of discourse is not yet set in stone. Its conventions and norms are in the process of being formed as such, and biography cannot depart from its genre because there is no such genre yet. A biography is an account of the life of an individual, usually someone prominent such as King Agesilaus, and is generally thought to be commendatory; however, I suggest that praise does not have to be its aim or purpose. Melina Tamiolaki regards Agesilaus (along with Jason and the two Cyruses, the Great and the Younger) as close to an ideal leader only after Socrates,[9] but I take a very different view. I suggest that it will become clear that the *Agesilaus* ironically defeats the expectation that biography should be of someone worth praising because Agesilaus was far from the ideal leader of Sparta.

Xenophon begins this work by stating that it is indeed not easy to write praise (ἔπαινον) which is worthy of his subject's virtue and glory, although he must try to do so. He goes on to state that it would not be well for a man to be so utterly good and not to receive praise (1.1). The statements would seem to commend Agesilaus and knowing what one does of Xenophon, if it does, it sets up the subject of this text to be the subject of a huge ironic disappointment. Or, one may ask, if it is not easy to praise Agesilaus because there is nothing commendable about him to praise? Agesilaus is of the line of Heracles (1.2), his family are leaders in the state (1.3), and although there was a struggle for succession, there were, Xenophon pronounces, signs (σημεῖα) that Agesilaus should be the king (1.5). The state decided that he should be king on the basis of his birth (443/442 BCE (Hamilton) or 445/444 BCE (Cartledge[10])) and character. Yet despite having declared that he will do so, the author does not give any detailed signs of Agesilaus' suitability for kingship beyond this general declaration.

Xenophon provides no remarkable occurrences at his birth or divine omens that one might expect, although these are certainly evident in other earlier and later narratives by other authors which discuss the life of Agesilaus. In his life of *Agesilaus* Plutarch tells of various divine portents surrounding the birth of Agesilaus. First, the divine Diopeithes cites an oracle which stated it contrary to the intention of the gods that a lame man will rule (Plutarch *Agesilaus* 3.4). So the signs suggest that he was not expected to reign as he was disabled: he had a bad leg from birth (cf. Plutarch *Agesilaus* 2.2).[11] But in Xenophon's text Agesilaus' claim to the throne is supported by Lysander, who argues that the 'maimed royalty' spoken of by the oracle refers rather to Leotychides, who was a bastard. At *Hellenica* 3.3.1–2 Agesilaus states that Poseidon had given evidence of Leotychides' supposedly illegitimate birth. Agis had been cast out his bedchamber by an earthquake and Leotychides was born some ten months later (also Plutarch *Alcibiades* 23.8; *Lysander* 22.3ff.).

Other authors, moreover, show what an auspicious birth should be like in the case of other individuals even though they may not be writing 'lives'. The marvellous birth of the Athenian statesman Peisistratos is one example of an ominous event that an author earlier than Xenophon relates. Herodotus tells a story that while Hippocrates, the father of Peisistratos, was observing the Olympian games and was offering a sacrifice, a cauldron full of meat and water boiled and foamed over without any fire being lit. Chilon the Spartan warned him not to take a child-bearing wife, or if he had one, to send her off. Furthermore, if he had a son, he was to disown him (Herodotus 1.59.1–2; see also Diogenes Laertius 1.68). Frost observes that Chilon was actually born around the same time as Peisistratos, but was probably incorporated into the story as someone who promoted an anti-tyrant policy at Sparta.[12] In another story involving fantastical signs, the Bacchiad rulers of Corinths were told by the oracle at Delphi that an eagle would give birth to a lion. Upon further investigation, they found that a certain Eetion (whose name means 'eagle') had married Labda and that they were expecting a child. Men were sent to kill the child, but they had pity for the child and were unable to find him because Labda had hidden him in a chest (*kypselê*). Called after the chest in which he had been hidden, the child, Kypselos, became tyrant of Corinth and committed many excesses and violences. His son Periander continued committing acts of violence, as we learn from Herodotus 5.92. The historian again reports in another story that Agariste, the wife of Xanthippos, dreamed that she had given birth to a lion. A few days later Pericles was born (Herodotus 6.131).[13] A much later author, Plutarch, tells of Romulus being suckled by a she-wolf in a cave which came later to be known as the Lupercal, after he and his brother were abandoned in the wild at the order of King Amulius (Plutarch, *Romulus* 6.5). The intervention of the she-wolf is to be regarded as a sign of Romulus' destiny to be a ruler.

It would appear that σημεῖα, 'signs', are generally ominous. They are remarkable happenings associated with the birth of a leader that indicate the individual to be marked out to have a notable career in the future, doing either notably good or bad things. Xenophon disappoints his announcement that there were auspicious happenings at the birth of Agesilaus at 1.5. There were none. All he states is that Leotycidas, son of Agis, and Agesilaus, son of Archidamus, struggled with one another for the throne and that the state appointed the latter king due to his birth and character (1.5). The ominous portents at the king's birth are missing and all we have is a rather mundane political act which made Agesilaus ruler in 398 BCE. In fact, Agesilaus' ascendency to the throne is rather surprising, if not unexpected. There is indeed nothing to mark Agesilaus as someone who should be a predestined or a remarkable leader.

IV

Xenophon does not narrate Agesilaus' youth, as C. D. Hamilton notes,[14] but then directly proceeds to deal with his exploits as king in chapter 1 of the text. There is no account of the Spartan education and training that might make a good warrior and statesman. Nevertheless, in particular, the author deals with Agesilaus' defence of Greece against the Persians with a view to subduing Asia and their ruler, Tissarphernes, offering a contrasting characterization of the Spartan leader as honest and true to his word and the Persian leader as deceitful. Agesilaus is able to draw many other nations, both Greek and barbarian in the empire to himself, while on the other hand, the Persian king sends Tithraustes to behead Tissaphernes, believing that he is responsible for the downturn in Persian affairs (1.35). Agesilaus gains more and more power for Sparta, but remains loyal to the state, returning to answer a call when needed there (1.36). The Greeks in Asia followed him and even pledged to be allied to the Spartan cause when needed (1.38).

But amidst this apparent praise there are a number of details which call into question Agesilaus' leadership as king, and his advocacy of Spartan ideals. Agesilaus may have been somewhat corrupt, seeking to enrich his friends through war. The reader learns that because the acquisition of plunder was so great, Agesilaus told his friends to buy goods at next to nothing due to their abundance. Auctioneers made up the list of prices and saw to it that the goods were delivered. Accordingly, without significant capital outlay or cost to the treasury, the king's friends made a prodigious amount of money (1.18). When deserters told the king about where plunder could be taken, Agesilaus told his friends to make the capture so that they would be enriched. Many people thus sought to be the king's friend (1.19). Surely, one must observe that this seeking after booty, especially among the more privileged classes as the king's friends must have been, stands in opposition to the original Spartan disregard for material wealth (cf. *Constitution of Sparta* 14.2-3). Booty is certainly not to be a concern for the Spartan elite, but is of interest as a supplement; for instance, for the pay of soldiers as it is in the *Anabasis* (cf. e.g. 7.3.10-1, 7.4.2 and *Anabasis* 7.4.2). Then, there is the curious fact that Agesilaus does not seem to support the Spartan culture which puts courage and exertion in war above all other concerns.

The reader is informed that it was not possible to conduct a campaign in Phrygia due to Pharnabazos' cavalry and thus, Agesilaus decided to equip a cavalry force so that he could go to war without running away (cf. δραπετεύοντα) (1.23). Agesilaus sees standing firm in battle as the ideal in keeping with Lacedaimonian ideals, but it is apparent that the Spartans have not always been standing firm. It seems from this passage that Spartans might flee a battle scene when they were supposed to value bravery and courage beyond other virtues: they were meant to prize dying in battle rather than returning home a coward. Indeed, according to the *Constitution of Sparta*, Lycurgus ensured that the Spartans severely punished citizens who were bad and cowardly (ἀνάνδρων) (10.6).

Furthermore, according to the narrative, Agesilaus enrolled the wealthiest men in Sparta as horse breeders – horses, which were after all a possession of the very rich – and thereby allowed them to exempt themselves from military service (1.23–4). In addition, Agesilaus is depicted as permitting those who furnish horses, weapons and cavalrymen the same exemption from service at *Hellenica* 3.4.15. We find that the existence of wealthy citizens at Sparta suggests a departure from the ideal in which wealth was not regarded as important for the citizen. In addition, the rich citizens eagerly equipped others for the cavalry as if they were finding someone else who would die on their account (cf. τὸν ὑπερ αὐτοῦ ἀποθανούμενον) (1.24). The Spartan wealthy question the ideal of the brave citizen of this city-state. As well, Agesilaus laid it as an obligation on other cities to supply his cavalry so that Spartans would not have to go to war. Certainly, it is the case that mercenaries are involved in the battle of Coronea (cf. 2.11).[15] This is the Sparta contemporary with Xenophon, the corrupt and degenerate city-state of *Constitution of Sparta* chapter 14, in which courage is no longer an honoured or a highly regarded virtue.

Yet Agesilaus' cavalry is successful as it manages to defeat a party of Thessalian and Theban horsemen at the plain of Coronea as the Spartan leader marches back to Sparta. Chapter 2 recounts the battle at sections 9–12, but there are qualifications in the narrative which suggest that Agesilaus may not have been the ideal military commander. At 2.7 Xenophon offers something of a *recusatio*: he will not come to declare that the king engaged in battle while he has fewer and inferior men, καὶ οὐ τοῦτο λέξων ἔρχομαι, ὡς πολὺ μὲν ἐλάττους πολὺ δὲ χείρονας ἔχων ὅμως συνέβαλεν. The author declares that he will not assert that Agesilaus went to battle with an inferior force, but this is a *recusation* which actually makes this pronouncement in the act of ostensibly rejecting it. He goes on to offer a damning assessment of the Spartan leader. If this were true – and it would appear to possibly be so – then the king shows himself to be senseless (ἄφρονα) and the author reveals himself to be an idiot (μωρόν) in seeking to praise a subject taking such a large risk (2.7). Xenophon then goes on to declare that he admires Agesilaus for bringing an army to war which is no lesser than the enemy brings, one which was arrayed in bronze and red. Interestingly, the author employs the verb 'he equipped' (ὥπλισέν), which ought to denote the supplying of weapons and armour, but which here denotes the provision of fine raiment. It would appear that Agesilaus is more concerned with the trappings of war than with the actualities of war. On this point, Rosie Harman has rightly observed that the Spartan leader engages in a reliance on deception and trickery in his military manoeuvres.[16] Agesilaus invokes visual trickery elsewhere as he uses the day as if it were night and the night as if it were day.[17] Sleight of hand currently takes precedence over sheer strength and courage where the Spartans are involved and although it may be commendable for other city-states to employ ruses, this runs counter to the stereotype of them as a military powerhouse to be reckoned with.

The narrative of the battle calls into question Agesilaus' leadership ability. At 2.12 Xenophon observes that one would undoubtedly name Agesilaus as 'brave' (ἀνδρεῖον) in the battle; however, he demonstrated a mindless recklessness. Instead of falling upon the Thebans from behind and annihilating them, he attacks them from the front so that many on both sides died, although some Thebans managed to escape to Helicon. Agesilaus won the battle but it is the case that he was wounded badly. Xenophon says that he had many wounds everywhere, ὁ δὲ καίπερ πολλὰ τραύματα ἔχων πάντοσε (2.13). The battle leaves the earth blood-stained, with dead friends lying side by side as corpses, and with smashed shields, broken spears and knives without their handles, whether on the ground, in bodies or still in hands (2.14). This is the aftermath of a horrific battle and Agesilaus marches home while the Thebans set about burying their dead (2.16).

The remainder of chapter 2 relates other military ventures under Agesilaus in which he captures Peiraeum (2.19), persuades the Archanians, Aetolians and Argives to enter into an alliance with Sparta (2.20), leads an expedition against Phleius (2.2.1), and marches against Thebes (2.22) so that the Spartans have a string of victories. At 2.23 Xenophon points out that there were disappointments or setbacks (σφάλματα) which, he comments, were not the fault of Agesilaus as leader: the king's friends were being murdered at Tegea and Boeotia, Arcadia and Elis had formed an alliance. Then, this alliance, together with the Argives and Phocians, attacked Sparta, while slaves were revolting (2.24). But one might ask: if Agesilaus was the king of Sparta, how could these events not be his fault? Agesilaus' friends and allies must have been an unsavoury lot to be murdered at

Tegea and he would have been responsible for the alliances and hostilities undertaken by the state of Sparta and for the treatment of the slaves at home. Hamilton concludes that Agesilaus was responsible for the collapse of the Spartan hegemony as under him Sparta alienated both subjects and allies, as this chapter of the biography seems to imply.[18]

David Kovacs unknowingly points to a notable irony at *Agesilaus* 2.26. The Spartan leader is now an old man and too aged to be a soldier, so he raises money for the state in his capacity as an envoy. A trophy stands (cf. εἱστήκει) in his honour due to a bloodless victory achieved when Autophrades fled from fear of Agesilaus after attempting to lay siege to Ariobazarnes, an ally of Sparta at Assos, but Kovacs notes that this monument is not for a victory that has been won and would therefore be unusual. Accordingly, this scholar asserts that there is need of a counterfactual ἄν that has disappeared due to haplography.[19] According to Kovacs, Xenophon intends to say that a monument *would have* been set up in Agesilaus' honour for this success, though he declares that it was not. My reading sees an irony in the text. I propose rather that a trophy was set up even though there was no fighting or battle involved and even though there was thus no occasion to merit the erection of the monument because Agesilaus was self-aggrandizing. Xenophon's suggestion is that the Spartan leader sought undeserved honours and recognitions.

Agesilaus has a career marked with serious miscalculations and misjudgements, and suddenly in the narrative at 2.25, he is an old man. Perhaps, Xenophon implies, the Spartan leader did nothing of serious consequence during his adulthood, or the 'achievements' of his old age are characteristic of Agesilaus throughout his lifetime; that is, inconsequential. Now he is no longer able to march or ride a horse, and turns his attention to raising money for the state and to working as an envoy (2.26). At 2.28, when Agesilaus is about eighty years of age, the king of Egypt seeks war with Persia, asking for help from Sparta (2.27). Agesilaus is, however, not given command of the army and the Egyptian king's forces revolt from the king and split in two. Agesilaus chooses the party he thinks will be better friends to Sparta, allies with them against Persia, and wins a resounding victory against that nation after which he sails home (2.31).

V

We are at the end of chapter 2 and it is the end of the account of the king's exploits. The reader might well ask: what has Agesilaus achieved up to this point in his narrative? The reader has been given a king who is not divinely marked out to be the ruler, and an individual who acts in military matters often in an unsatisfactory manner as he takes unnecessary risks in battle, which he certainly does at the battle of Coronea when he goes to battle with a smaller force of inferior men including a mercenary force, and also permits a culture of non-responsibility as far as participation in the military is concerned. What this means is that most of the *Agesilaus*, a further nine admittedly briefer chapters, is a gerontology, an account of the aged king, but specifically a supposed account of the virtue of his soul through which he accomplished all that was fine and chased away all that was base (3.1). In chapter 3 one learns that he was pious and always good to his word (3.2–5); in chapter 4 Xenophon celebrates his honesty in financial dealings: he did not steal, that is embezzle, from the city (4.3). Yet, he would benefit others by taking money from other people (4.3), a fact which suggests that Agesilaus was not so generous and kept his own money for himself but used the resources of other individuals. The critique is perhaps subtle.

In the next chapter we read of the king's moderation, his avoidance of drunkenness, of greed where food is concerned (5.1), his avoidance of too much sleep (5.2), and his ability to withstand heat and cold (5.3), which together speak of someone who undertakes hard labour. Xenophon devotes most of the chapter, however, to discussing Agesilaus' relationship with Megabates, a Persian youth (5.4–6). Agesilaus resists a kiss from the youth and later tries to persuade Megabates to kiss him again (5.5). When asked if he would kiss Megabates if he yields, Agesilaus strongly rejects the suggestion (5.5) and Xenophon very tantalizingly observes that he is not unaware of the opinions that some people hold on this matter, which perhaps intimate that the contrary is the case, καὶ ὅτι μὲν δὴ ὑπολαμβάνουσί τινες ταῦτα οὐκ. The author goes on to propose that it is harder for most people to control their impulses than to defeat their enemies (5.6), and it is the case that no one has ever seen the Spartan leader in any amatory dalliance and he in any case had public and open dwellings when abroad. But, I ask, what did Agesilaus do at home? The suggestion is that the Spartan leader was perhaps not the restrained, modest figure that some might make him out to be. Xenophon proposes that such was the case when he comments that 'by far many more people are able to overpower the enemy than such [desires]' (5.6).

Chapter 6 addresses Agesilaus' courage and his wisdom. Here the author ostensibly commends his bravery, commenting that the Spartan king always fought in the forefront against the enemies of Sparta and of Greece (6.1). He gained many trophies for his state (6.2–3). I suggest, however, that praise of

Agesilaus' courage has been qualified by the account of his recklessness with the Thebans, which resulted in him being gravely wounded all over his body at 2.13, while the decision to attack these individuals from the front rather than the back in this same encounter must qualify any praise of his apparent wisdom at 6.4–7.

The following chapters of the work praise Agesilaus' loyalty (cfφιλόπολις) to Greece (chapter 7), his general refinement and possession of self, which enabled him to look after his friends, although we have seen that this resulted in him enriching his friends by allowing them to buy and sell war booty (cf. 1.18–19) and in avenging anger and hatred against his friends, which resulted in their slaughter at Tegea (2.23–4). Xenophon sets up a contrast between the Spartan and Persian kings, with the former apparently helping his fellow Greeks and the latter seeking to enslave them (7.6–7), and with the former living simply while the latter seeks all things gold, silver and what is most expensive (8.6). Chapter 9 continues to extol Agesilaus for his simplicity as opposed to the Persian king, who has his men search for the most exquisite and extravagant food and drink (9.3). But there is a qualifying moment in the chapter, for at 9.6 we learn that Agesilaus adorns (κοσμεῖν) his own home with works and possessions, keeping many hunting dogs and war horses. The verb κοσμεῖν suggests that the king decorates his home with more than the necessities. What suggests that one reads κοσμεῖν as denoting excess is that he encourages his sister Kyniska to keep chariots because they demonstrate that their owner is marked not as a person of courage and bravery (ἀνδραγαθίας) but rather as an owner of wealth (πλούτου) (9.6). Agesilaus here shows a concern for money and possessions that should run counter to the Spartan ethos of parsimony and sparing. The king encourages his sister to be a conspicuous consumer, a notable owner of a possession only the wealthiest in society can hold. Typically, after this detail, which calls into question the status of the *Agesilaus* as encomium, Xenophon proceeds to offer a qualifying detail. Victory in horse races actually means nothing; it is rather in serving his fatherland and friends and in punishing his enemies that an individual would gain the greatest and finest victory and in which he would gain the greatest fame whether he was dead or alive (9.7). Dealing properly with one's friends and enemies constitutes the race or ἀγών, which he is ideally to win as his use of the verb νικῷη in this segment of the chapter suggests.

The final two chapters of the *Agesilaus* pronounce that the current discourse has been encomium (cf. ἀλλὰ πολὺ μᾶλλον ἐγκώμιον) rather than standing the words of a funeral dirge (10.3). He is in Xenophon's estimation, at least as ostensibly stated here, a blessed and successful warrior king. The final chapter lists all the positive attributes of the king, which include: piety (11.1–2, 8);

cheerfulness (11.2); righteousness (11.3); goodness to friends (11.4); openness to candour (11.5); courage with wisdom (11.9); urbanity (11.11). The author presents apparent praise but he has suggested otherwise to the reader who considers his text perceptively. Actions which Agesilaus has committed during his lifetime, whether during his military career or in his life more generally, call into question whether or not the Spartan king is such a paragon of virtue.

John Dillery has demonstrated that Agesilaus is an extremely problematic Spartan leader in the *Hellenica*. He is after all found to be the force behind activities which cause criticism of the Spartans for their war crimes in Book 5 of the *Hellenica*, and he is seen to help tyrants come to, and consolidate, their power in the matter of the siege at Phlius at 5.3.16 and 5.4.13.[20] Because of self-interest, I find it hard to see Agesilaus as a panhellenist in everything that he does, as G. L. Cawkwell prefers to.[21] In the latter passage, it is, however, the case that Agesilaus remains in Sparta precisely in order to avoid being accused of giving his help to tyrants by leading the citizens into war. If Xenophon is implicitly critiquing Agesilaus, then he is also critiquing this individual's state, for the negative evaluation of the one always implies the negative evaluation of the latter, as Dillery has argued.[22] Certainly, it is the Spartans as a whole who are faulted by the author for seeking to control Thebes and for being punished by the Thebans (5.4.1). Xenophon regards this a divine retribution for Lacedaimonian wickedness.

And so, in conclusion, one might ask: is the *Agesilaus* really an encomium of the Spartan leader? And is there indeed such a disjunction between the negative portrayal of the *Hellenica* and the supposedly more positive one of the *Agesilaus*? Or, is the *Agesilaus* rather an apparent encomium that ironically shows up the problems of this figure, and perhaps, of the whole Spartan system as it has latterly become? For example, Trego regards the *Agesilaus* as showing partiality for the ruler because it is an encomium of this figure.[23] Others have regarded Xenophon as Agesilaus' friend, fighting in his army and receiving the estate of Scillus from the leader, and therefore, most likely to be well-disposed towards this individual.[24] Yet and in contrast, the Agesilaus of this work is not an unproblematic figure, as I have attempted to argue and as Marincola suggests; indeed, he is less than ideal, as he also is in the *Hellenica*.[25]

VI

Sparta is where Xenophon fled to after his episode of treachery against Athens, and it is the Spartans under Agesilaus with whom Xenophon served on the march of the Ten Thousand. It would appear that this closer association with Sparta is the basis for disillusionment, for it would seem that the city-state is not so ideal after all. The carefully restrained and warlike Sparta which Lycurgus founded with his legislation has decayed to become the greedy state in which bravery is no longer highly sought after and cultivated. The city-state has come somewhat to resemble contemporary Athens. And Xenophon shows this to be the case in his portrayal of a subsequent Sparta in the *Agesilaus*. This work shows that Sparta and its latter-day leader Agesilaus disappoint. Sparta is not the city-state that Lycurgus had planned it to be as avarice and cowardice have taken hold of the population some three hundred years later, and Agesilaus, a king in the fifth century, is not the ideal leader that Lycurgus might have imagined. Club-footed, he is not destined to be king but he engineers it so that he becomes such. Foolish and foolhardy in battle, he evidences signs of greed and displays preferential treatment with regard to his friends, both of which make him a despot rather than a righteous king.

10

The *Hellenica* and the Irony of War

The *Hellenica* is a long work by Xenophon which deals with the Greek states at war with one another. Composed near the end of the author's life (he died in 354 BCE) when he had supposedly moved away from Sparta after its defeat to Corinth, it picks up the narrative where Thucydides' *History* ends and continues to 362 BCE or perhaps 359 BCE. It narrates the various skirmishes and battles which the different sides have with one another in order to achieve supremacy in the Greek world. It pays attention to the roles that various leaders – for instance, Alcibiades on the Athenian side, Sphodrias, or Agesilaus and Archidamus on the Spartan side – have in the proceedings in lawcourts and councils, on land and on sea, to their downfalls and successes, and to the destruction wreaked on various communities during the hostilities.

The narrative is not a singular one, for it reveals the various perspectives of the different players: Spartans, Athenians, Persians, Corinthians, Thebans, Eleans and even the Phliasians.[1] Furthermore, John Marincola observes that like the *Anabasis*, the *Hellenica* does not readily reveal the author's motives or reasons for writing the text – there is no preface.[2] I suggest in view of the rest of the corpus that irony may be the key to discerning the work's purpose. And, if the *Hellenica* is an ironic text as the rest of the Xenophontic corpus has shown itself to be – otherwise, it would an extremely peculiar and idiosyncratic text as far as Xenophontic writing is concerned – then its irony is connected with the horrors of war, which were apparent to all who experienced them. Irony, it must be remembered, lies in the differing levels of perception. Some perceive reality and therefore perceive irony, while others, usually the majority, fail to do so. After seven books of war narrative, Xenophon portrays a realization among some of the peoples in his narrative that war is not for the benefit of Greece nor its peoples, and this realization ironically shows up the whole condition of Greece in conflict as one that is misinformed and unconsidered.

I

The *Hellenica* positions itself as an intense and engaged work. It famously begins with the words μετὰ δε ταῦτα, entering the narrative *in medias res*, although some scholars mistakenly think that these words indicate that the beginning of the work has been lost.[3] As has been widely commented on by a number of individuals,[4] these words identify the *Hellenica* as a work that continues the narrative of Thucydides' earlier *History*, which itself ends mid-sentence either with a report of Tisserphernes arriving at Ephesus and making a sacrifice to Artemis or with a statement that the twenty-first year of the war was concluded, which is thought to be an extraneous piece of text rather than a genuine summation of the narrative (see 8.109.2). Leo Strauss mistakenly thinks that because he was so influenced by his recollections of Socrates, Xenophon did not take history, which was comprised of the 'public speeches and deeds of the perfect gentlemen', as seriously as Thucydides did, and in his view the *Hellenica* is therefore not intended to be a continuation of the latter.[5] Xenophon is not the only continuer of Thucydides because as a student of Isocrates, he wrote a history of Greek affairs in the Peloponnese at this period, perhaps in a work called the *Hellenica*. Yet *pace* Strauss, like Theopompus, Xenophon perhaps aspires to be the new Thucydides,[6] despite having his own distinctive approach to writing history. I propose that there is indeed a continuity in the context which Thucydides' work provides for the *Hellenica*, for the former is a text that offers a critique of Athenian politics in the fifth century during the Peloponnesian War from the point of view of a responsible elite member of society. The *Hellenica*, it will become apparent, narrates the final seven years and aftermath of the Peloponnesian War and is also a critique of the politics of its moment.

Indeed, if Xenophon's work is cast as a continuation of Thucydides' *History* – and so, Vivienne Gray calls the text 'continuous history'[7] – then one might expect the same sort of scrutiny of political and military events but in a manner which we have come to know to be characteristic of the author. It is also important to recall once more that Xenophon was one of the socially and economically privileged class at Athens that would have rejected involvement in the politics of the city-state and probably also would have rejected the state going to war. Certainly, his implicit censure of the culture of the Athenian cavalry in *On Horsemanship* and *On the Cavalry Commander*, and his view that Athens' finances would be greatly increased in a state of peace rather than war in the *Poroi*, suggests as much. Accordingly, since the *Hellenica* is a work about conflicts and wars in the Greek world which appear to have no decisive outcome, one can expect that he would be critical of the situations that he is portraying. War proves itself to be a futile undertaking. Yet Xenophontic criticism is never overt. It is for the reader who is like-minded with the author, the fellow elitist, who can recognize where inconsistencies and *non sequiturs* arise and thus, where the ostensible picture which is being presented collapses. Thus, Xenophon makes observations without needing to offer any explicit evaluation of what is reported and it is when observations prove to be in conflict with one another that criticism is implied. Where Thucydides deals with the condition of politics at Athens alone, the latter does so in a larger, Hellenic context. The *Hellenica* is seven long books of war and unrest in the Greek states, with each book narrating the events of a year of the conflict: conflict, rather than peace, is the unfortunate normal state of being for them.

II

Because the critique offered is one of the Greek states as a whole, the *Hellenica* begins at 411 BCE and the reader is not at Athens, but in the Hellespont. The narrative offers a bald account of the conflicts as they arise between the Athenians and the Spartans, who are occasionally assisted by the Persians. For instance, the first event presented has the Athenians, who are under the command of Thymochares, meet the Lacedaimonians, who are under Agesandridas, in a naval battle and the former suffer defeat (1.1.1). But in the following chapters they win some battles and lose others under the leadership of Alcibiades, who was a prominent character in Thucydides' work (1.1.5). Later in the chapter we learn that under Thrasyllus, the Athenians enjoy success against the Spartan Agis, who is at Decelea, and that they then pledge their support to Thrasyllus (1.1.33–4). Tissaphernes, who also features at the end of the *History*, appears at 1.1.9, having been ordered by the Persian King to make war on the Athenians.

Thrasyllus continues to have successes with his troops as he sets sail for Samos (1.21). The Persians under Tissaphernes muster at Ephesus in order to stop the Athenians (1.2.6). The Athenians and Persians meet and about three hundred Athenians are killed with the rest put to flight (1.2.9). At 1.3.5–6 Thrasyllus fights the Spartan Hippocrates and his men with the aid of the Persians. Alcibiades comes to their aid and Hippocrates is killed (1.3.6). Alcibiades tries to get help from the Persian Pharnabazus, seeking twenty talents (1.3.8) and manages to secure an oath with the Persian leader at 1.3.12. The Athenians attack Byzantium, where there are some Spartans (1.3.14). Unable to make progress by force, the

Athenians try to get the Byzantians to betray their city (1.3.16). Alcibiades is eventually let into the city (1.3.21) as the Spartan leader Clearchus goes to meet Pharnabazus to get the pay for his soldiers (1.3.17).

The first few chapters of the *Hellenica* are characteristic of the whole war, revealing that the conflict was one in which no side demonstrated a clear advantage. Athens would win some skirmishes and Sparta would win others in turn. The city-states either praised or blamed their generals for their victories or defeats and sought to either reward or punish them. Individuals changed allegiances, or left the conflict, as in the case of Protomachus and Aristogenes (1.7.1), if it profited them to do so. Many, of course, perished, such as Phanosthenes (1.5.19) and Callicratidas (1.6.33), and some died as a consequence of being condemned to death at trial, including the Athenian generals who failed to rescue their drowning sailors at Arginousae (1.7.34), due to their perceived misconduct in war.

Perhaps one of the most significant and important figures to appear in the first book of the *Hellenica* is Alcibiades, who was depicted as a self-interested warmonger and popular orator, in other words as a polypragmatist, in Thucydides and thus, as a *persona non grata* as far as this author was concerned.[8] The concern with Alcibiades in Xenophon is perhaps another mark of continuity with Thucydides, who was generally interested in the role that individuals had in the Athenian city-state. For Xenophon, Alcibiades is an individual who exerts at Athens a remarkable influence that is not always in the best interests of the city-state regardless of what its citizens may think. Furthermore, he is an individual who either attracts crowds or repels them, and so, is a focus around which the city moves. At 1.4.13 the author declares that the general sails into the Piraeus with a crowd wishing to catch sight of him. He is a figure of some controversy and some citizens claim that he is the best citizen and was banished without proper cause. They also state that individuals with less power and less speaking ability banished him with a view to their own private gain despite the 'fact' that Alcibiades always worked for the common good. These citizens also claim it was correct that the trial of the Eleusinian Mysteries, in which the general was indicted, was postponed although Alcibiades found himself robbed of his Athenian citizenship (1.4.14). As a consequence of his exile, Alcibiades is now said to be forced to court those he does not respect and is unable to help Athens (1.4.15).

On the other hand, and against Alcibiades, there are others who say that he alone was the main reason for Athens' present and future troubles (1.4.17). (One recalls that he was a student of Socrates and the negative perceptions of him certainly influenced the outcome of the trial against the philosopher.) Yet he is still able to win favour. He speaks in his own defence in the Senate and the Assembly, and is so effective that he manages to be appointed general-in-chief with complete authority at 1.4.20. Then, he has a minor victory at Gaurium over the men of Andros and over the Spartans (1.4.22). When Alcibiades warns Antiochus not to attack the Spartans when he goes to see Thrasybulus in the Hellespont at 1.5.11 but when Antiochus in any case attacks Lysander's ships (1.5.12), the Athenians lose fifteen triremes at Notium and they become angry at Alcibiades for supposed neglect of duty and appoint ten generals to take his place (1.5.16). The reader is informed that he is also in disfavour with the army and that he sails away to his castle in the Chersonese (1.5.17).

Thus, it would appear that Alcibiades is a figure who is either much admired and loved, or much hated. His oratorical ability keeps him afloat, but mismanagement of affairs by others in the military sphere endangers his position and reputation at Athens. What this shows is the instability of politics in the late fifth century. Differing assessments of the same person existed as a consequence of public speech and popular opinion, and it is popular opinion which ultimately moves events. I have related some chief events of the first chapter of the first book of the *Hellenica* to show that war does not really achieve anything for any of the protagonists except death and destruction for one or the other side. One side has a victory, then a defeat at the hands of the other side. Men die and the people whose communities are attacked experience hunger, exile, dispossession, and death.

III

I suggest that chapter 2 of the second book depicts the pointlessness of conflict between the states because external war becomes an internal war: indeed, Athens ends up turning in on itself rather than fighting a common enemy. Xenophon declares that most of Greece, with the exception of Samos, had turned away from Athens, leaving the city-state isolated. At 2.2.10 the Athenians run out of food, as Lysander had given safe conduct back to the city-state to any Athenians abroad with the result that provisions in the city were more quickly exhausted (2.2.2), and at 2.2.11 they seek to form an alliance with their enemy Sparta. If there is no alliance, the prospect is that the city will be starved and reduced to slavery (cf. 2.2.16) and that its walls will be torn down (cf. 2.2.15). The Athenians seek peace and many of the Greeks agree with the terms of the proposal, although the

Corinthians and Thebans want the destruction of Athens (2.2.19). The Spartans, however, refuse to enslave a city that did so much for Greece in the Persian war and offer peace if the Athenians should destroy their own walls (2.2.20). The current absence of war is the outcome of the conflict to this point.

MacLaren, amongst others, has argued that the *Hellenica* was not written as a continuity but demonstrates a division at 2.3.11.[9] He observes that the first part ending at 2.3.10 was one of Xenophon's earliest works,[10] while John Dillery sees 2.3.11 to the end of the work as being written together after the Battle of Mantinea in 362 BCE.[11] The second part of the work demonstrates, for instance, more humour and deeper characterization of its personalities.[12] It is also the case that the government at Athens now takes a very different form after this point in the work. The situation at Athens leads to the establishment of oligarchy, as the Thirty come into power for the purpose of establishing a constitution under which the government could function and this group of oligarchs becomes the concern of the text from 2.3.11 to 2.4.43. This political change has unfortunate consequences for the state. Xenophon has the tyrant Critias observe at 2.3.32 that a change in government leads to loss of life: the common people have killed a number of oligarchs, while the aristocrats have been responsible for the slaughter of a large number of democrats. There is civil strife at Athens, which ends at 3.1.1. The Thirty are greedy and have no self-restraint.[13] Thus, oligarchy is a degradation from, and worse than, the democratic city-state, even if democracy as it is currently manifest at Athens is less than ideal. Theramenes, who is characterized as being good and moderate,[14] declares that the Thirty are unjust towards men and impious towards gods (2.353). The Thirty are despotic and autocratic rulers;[15] they seek to do as they wish, and here they want to get a Spartan garrison to stay at Athens to help them (2.3.13). Furthermore, they enrol another three thousand individuals, the Three Thousand, to create an impression of a more widely based government (2.3.18–20). Thus, enhanced by numbers, the Thirty kill many Athenians, including Theramenes, out of enmity and for their money (2.3.21).

The culture of war is quite literally an unproductive one. Agesilaus may have turned the city-state Ephesus, in which he stayed on his journey towards Phrygia, into a virtual workshop (ἐργαστήριον) of war. But the true productivity of this factory must be called into question. The marketplace is full of horses and weapons, and the artisans are all engaged in making the equipment required for war (3.4.17). The gymnasia, furthermore, are full of men exercising for war; the hippodrome with cavalrymen riding and javelin men and bowmen are practising their skills (3.4.16). This is a city which has become primed for war and is entirely in keeping with the Spartan military ethos. The text is probably a repetition from *Agesilaus* 1.26, where Xenophon notes that when the Spartan leader was quartered at Ephesus arms and horses were on sale and the craftsmen were busy making weapons for war so that the city became a workshop of war (πολέμου ἐργαστήριον). In the previous section of this work he also notes that cavalrymen and heavy infantrymen were engaged in competitions while archers and javelin throwers practised. But the community entirely concerned with war cannot be sustained. One notes that there is no growing of crops, no market from which people can get what they need to live, no art and no culture. Xenophon is implicitly criticizing Agesilaus' 'workshop of war' as a nihilistic community.

In Book 3 the Athenians enjoy a victory at 3.5.9–10, while the Spartans have success against the Thebans and Corinthians in the following book, at 4.2.22. Then, the Spartans lose a naval battle (4.3.10) and are again defeated by Pharnabazus and Conon at 4.8.1. The same sides do a great deal of winning and losing in the war: gains and defeats are the order of the day so that no one side seems to come out ahead. Each side attempts to gather allies to strengthen its position, with the Athenians gaining for their side the Thebans for a while (6.3.1), the Corinthians gaining the Plateans (6.3.1) and winning the support of Jason of Pherae (cf. 6.4.2), and the Spartans gaining the support of the Persians and most of the rest of Greece.

IV

Narration of war amongst the Greek states consumes seven books in total with battles on land and in the sea. Many lives are lost and property is destroyed, and there is no obvious winner of the conflict (as we shall see from Xenophon's assessment of the wars in the final book of the *Hellenica*). Along with other scholars, Hau has observed that Xenophon is a moralist almost to the point that his historiography is impaired.[16] Rahn offers a different view, suggesting that being at the height of one's power may initially have made an individual or state noteworthy for Xenophon, but that the author becomes fascinated by the behaviour of lesser individuals and small states, for instance Phlisia, as his historiography develops.[17] I suggest that Rahn assists our understanding of irony within the text, for irony in the *Hellenica* is most pronounced in the futility of war within the Greek states, and especially in those which are more powerful and can therefore do greater damage. (And indeed, the identification of irony is certainly in keeping with the recognition of Xenophon's identity as the economically privileged individual, who attempts to diminish his ostensible role within the state, precisely by assuming the pose of the non-aggressive quietist.)

As the war progresses into the final two books of the work, there is a growing sense that peace between Athens and Sparta and their respective allies is more desirable than war, which has resulted in the deaths of many soldiers and citizens, in hunger as crops cannot be planted and grain cannot be shipped from state to state, and in a general political instability, which allows tyrants such as Jason and Alexander to gain power if only for a short while (cf. 6.4.32–7). War achieves nothing except destruction in the Mediterranean of the fourth century BCE. So at 6.2.1, which tells of events in 374 BCE, we see that when the Athenians perceive that the Spartans and their allies are mustering in Phocis, that the Thebans are continuing to fail to contribute money to their fleet, and that they were being worn out by taxes, by plundering raids from Aegina and by guarding their own territory, they wish to stop being at war and send ambassadors to Sparta to conclude a peace. It is evident that Athenians seek peace as an act of self-preservation in order to prevent any further harm to the city-state.

Achieving peace is a long and difficult process. When the Athenians first seek a cessation of war, there is a setback as the Zacynthians send a party to Sparta to complain of mistreatment at the hands of the Athenian general Timotheus (6.2.3). The Lacedaimonians perceive the Athenians to have done wrong and immediately prepare a fleet of sixty ships from Sparta and from her numerous allies, seeking to attack Corcyra so that the city would not come under Athenian rule. As a consequence, the Corcyreans suffer terribly from hunger and attempt to desert the city only to be faced with the punishment of being sold into slavery (6.2.15). Indeed, in the final book, 7, the Athenians and the Spartans meet at Athens to determine the terms of a peace, which is to be on equal terms for both sides. Procles, the Phlisian, is the intermediary and addresses both parties. He proposes that the Athenians should have naval supremacy and the Spartans supremacy on land as this is due to divine arrangement and ordering (7.1.2). The Athenians after all are adapted to have supremacy on the sea and they have a fleet of triremes to which they keep adding more ships (cf. 7.1.3), while the Spartans are much less experienced at naval matters even though they managed to capture the Athenian fleet at Aegospotami and effectively, to end the war (cf. *Hellenica* 2.1.20–32). The Spartans, in contrast, are land-based and win the majority of their military encounters on the land (cf. 7.1.10). Procles' speech characterizes each of the states adequately and accurately, and as a result both Athenians and Spartans applaud his speech energetically (7.1.12). Following this, Cephisodotus proposes that both Athenians and Spartans should hold leadership of the fleet and of the army each by turn for five days at a time (7.1.14).

But if the Athenians and Spartans achieve a peace, it is the case that other Greek cities begin agitating for power amongst the Hellenic states. And this is where Athens and Sparta stand when the Thebans begin their aggressions, which continue until 7.1.21. The Thebans attack a Spartan garrison at 7.1.15 and they advance against Sicyon and Pellene, lay waste to Epidaurus and rush at the gates of Corinth at 7.1.18. At 7.1.27 they take issue with Messenia, which is a Lacedaemonian territory, and Philiscus collects a mercenary force to make war on the Spartans. The Athenians plan to go to Thessaly to help their new allies, the Spartans (7.1.28). Allied with the Thebans are the Arcadians, who have already invaded Sparta at 6.5.23, and the Argives and the Thebans subsequently attempt to get the Persian King on their side, sending a delegation to him at his court (7.1.33ff.). When the Corinthians, who had sought help from Athens against the Thebans in the previous book at 6.5.37, refuse to take an oath to the King in support of the Thebans, the bid of the latter for supremacy in the Greek world comes to an abrupt end (7.1.40). Meanwhile, in Sicyon Euphron aggressively takes out supporters of Sparta and becomes something of a tyrant. Amidst the peace between Athens and Sparta, there is thus considerable instability and grappling for power as there is a shift away from the struggle between these two states as Thebes becomes greedy for its own authority and status in the Greek world.

The Athenians and Spartans are united by their enmity with the Thebans, who attack in 369 BCE and who continually seek the leadership of Greece (cf. 7.1.33), which Xenophon narrates at 7.1.18ff. At 7.1.27 Philischus of Abydus has the Thebans and the Spartans meet to discuss the possibility of peace. Xenophon observes, however, that the fact neither side consulted the god as to how this peace was to be achieved was a serious problem for the success of this venture, and the Spartan claim on Messenia remained a major sticking point to any agreement that might come about. The author was pious, as we know from his other works, and the failure to consult the gods would suggest a consequential coming up short where peace was concerned. Yet the Thebans seek an alliance with the Persians and attempt to persuade their allies to assume the same stance, although the Arcadians distance themselves from this proposal in a huff (7.1.39).

The Greeks find the arrogance of the Spartans hard to bear so that there is a general resistance against the latter (7.1.44), while the Argives and Arcadians invade Phlisia, upon whose citizens Xenophon lavishes praise for their military successes and for their loyalty to their friends at 7.2 (also cf. 7.3.1) in 368 BCE so that there is a general unrest in Greece even as the two major city-states have come to a position of peace and co-operation (7.2). There is also the case of Euphron, tyrant of Sicyon, who, when the common people and aristocrats in his city-state come to strife, attempts to bribe the Thebans to return the state to his power (7.3.4). Learning of his plan, Sicyonian exiles kill him in the Acropolis (7.3.5). One of the murderers notes that Euphron had emptied the city's coffers of its gold and silver, shifted from an alliance with the Spartans to one with the Thebans, and killed, banished and robbed citizens (7.3.8). Yet the final verdict on the tyrant is uncertain: the Thebans deem him to have met his death rightly, while the citizens of Sicyon regard him as a benefactor and bury him with honours (7.3.12). The desire for power (on Euphron's part) and civic strife characterize affairs in Greece at this point in time, but the assessment of these states is open to interpretation.

Peace comes to Greece gradually in bits and pieces, and is generally a consequence of one party feeling they are disadvantaged or finding that they are losing in a conflict. As early as Book 4 we find the Corinthians seeking a cessation of war. They see their land being laid to waste and that many of them are being killed because they live close to the enemy, while their allies live in some state of peace (4.4.1). Yet it is not to be as the Argives, Athenians, Boeotians and some Corinthians, who receive money from the Persian king, see the possibility of the city-state going over to the Spartans again. Thus, they undertake a slaughter of those who want peace at Corinth at a religious festival, the Euclea, which Xenophon denounces as the most sacrilegious (ἀνοσιώτατον) action (4.4.2). This is possibly an oligarchic-led attack against the majority.[18] The attackers, whom the author describes as most impious (ἀνοσιώτατοι), completely disregard custom and slaughter people even at the holy places (4.4.3). There is divine retribution as the Spartans come and massacre those involved in the killing of the pro-peace party at Corinth (4.4.11–13). Hence peace is stalled by concerns over who would own the territory.

Much later in the work, the Athenians under Demotion appear to be negotiating a peace with the Arcadians at 7.4.4. The Corinthians, having been defeated on land and having collected enemies including the Athenians (cf. 7.4.6), approach the Spartans asking them to conclude a peace at 7.4.8. The Spartans agree, requesting also that their allies abide by this arrangement (7.4.9). The Corinthians then approach the Thebans to seek a peace with them at 7.4.10. The Thebans want more than peace, for they seek an alliance, which the Corinthians regard as an exchange (μεταλλαγή). Pleased with this arrangement, the Thebans then grant peace to the Corinthians, the Phlisians and to their allies on the condition that each keeps his own land (7.4.10).

The constant fighting between the various city-states leads to a desire for peace between the opposing parties at times. The Arcadians are the new aggressors in Book 7 and they attack the Eleans at 7.4.13. Furthermore, they capture Acora and Margana, betrayed by some of its citizens, but they are driven out by a number of the Eleans from Olympia (7.4.14). The Arcadians make a further attempt on the territory of the Eleans, who are assisted by the Asheans, and they retreat from that place without accomplishing anything (cf. 7.4.17). The Arcadians then capture the city of Olorus (7.4.17) and the Pelleneans enter the conflict at this point to repel them (7.4.18). Meanwhile the Pelleneans and Eleans have become allies of the Spartans (7.4.17–9). The Eleans subsequently even ask the Spartans to take the field against the Arcadians at 7.4.20, who then besiege Cromus in the following section of the work. 7.4.24 finds the Spartans despondent as their leader Archidamus is wounded and they have just heard the names of the dead, while the Arcadians are in high spirits because they have defeated an enemy. What happens as a consequence in the ensuing narrative is that one of the older men, presumably a Spartan, calls out for peace and a truce. It turns out that the opposing sides are pleased with this suggestion and they make a truce. The Lacedaimonians pick up their dead and leave, while the Arcadians return to the place from which they had set out and set up a trophy. War in this way may engender peace.

At 7.4.35 the Arcadians are failing in the war effort again and once more this leads to a call for peace. It seems that lack of success in war educates and gives a knowledge of its horrors, which the victors cannot, and do not have. It offers a recognition that constitutes irony as the supposed 'winner' fails to grasp the reality of war. At 7.4.30 the aggressive Arcadians, together with their allies, the Argives, have been defeated by the Eleans, whom they never imagined would attack them (cf. 7.4.29). Then the Arcadians declare that having no desire for war, they are willing to surrender the presidency of the temple of Zeus (cf. 7.4.35). Because the Eleans want the same things, a peace and truce are concluded between the two sides. In the following section, it would appear that all the states are desirous of peace. The Tegeans and the Theban governor conclude the peace and have a feast to celebrate this event (7.4.36). The peace is, however, not an easy one as the Arcadians sense that the Thebans want the Peloponnese to be as weak as possible so that they may reduce it to slavery (cf. 7.5.1–2). There are further skirmishes too with the Athenians defending the Mantineans in their own territory at 7.5.16–17.

At 7.5.1 Xenophon observes the Acheans and Eleans realizing that the Thebans want the Peloponnese to be weak so that they can enslave it. The

Thebans thus want the Peloponnesian cities to make war with one another, as they are actually and already doing. Accordingly, the Peloponnesian cities send to Athens for the latter's aid, while the ambassadors from Lapiriti approach the Spartans for assistance in case any other city should attack the Peloponnese (7.5.3–4). Furthermore, the Battle of Mantinea, which these matters precede, shows up very clearly the pointlessness of war. At 7.5.23–4 Epaminondas, the leader of the Thebans, who has been largely ignored up to this point in the narrative,[19] leads his men to an apparent victory, causing the enemy to flee. The Theban leader, however, himself falls, the survivors were unable to take full advantage of their victory and failed to kill any of the enemy or to advance even though the opposing force had fled (25). Xenophon observes that things turned out to be the opposite of what was expected. The victorious and the defeated did not behave as expected but each set up trophies as if they had won and the dead were returned to their respective sides. Neither side gained any more land, and there was more disorder and confusion than before (27).

Epamonidas' engagement marks the last battle and, in fact, the end of the *Hellenica* and Xenophon's assessment of the final state of affairs proves to be a condemnation of war, and particularly this war, for its futility. The Thebans as a whole experience success against their opponents, causing them to flee where they attack (cf. 7.5.24). Epamonidas dies in this attack and while his men have been victorious in gaining the upper hand, the success of the Thebans is curiously and hugely understated. They fail to advance any further, their hoplites do not manage to kill a single man of the enemy, and their cavalry also do not have success in killing anyone. The Thebans slip back in fear as if they had been defeated and their foot soldiers and peltasts, who made their way as victors to the enemy's flank, are killed by the Athenians (7.5.25). Victory is somewhat compromised by the mood and temperament of the winners. Furthermore, the end result of conflict is not what everyone assumed it would be. In fact, the opposite of what everyone expected occurs. It would seem that the victorious in a battle should end up as the rulers, and the defeated as their subjects. But Xenophon observes that the deity ordained it such that both parties set up a trophy as though each of them had been victorious without either attempting to stop the other from doing so, and both parties handed back the dead to the other side as though they were victors and both received bodies as though defeated. Each party claims an empty victory (7.5.26).

The outcome presented in this penultimate section of the *Hellenica* defeats what people assumed to be the case. There appears to be no distinction between winning and losing in the war: both sides are at once winners and both sides are, simultaneously, losers. In the next and final section of the work the author observes that neither side was found to be better off than the other, having gained no further territory or influence than before the conflict. Xenophon concludes that there was even more disorder and confusion after the fighting than before (7.5.27). The point is that war achieves nothing for any of the Greek states involved in it, since no one gains any more territory than before they fought. And because there is no clear loser or winner, no party has acquired knowledge as a consequence of losing. As a result, the author is the only figure in the *Hellenica* who knows what war and its consequences are and consequently, he is the particular individual who must reveal the irony of war to the reading audience – it is futile despite, or perhaps especially because of, the effort, the expense and the loss of life that it involves. Apart from the pointlessness of war, Xenophon observes that there is greater confusion and turmoil in Greece than before. The attempt to establish peace is not after all completely successful. The author ends his work by noting that he has written this much and that perhaps another person will be concerned with subsequent events. He presents the *Hellenica* as part of a narrative relay, one that has taken off from Thucydides and may be continued by a different author.[20] Possibly, as Pelling suggests, this is not yet the time to see what shape the history of the Greek city-states will take and any firm vision is to come from Macedon.[21]

V

I want to suggest that the final chapter of the work presents the author's opinion of what the conflict in the Greek states has achieved: that is, essentially, nothing. Nobody is the outright winner or the loser; nobody has gained land, and in fact, the cost in lives, property and money to conduct this conflict has rather been immense (7.5.27). And this is where the irony of the *Hellenica* must lie: such effort goes to produce no gains for any party in the Greek world and in fact, there is only loss and destruction. This is an outcome that suggests an advocacy of quietism, which Xenophon may be ascribing in light of the outcome of Hellenic conflict.

Moreover, Xenophon owns this articulation of this irony, proposing his perspective on events as his own effectively by making his authorial presence more apparent as the work continues to its conclusion. Indeed, Christopher Pelling has observed the narrative proceeds 'with the personal voice sounding louder'.[22] The work begins by identifying itself as a continuation of Thucydides' account of the turmoil and political trouble at Athens. War in the Peloponnese is the outcome of this scenario, and this is what the *Hellenica* narrates. If there is an authorial presence identified here, it is that of Thucydides. Xenophon, however, has to assume his place and own the narrative, as he does by the end of the work. The narrator of the *Hellenica* initially casts himself as impersonal and he will proceed to focalize the events he tells through different perspectives, whether they are Greek as a whole, or only Spartan, Theban and so on. But it is the case that as the narrative continues, Xenophon becomes more of a presence in the text as the narrator. For instance, at 6.1.19, he announces that he will return to the point where he left off his story, when he took up his account of the deeds of Jason. Later at 6.5.1 he again signals a similar return to his main narrative after a diversion on matters concerned with Thessaly and Jason down to the rule of Tisiphonos. Xenophon thus shows that he has complete control of the narrative in order to signify that views presented in the text are completely the ones that he has chosen to put out.

There are other indications of authorial presence in the later part of the work. At 6.2.32 he presents himself as an expert on military affairs. He states that he knows (cf. 'I know', οἶδα) in which matters men must achieve training and practice when they seek to undertake naval battle. As a result, he praises (cf. 'I praise', ἐπαινῶ) Iphicrates for ensuring that his men were not unskilled in naval war or slower at arriving where they needed to be. At 6.2.39 he continues to be fulsome in his praise of Iphicrates for choosing as his colleagues the orator Callistratus and the general Chabrias, who otherwise seemed to be his opponents. Choosing them as his advisers (συμβούλους) reveals him to be a man of great-heartedness or confidence (cf. μεγαλοφονοῦντος ἐφ' ἑαυτῷ τοῦτό μοι δοκεῖ ἀνδρὸς εἶναι). At 6.5.51 the author states that he can find no fault (cf. οὐ ψέγω) with Iphicrates at all for his good generalship. But as far as his leaving unguarded the best pass, which went past Cenchrea, Xenophon finds (cf. εὑρίσκω) that the general's actions were either to no avail or unhelpful. Overall, Xenophon praises Iphicrates' actions in the conflict, showing that he is willing to side with certain actors and presumably, that he may disapprove of others. He establishes himself as a moral onlooker to events, something that is pronounced in the final chapters of the work as he pronounces on the overall outcome of conflict in the Greek world.[23]

Xenophon becomes an even more prominent presence as the observer and narrator of the events recounted later in the work. The first person pronoun becomes more evident as the work progresses. Certainly, in the final book of the *Hellenica* the narrator's presence becomes more pronounced. At 7.2.1 he announces that it seems right to him (cf. ἐμοὶ δὲ δοκεῖ) and more deserved to tell of a small state accomplishing many fine deeds than of big cities doing the same thing.[24] Thus, he gives attention to the actions of the Phlisians, who were allies of the Spartans. At 7.3.1 he summarizes his account of the Phlisians, observing that he has shown how they were faithful to their friends and remained courageous in the war. He then follows this with a narrative which provides a stark contrast to the faithfulness of the Phlisians. At 7.3.4 the narrator persona asserts itself as Xenophon states that since he has begun (cf. ἠρξάμην), he wishes (cf. βούλομαι) to complete his account of Euphron. He departs from chronology to offer an example of the punishment of this unsavoury and immoral character. With the help of mercenaries Euphron seeks power at Thebes (7.3.4), but he is killed in the Acropolis by those who fear what he wants (7.3.5). A speech given about him after his death shows him to be greedy, as he robbed the shrines of gold and silver and was treacherous as he sought the aid of Athenian mercenaries after pledging himself to Sparta (7.3.8). At 7.4.1 Xenophon declares that he has now told the story of Euphron and he now returns to the point where he left off his narrative, cf. ἐγὼ δὲ ἔνθεν εἰς ταῦτα ἐξέβην ἐπάνειμι. Xenophon emphasizes that he is in control of the story he tells by emphatically stressing his subjectivity with the first person pronoun ἐγώ.

Xenophon asserts himself as an evaluative presence of events and persons in the conflict at 7.5.8. He declares that he will not say whether the Spartan's Epamonidas campaign in Tegea was successful (εὐτυχῆ μὲν οὖν οὐκ ἂν ἔγωγε φήσαιμι τὴν στρατηγίαν αὐτῷ γενέσθαι) but he declares the general's foresight and daring were commendable in every way. The author praises (cf. ἐπαινῶ) Epamonidas for pitching camp within the city walls of Tegea, as it was safer than being outside and because he could provide his troops with all the supplies they needed from within the city. Furthermore, he was able to observe the movements of the enemy outside the city. Xenophon presents his very positive and affirmative assessment of the general again later at 7.5.19, when he declares that it does not seem to him (cf. μοι δοκεῖ) very remarkable that Epamonidas should choose to die in battle as he was seeking to make the whole Peloponnese come under the control of Sparta. Pelling observes an 'old-fashioned virtue' in the general as he considers his men first while being open to living or dying in battle.[25]

The establishment of the narrative persona in the latter part of the work ensures that Xenophon emphatically owns the opinions expressed in the *Hellenica* – war is destructive and of no use to anyone – and he lays claim to the irony of seven books that depict conflict and the circumstances which accompany conflict as producing no clear or distinct end result for any of the warring parties.

The author presents the futility of war as its ultimate reality: nobody can win amidst the destruction that is rendered on the Greek communities. Thus, war should be anathema to the Hellenic world.

VI

With its first two books probably composed during the war and the remaining books written much later, in the 360s and perhaps the 350s,[26] the *Hellenica* is a work with a long-term view and it has a strongly moral perspective beyond its judgements on individuals or city-states as regards their loyalties and interactions with one another. It is perhaps Xenophon's most forceful articulation of a non-imperialist position, a stance that is also suggested in the *Poroi* and in the works on horsemanship. He narrates the conflicts of the Greek states for seven books only for the participants – the Athenians, Spartans, Thebans and Tegeans and so on – who have experienced this conflict to declare the futility of fighting. The text is not ostensibly pro-Spartan but it is certainly anti-imperialist and all that being anti-imperialist implies. As a consequence of fighting, nobody has gained any more territory. War is the condition that impoverishes and destroys peoples and lands; peace is what rather enriches them.

Part Four

Persia

11

Xenophon's *Cyropaedia*: Disfiguring the Pedagogical State[1]

I

The Persia of Xenophon's *Cyropaedia* is an ironic text because it is (or rather, should have been) an important site of political pedagogy, providing a historical scenario for a ruler's education and then a reference point for subsequent sites of instruction in power – and it is *not* so. (As I shall suggest – it possibly also offers an implicit aetiology of the younger Cyrus' rule and early demise in the *Anabasis*.) Cicero informs us that Scipio Africanus kept the *Cyropaedia* by his side to supply himself with an image (*effigies*) of just empire (*Ep. Quintum* 1.1.25; also *Ep. Ad Fam.* 9.25 and *De Senectute* 79–81).[2] Later, Renaissance scholars regarded Xenophon's work as a prescriptive account of how to produce an ideal ruler for an ideal state, and prior to Machiavelli, as the most influential 'mirror for princes'.[3] Modern readers add their voices to this regard for the work, continuing to find in Xenophon's portrayal of Cyrus the Great and his career a paradigm of ancient kingship and the system that produced it.[4] In this chapter, I want to suggest, however, that this is not the only narrative provided by the *Cyropaedia*. If the work as a whole affirms the link between education and political authority, it also qualifies it. Xenophon's text presents a system of education which precipitates the collapse of a kingdom, not least because it tolerates a series of discontinuities between the knowledge Cyrus requires to be a good leader and the knowledge he actually possesses. And it is here in the work, I suggest, that the irony lies.

II

In the first book of the *Cyropaedia* Xenophon provides the idealizing image of pedagogical Persia whose authority is to be called into question. Power, most simply the capacity to rule oneself and others,[5] is predicated on knowledge, specifically the knowledge of how to rule. Persia is a state where knowledge and political status are conceived as separable from one another and where the figures of didactic and political authority, namely the teacher and the ruler, refer to, and are elided, into one another. In pedagogical Persia adult citizens are required to accord the same respect to those in charge of the state, and particularly to the leader (ἄρχων), and to those who oversee the παιδεία of their children (1.2.12). The pedagogue is endowed with a privileged political identity, which the author goes to some length to reinforce and elaborate. In Book 1 Xenophon reveals that the task of the pedagogue is to rehearse his pupil in obedience to and in reverence for the state's rulers. The teacher instructs his young charges to obey (πειθέσθαι) their leaders (τοῖς ἀρχοῦσι); (1.2.8, cf. 1.6.20). His role is to mediate the ruler's power with the assistance of other individuals whose authority also refers and defers to that of the king. When the teacher trains his young pupils to control their appetites for food and drink, he permits them to eat only after receiving a signal from individuals named 'leaders (ἀρχόντες)' (1.2.8). As ephebes, the youths are again watched over by other individuals also named ἄρχοντες (1.2.5; 1.2.9; 1.5.1).[6] Chrysantas, a figure commended for his acumen (cf. 2.3.5 and 4.1.4[7]), stresses the continuity between pedagogical and political authority when he assigns to both teachers (διδάσκλοι) and rulers (ἄρχοντες) the task of giving good directions and habituating those under their authority to act reputably (3.3.53). The training of the youth comes to an end with a hunt led by the overall 'leader' of the state, the king. The hunt is present as a rehearsal for war (1.2.10[8]) but also implicitly as a climax affirming the goal of Persian education to be the training of the subject.

Persian education is far more than a temporary intervention in an individual's life if only because it entails the inception of a social identity which continues to be enacted and sustained by an individual throughout his life as a member of a community. Carlier observes that παιδεία in the *Cyropaedia* is coterminous with the political organization of the fatherland.[9] Indeed, it is a process of socialization that extends throughout a citizen's life, spanning childhood and old age (cf. Aristotle *Pol.* 1337b4–5; 1337b36).[10] Both Due and Tatum observe that when Xenophon writes of Cyrus being 'educated in the Persian laws'[11] the author points to a blurring of the distinction between citizenship and education. As the state's ruler and teacher, the king continues, or rather completes, the work for the teacher, 'instructing' his subjects as if they were his pupils. Accordingly, Xenophon later figures the exercise and articulation of the Persian king's power as a form of 'instruction'. Cyrus 'teaches' his army and subjects when he addresses them: the verb διδασκεῖν recurs through the work as a description of the leader's speech act.[12]

Barry Strauss has drawn attention to what he understands to be the 'intrinsically *political* nature of the father-son relationship' in Greek thought, where the father stands for the lord (κύριος) of the household (οἶκος) and the son is his successor.[13] It is the father's obligation and a sign of his authority that he instructs his 'children' in virtue, particularly moderation, as the taxiarch Aglaitadas highlights at 2.2.14. According to Xenophon, the king's pedagogy is also the teaching of the 'father' of the state. He observes that the Persian leader regards his subjects as if they were his children, while they in turn revere him as a 'father' (8.8.1; cf. 8.1.44; 8.2.9).[14] In Book 8 the sagacious Chrysantas declares the good leader (ἄρχων) to be similar to the good father, as both concern themselves with the well-being of those under their authority and care (8.1.1). The ruler-father serves as a source of knowledge and a paradigm for imitation by his 'offspring' (cf. 7.5.85–6; 8.7.24). Cyrus' own father, Cambyses, provides the work's ideal example of the paternal king as teacher. In the second half of Book 1, in the most obvious of Cambyses' *paideutic* interventions in the work (also cf. 1.6.20 and 8.5.22–7), Cambyses, significantly designated 'father (πατήρ)', instructs his heir and son (παῖς) in the art of warfare (1.5.14).[15] Later Tigranes, the son of the Armenian king, corroborates the pedagogical obligations of Cyrus' royal father, echoing what seem to be banalities regarding paternal authority.[16] Tigranes advises the youth to imitate (μιμεῖσθαι) his father if he admires the latter's plans and actions (3.1.15).

Cyrus at least ostensibly follows this advice when he inherits the rule of civic educator from his father Cambyses. He instructs subjects to educate their children (καὶ τοὺς παῖδας . . . παιδεύομεν, 7.5.85–6), while in the final book he is depicted as telling his own sons Cambyses and Tanaoxares, that he educated (cf. ἐπαίδευον) them to honour those above them in rank and to be honoured by those beneath them (8.7.10). Cyrus reinforces the ideal of παιδεία as a lesson in the structure of social ranks and its obligations.

III

Plato proposes that there was a discrepancy between the ideal pedagogical state and the real Persia. In *Alcibiades I* Socrates praises Persia for ensuring that its future kings are educated by individuals who are most wise, just, moderate and courageous (121e). In his dialogue Plato portrays the barbarian state as one in which the leader has been prepared for his position of political authority and responsibility by a rigorous training in virtue. In the *Laws*, however, the author offers a critique of Persian education. Here Plato's Athenian Stranger pronounces the education of Cyrus the Great 'incorrect' and finds fault with the king for not educating his children properly (3.694c). The Stranger declares that the sons of Cyrus have been 'educated' into corruption and luxury, and not into virtue (3.695b). For Plato, the historical Persia of Cyrus and his heirs is an example of the improperly enacted pedagogical state.

Ancient and modern scholars locate the critique of the education of Cyrus in the Laws within a larger narrative about the relationship of Plato to Xenophon. Aulus Gellius observes that some people regard the *Cyropaedia* as a response to the *Republic* (14.3), while Diogenes Laertius regards both as works which depict ideal constitutions (3.34). Athenaeus, followed by modern readers, perceives the *Laws* to be Plato's response to the *paideia* of Cyrus as portrayed in the *Cyropaedia* (504e–505a).[17] In fact, at *Laws* 694c the Athenian Stranger faults Cyrus for not educating his own sons, failing to comprehend what a correct education is.[18] Yet, this narrative, which attempts to give Plato the last word over his contemporary, ignores the polemical conclusion of Xenophon's work, which supplies the reader with a catalogue of problems following the death of Cyrus and thus seems to assent to the verdict of the *Laws*. Here the author points to strife amongst the king's sons, the empire's cities and peoples (8.8.2), a decay of religious piety (8.8.3–5), a relaxation of morality, demonstrated in the Persians' now indulgent attitudes towards food and drink (8.8.6–12), abandonment of the rigorous outdoor training of children (8.8.13–14) and an ensuing decline in military standards (8.8.19–26). Perhaps most significant of these problems is the easing of the formerly strict system of education, which constitutes the removal of one of the crucial supports of the pedagogical state.[19] Indeed, Carlier argues thus that Cyrus' monarchy was bound to fail because it was not concerned to educate the leader's sons.[20]

Because this concluding passage calls into question the ideal delineated in the first book, individuals attempt either to deny Xenophon's authorship or else to downplay, by qualifying, its obviously critical tone. As Tatum notes, until the nineteenth century, the work's epilogue was regarded as authentic and seen to be an instance of the 'decline of empire' motif.[21] Later critics turned their attention to it, often to treat it as a textual problem rather than as one of sense. Bizos and Hirsch, for instance, argued that the apparent inconsistencies and contradictions between it and earlier parts of the work meant that it must be apocryphal.[22] Others, such as Eichler, who produced a dissertation on the problem of the

Cyropaedia's ending, and Miller, the editor of the Loeb text, were either puzzled by it or coped by ignoring it.[23] Weathers maintained the authenticity of these chapters but saw them as affirming the greatness of Cyrus in that they report political difficulties only *after* the leader's death,[24] while Delebecque, regarding them as genuine, accorded them the status of afterthought.[25] Due insists that they were an integral part of the author's plan, though he perceives the critique to be limited to the Persia of Artaxerxes II rather than to the Persia depicted in the work as a whole.[26] He justifies his position by insisting that Xenophon is providing a picture only of Persia's leader, Cyrus, and not the state's overall system, despite the fact that Wood has shown that for the author good leadership proceeds from the good organization of society.[27] For Due, Persia's more ideal period under the leadership of Cyrus the Great signals the possibility that the present and the future can be better again. Tatum and Gera, prepared to tolerate the explanations of pre-nineteenth-century critics, seem to accept the epilogue at face value. Tatum suggests that Xenophon's work turns at the end into a 'novel of disillusionment',[28] while Gera sees the last section as pointing to a decline of moral standards in Persia after the conquest of Babylon, implicitly rehearsing the truism that 'power corrupts' and 'absolute power corrupts absolutely'.[29] Even more recently and without commitment, Field sees the conclusion of the *Cyropaedia* as leaving it open to question as to whether Cyrus was of such a nature that a different education might have reformed him.[30]

If the reader is uncomfortable in accepting the implications of what the final chapters of the *Cyropaedia* seem to be saying this is due above all to the apparent contradiction with the preceding narrative and its image of an ideal Persia. The instinct to suppress any discourse which might negatively qualify the image of the pedagogical state and of its leader is strong. Thus in the *Oeconomicus* readers assume that the conflation of the portrait of Cyrus the Great with that of the much less impressive Cyrus the Younger must be to the credit of the latter.[31] A Straussian 'reading between the lines' is the mode of reception which currently and notoriously tolerates apparent discrepancies in Xenophon's texts.[32] So in this vein of reading, Higgins proposes that Xenophon produces a gap between what is apparently being said and what is in reality the case, with an effect which the former terms an 'ironic humour', regarding the *Cyropaedia* as a representation of an ideal government which shows up the failure of contemporary political structures.[33]

Yet Straussian 'reading between the lines' is a mode of interpretation which takes enormous liberties, and I would argue that the discrepancies in the *Cyropaedia* are sufficiently explicit to demand that we read the lines themselves, that we take the epilogue as an integral and necessarily disturbing element of this work. The critique of contemporary Persia at the end of Book 8 is a rupture only inasmuch as it is far more obvious in its point than the narrative which precedes it: the conclusions make clear the consequences of the youth and subsequent actions of Cyrus. Against previous attempts to present the work as a eulogy of Cyrus, I maintain that Xenophon displays his subject's deficiencies, first as a student and then as a ruler-teacher, to account for the non-fulfilment and collapse of the pedagogical state. The work is evidence of the point that the author makes in the text's very first chapter, namely that all constitutions – whether they are democracies, oligarchies, or tyrannies – are bound to disintegrate unless those who rule them (ἀρχόντες) are wise and fortunate (1.1.1).

IV

We now need to go back to the beginning of the work to discover that this is the case.

Xenophon informs the reader that Cyrus is educated in the conventional Persian manner until the age of twelve or so (1.3.1). After this, Cyrus is taken by his mother, Mandane, away from Cambyses, the father-king who can best provide him with the knowledge of how to rule (cf. 1.5.14), and to the Median court of his grandfather Astyages (1.3.1). Due asserts that Cyrus is not compromised by his time in Media,[34] while Tatum, adhering to the Herodotean characterization of the Persian leader as someone who cannot be tempted by luxury (cf. Herodotus 9.122), optimistically argues that the youth resists the bad model offered to him by Astyages.[35] Because they are bound to the idealized image of the mature king, these scholars actually disjoin Cyrus' youth and adulthood in a manner that is questionable. They ignore both unfortunate influences upon the boy and aspects of his behaviour which should call into question his subsequent authority as Persian leader.

Immediately troubling for the idealizing reading are the young Cyrus' interactions with his grandfather's beloved attendant and favourite, Sakas.[36] When the prince first arrives at Astyages' court, he finds access to his grandfather hindered by Sakas. Sakas maliciously prevents the youth from running up to Astyages, deliberately inventing excuses to keep him away from the Median monarch (1.3.11). Although initially critical of the servant, Cyrus himself later assumes the roles of favourite and of 'gatekeeper' within the palace. First, the prince takes over Sakas' duties as wine-pourer in jest (1.3.9); then and more importantly, Cyrus finds himself needing to convince Astyages of his maturity when he wishes to go on a hunt with the king. He realizes that he can no longer beg as if he were a child (ὡς ἂν παῖς μηδέπω) or ask permission spontaneously (cf. 1.3.8) and that he must make cautious overtures to his grandfather. Cyrus adopts the posture of the sycophantic courtier, as he learns to anticipate the rhetorically privileged moment of opportunity (καιρός) for his request to be heard and acquires knowledge of how to fawn (cf. ὑποπτήσσων, 1.3.8). The prince controls and regulates access to his own grandfather, as Xenophon wryly observes, outgrowing childhood to become his own Sakas (1.4.6,[37] 1.3.8).

Markedly unlike the sober and virtuous Cambyses, Astyages is a figure who, in Xenophon's characterization of him, makes us acutely aware of the absence of paternal and pedagogical authority at the Median court. As leader of Media, he comes to represent his state as a deeply feminized land of luxury and laxity, and so as a land which stands in marked contrast to the ideal of a moral, temperate Persia. As Tatum notes, even Astyages' own daughter Madane is adamant that Cyrus will be unable to learn about justice (δικαιοσύνη) in the tyrant state of Media (1.3.16–18). When the Median king first appears, he does so in oriental finery, which prompts Cyrus to declare him 'beautiful (καλός)' and 'most beautiful (κάλλιστος)' (1.3.2). It is, perhaps, significant that the only other individuals described by this adjective are the slaves Sakas (1.3.8) and Abradatas' gorgeous wife, Pantheia, that is, figures who are other than the free-born male and who are subordinate within the structure of Median tyranny (4.6.11; cf. 5.1.4ff.).

Astyages is a poor example for his subjects and for his grandson because he continually contradicts his words by his actions. As Cyrus perceptively charges, the king and his companions do precisely what they do not permit their children to do, with the result that those around him have forgotten that Astyages is the state's king and ruler (l.3.10[38]). The king's political position is compromised by his inability to offer himself as a paradigm of virtue to others. On the one occasion that the Median king is depicted as assuming the discourse of the teacher-ruler, it is hardly as the benevolent father-teacher of his subjects idealized in the initial chapters of the work. In response to his mother's, Mandane's, observation that he would be severely punished if he showed signs of Median softness in Persia, Cyrus ventures that Astyages 'instructs (διδάσκειν)' his subjects to be content with the wealth that they have. But even in Cyrus' account, it becomes clear that the Median leader uses pedagogical discourse to articulate his own superiority as he 'teaches' his subjects that they should own less by virtue of their inferior position with respect to their king (1.3.18). Cyrus' reference to his grandfather as Mandane's πατήρ, as father of a daughter (not a son) at this moment in the narrative draws attention to the fact that the ideal of the father as a locus of pedagogical and political authority has been undermined (cf. 7.5.86; 8.7.24): to his children-subjects, the Median king is a father who fails to justify his position of responsibility by his behaviour.

Cyrus may criticize Astyages for undermining his own 'teaching', and consequently his political position at 1.3.10; however, the prince takes his grandfather as an implicit role model for his own actions. Media also trains Cyrus in an extravagance which will manifest itself at later points in his life. Astyages organizes for his grandson a grand feast which he hopes will whet the youth's appetite for the Median way of life. The youth initially appears to resist luxury. He questions the need for such excess, and draws a contrast between the numerous delicacies which the diner has to go to great trouble (cf. πράγματα) to reach and the simplicity of the Persian meal (1.3.4–5). Cyrus ostensibly espouses the Persian attitude of parsimony towards food and drink, which Xenophon describes elsewhere in the work. The author informs the reader in Book 1 that the Persian citizen is educated to endure a diet of bread and water; the only delicacy permitted the Persian is cress (κάρδαμον, 1.2.8; 1.2.11–12; 1.15.12 cf. Herodotus 1.71). Later Gobryas, the Babylonian general, affirms that no educated Persian would be caught snatching food while on campaign nor allow his meal to become an overriding passion (5.2.17). At 4.2.45 Cyrus reveals what appears to be his commitment to self-control.[39] He encourages his men to make a display of their education (cf. ἐπιδειξαίμεθ' ἂν τὴν παιδείαν) by restraining their appetites and reaffirms the educated Persian's view that self-denial is a form of gratification. The verb ἐπιδειξαίμεθ invokes the ἐπίδειξις, the sophist's self-advertizing performance of his skill and wisdom. Repeating the teaching of his father Cambyses (cf. 1.5.12), he tells his army that hunger is a delicacy (ὄψον) and that they should enjoy drinking water from a flowing river (4.5.4). The Persian leader attributes carousing and drunkenness to the defeated Babylonians, tacitly characterizing them as undisciplined and therefore susceptible opponents (7.5.15–21).

Due astutely observes of the feast episode at 1.3.4–5 that narrative compression has occurred despite the reader's impression that Cyrus is newly arrived in Media: the youth's familiarity with the palace servants, especially Sakas, discloses that he has already spent some time at the oriental court.[40] I suggest that this narrative economy helps to emphasize the discrepancy between Cyrus' critique and his subsequent actions, for Cyrus' own later practice with food is radically different from his 'teaching' on moderation. The Persian prince relaxes the strict dietary regimen for his Persian army. Although it is customary for a Persian to eat only after he has worked up a sweat (2.1.29 and 2.4.6), the leader summons his taxiarchs to the meal only after gentle instruction (cf. τῆς τε πραότητος τῆς διδασκαλίας, 2.3.21). Even the exhortation that Cyrus gives on the virtues of drinking water and eating bread while on campaign at 6.2.6ff. suggests that the leader has undermined the ideal of Persian moderation. Cyrus tells his men to carry sufficient wine with them (6.2.29). The implications of this directive are that wine is the preferred drink, and perhaps even that the Persian army has become used to drinking wine under Cyrus' command. Disregard for dietary restraint is more obviously revealed elsewhere in the work. In Book 4 we learn that the Median army under Cyrus' command indulges itself on plundered food and drink during victory celebrations, while his uncle Cyaxares gets drunk with his men (4.5.8). If on this occasion Cyrus can be excused by his absence from the festivities as he sets out to catch looters, the reader is given the impression that Cyrus' army later marches ultimately and above all on its stomach rather than on virtue and restraint. Xenophon implies that an enormous retinue attends the army in order to supply its meals when he draws an analogy between the military outfit and the different individuals needed to prepare meals in a household at 8.2.6.

The youthful Cyrus undermines his subsequent identity as a reliable spokesperson for Persian morality and virtue in other respects. According to the account of a Persian child's education given in Book 1, the hunt has a pedagogical function, offering the king an opportunity to exercise his authority and his youthful subjects, an opportunity to obey it in rehearsal for war (1.2.10; cf. 8.1.34). But Cyrus' conduct on his first hunt is troubling. The prince had previously accused Astyages of *forgetting* (cf. ἐπελέσθε) his position and obligations as a king (1.3.1), but as soon as the prince sees his prey he forgets everything (cf. πάντων ἐπιλαθόμενος, 1.4.8), rather following the creature wherever it leads him (1.4.8). Philip Stadter thinks that this episode conveys 'Cyrus' powers and determination to excel' even if the young man fails to display wisdom.[41] But Stadter makes too many allowances for the young Cyrus. In response to this indiscipline, his uncle Cyaxeres tells him to do as he wishes (cf. Ποίει ὅπως βούλει) since he now seems to be the king (βασιλεύς) of the hunt, implying the youth has improperly and prematurely assumed the position of leadership in the expedition (1.4.9–10). That the youth disregards the instructions of his elders signals a refusal to be ruled by others and to rule himself, both of which are necessary prerequisites for good leadership (cf. σαυτῷ πείθεσθαι,

1.6.20; 2.2.11). Accordingly, Xenophon undercuts Cyrus' achievements in spearing a deer with an exaggerated description of the creature as 'a fine and great thing (καλόν τι χρῆμα καὶ μέγα)' (1.4.8). The author shows up Cyrus as the killer of a harmless animal, perhaps misappropriating to the slain creature Herodotus' description of the menacing Mysian boar as a 'great thing (cf. χρῆμα ... μέγα)' (*Histories* 1.36.1).

Because the hunt is a military rehearsal, Cyrus' behaviour determines subsequent shortcomings on campaign. The lapse of memory which Cyrus suffers at 1.4.8 is reenacted at 3.3.62 when, as the general of his army, he forgets (ἐπιλαθόμενος) a military formation. Later, as the leader of the Persian army, he reveals himself willing to tolerate similar carelessness in his subjects. The reader is told that Cyrus makes allowances for his soldiers *forgetting* their provisions while on campaign. He decides to establish his camps close to one another with the intention of making retrieval of neglected items easy (6.3.1;[42] cf. cf. 8.8.11). But the hunt also marks Cyrus' more worrying tendency to act prematurely. In the assault on the Assyrians that is narrated later in Book 1, Cyrus again acts precipitously, rushing at the enemy as soon as he sees them and prompting his men to act similarly (cf. ἀπρονοήτως, 1.4.22). Xenophon compares the impetuous youth to an inexperienced dog who tracks a boar without foresight (ἀπρονοήτως, 1.4.22), and the metaphor proposes an analogy between the present military manoeuvre and the earlier hunt. The adverb ἀπρονοήτως highlights the absence of προνοία, the quality which, together with φιλοπονία, distinguishes the leader from those he leads (1.6.8; cf. 4.5.10; 8.1.13; 8.2.2). Thus, the otherwise doting and anti-authoritarian grandfather uncharacteristically intervenes to restore order to the hunt situation in Book 1, blaming his grandson (cf. αἴτιον μὲν ὄντα) for the fiasco (1.4.24).

V

Shortly after his return to Persia from Media, Cyrus is named general (ἄρχοντα) of the Median army by Cyaxeres (1.5.5). It is at this point that Cyrus receives a Persian education. He invokes Cambyses' identity as father-teacher *par excellence* in order to learn (μάθων) about the art of war (1.5.14). What he receives from the king is an important lesson on how to possess and justify actual political authority rather than merely to appear to have authority. Cyrus' inquiries about how a leader should appear to be wise to the individuals he leads (φρονιμώτερον δοκεῖν εἶναι, 1.6.22; cf. 1/6.21) prompts from Cambyses a disquisition on the value of virtue. Apart from demonstrating forethought (προνοία) and love of labour (φιλοπονία) (1.6.8), actual authority requires that one must manifest real virtue. Cambyses declares that the most effective way of appearing to be wise (δοκεῖν φρόνιμος εἶναι) is actually *to be* wise (τὸ γενέσθαι . . . φρόνιμος). Reality is privileged over appearance to such a degree that the good Persian leader will employ deceit (ἐξαπατᾶν) only when he deals with enemies rather than with his friends: deceit operates in terms of a dichotomy between appearance and reality, undermining true power as far as Cambyses is concerned (1.6.29; 1.6.33).

Cambyses' 'lesson' on political leadership is intended to serve as a standard for Cyrus' subsequent conduct as general and king, and Tatum notes that the youth shows himself mindful of the teachings articulated by his father (cf. 1.6.3; 1.6.5; 1.6.6; 1.6.8).[43] Yet if we accept that character development is a concept alien to antiquity, any apparent change in an individual is to be explained as the character *revealing* him- or herself for the person he or she really is.[44] Accordingly, Cambyses' pedagogical interventions are of little effect: the child in Media is essentially the same as, and prefigures, the mature adult and his subsequent moral condition. There is a sense in which the son invites his father's teaching, only to ultimately reject it. The prince establishes his political identity and position above through the very strategies of display and empty gesture which he had learned in Media and which Cambyses rejects as the basis for true authority.

The extravagant and beautiful garments of Astyages, which delight the child and grasp his attention when he initially arrives at his grandfather's court (1.3.3), become the whole foundation of Cyrus' power as the youth holds on to and develops the politics of display as the basis of his subsequent power. Astyages gives Cyrus his own set of Median clothing before the latter returns to Persia. In retrospect it will appear that he gives the latter an apparent authority, a 'fashion system', through which to construct the basis of totalitarian power in his fatherland (1.4.26).[45] That the young prince already understands the significance of this gift is made clear when he proposes to Cambyses that a leader should distinguish himself from his subjects by a demonstration of privilege: he should dine more sumptuously than his subordinates, display his great wealth, and be seen to lead a more leisurely life (1.6.8). Cyrus, as teacher-leader, gives a new twist to the notion of 'nutritionist' pedagogy, providing bodily rather than intellectual sustenance.

Cyrus first invokes the politics of appearance when he asserts his superiority over his Median uncle Cyaxeres during the Assyrian campaign. In Book 2 Cyrus fails to attire himself to impress the leader as Cyaxeres had commanded

(2.4.1–8); however, in Book 5 the prince takes a cohort of allies, including Medians, Armenians, Hyrcanians and others, to impress and in this way to disclose his power (τὴν δύναμιν) to his uncle when he meets him (5.5.5). So effective is this display of power that when Cyaxeres observes his nephew's army, he considers himself dishonoured (ἄτιμον) by his own motley retinue (cf. ὀλίγην τε καὶ ὀλίγου ἀξιίαν θεραπείαν) (5.5.6). The uncle affirms the potency of appearance, claiming himself ready to die ten times over to avoid being seen to be worthless (cf. ταπεινός) and to avoid being mocked by his relatives. It is no coincidence that, where Cyaxeres had previously competed with Cyrus, following this episode Xenophon makes it clear that the uncle now defers to his Persian nephew (cf. 5.5.39).[46]

The narrative of Book 8 establishes even more securely the politics of theatricality and it is here that Carlier notes the tone changes to one of criticism as Persian traditions are perverted.[47] Wood understands clothing as supplementing and signifying actual ability; however, I would argue that the Persian leader encourages his state officials to articulate their position and influence wholly through a rhetoric of dress: attire is what fundamentally distinguishes the rulers from those they rule (8.1.40).[48] Cyrus' leaders are made to wear shoes which make them seem taller than they really are (ὥστε δοκεῖν μείζους εἶναι ἢ εἰσι); they wear make-up which causes their eyes to appear more handsome than they actually are (ὡς εὐφθαλμότεροι φαίνοντο ἢ εἰσι); in short, they are dressed so as to seem more impressive than their true natures (cf. ὡς εὐχροώτεροι ὀρῶντο ἢ πεφύκασιν, 8.1.41). The contrast between appearance and actuality, sign and reality, marks the arbitrariness of the rhetoric of fashion and its politics. Cyrus requires the leaders of his empire to be able to 'charm (καταγοητεύειν)' their subjects. The verb καταγοητεύειν suggests deception and it identifies Cyrus' rulers with the stereotype of the fifth- and fourth-century sorcerer-rhetorician, the figure who charms, deceives and overpowers his audience through his skill at deploying a cultural language, above all words.[49]

In this Persia the privileged cultural language is cosmetic appearance. As Cyrus devises an empire in which the only recognized power is apparent power, he abandons the pedagogical state with its foundation of power on knowledge. Later in Book 8 the Persian leader plans a public procession which employs the appearance of solemnity (σημνότης) to reinforce respect for his government (ἀρχήν, 8.3.1). Xenophon tells us that the Persian leader hands out extravagant Median attire, red and purple cloaks, to the Persians and to those allies who hold positions of authority (ἀρχάς), both to wear and in turn to distribute to their friends to wear (8.3.5). These gifts of clothing are the means by which Cyrus now bestows honour and status upon his subjects (8.2.10) so that they in turn can purchase the goodwill and deference of their subordinates (cf. τῷ δωρεῖσθαί τε καὶ τιμᾶν, 8.2.10; cf. 8.3.7l, 8.4.36). This whole episode is a significant turning point, for it is the first occasion on which the Persians en masse assumed Median clothing (8.3.1[50]) – later on the army will also be dressed in Median fashion (8.5.17; cf. 8.8.15). Xenophon marks this moment as a betrayal of the Persian way of life, contradicting Isocrates' observation that it is Cyrus' Persia which conquers Media (*Evagoras* 37). In the *Oeconomicus* Ischomachus proposes that, if he or his wife were to use make-up, it would constitute a deception between intimates (10.2–8). The author's implication is that Cyrus resorts to the very deceptive devices which Cambyses insists should only be used against one's enemies and never against one's own people on his subjects (cf. τῶν τεχνῶν ... τῶν μεμηχανημένων, 8.3.1; also see 1.6.38–9 and 7.5.37–8). Cyrus' emphasis on the clothing of his officials implies that the prince has succeeded in alienating his subjects, perhaps just as one might expect of a tyranny such as that portrayed in the *Hiero*.[51]

In the theatre of power Cyrus gives the starring role to himself. The Persian leader designates the status of his officials through splendid dress, but he employs even more extravagant attire to construct his own pre-eminent position. At the beginning of Book 7 Cyrus appears arrayed for war as a latter-day Achilles with gold armour gleaming like a mirror and surrounded by a retinue clad in purple cloaks and bronze armour (7.1.12; cf. *Iliad* 19.364–99). At 7.5.37 Cyrus is said to desire to dress himself as he deems appropriate for a king (cf. ὡς βασιλεῖ ἡγεῖτο πρέπειν). What this entails becomes evident from the grand procession described in the following book. Here Cyrus processes on a chariot with a crown and purple cloak which signify his kingly status. Xenophon declares that 'Cyrus appeared much larger (μείζων δ' ἐφάνη πολὺ Κῦρος)' than his charioteer and goes on to qualify this statement with the words, 'whether in reality (τῷ ὄντι)' or 'by some means (ὁπωσοῦν)' (8.3.14). While the author's comments make the point that physical appearance creates political status by dramatizing it – Cyrus appears to be, and so is greater, than his lowly driver – his uncertainty as to whether the king is actually greater in status than those around him or whether he has devised and fabricated his superior size also suggests the impossibility of distinguishing between true and apparent power in the theatrical state.

Michel Foucault has discussed the role of observation and the use of technologies of observation as a means of exercising one's own power and constraining the power of others.[52] In Cyrus' Persia, power is consolidated and realized when the external trappings of position are displayed by the leaders of the state and viewed by their subordinates. To ensure that such is the case, the Persian leader purchases through gifts and honours the loyalty of spies and eavesdroppers, his 'eyes' and 'ears' (8.2.10). The numerous 'eyes' and 'ears' watch for insubordination (τὰ μὴ σύμφορα βασιλεῖ) and unrest amongst Cyrus' subjects, with the result that the subjects live in constant wariness and apprehension (8.2.12). Xenophon takes pains to insist that the king has numerous 'eyes', and not just as some people think, since one individual would not be able to see or hear as much as many 'eyes' (8.2.11). The king's 'eyes' and 'ears' enable him to watch the watchers and, in so doing, to disseminate his authority throughout the kingdom. Cyrus creates a 'panoptic' state, one in which power is maintained through surveillance rather than through more overt violence or force. He contrives observation as a means of exercising his own power and constraining the power of others. The point is that the king's informers, in keeping with the metaphorical description of them as 'eyes' and 'ears', extend the physical presence of the monarch's body politic, perhaps just as clothing augments the corporality of Cyrus' favoured Persian officials.

The power of Cyrus' whole visual apparatus is affirmed by the response that his subjects give to the procession described in the final book. Xenophon identifies this as the first occasion that any Persian prostrates himself (cf. προσεκύνει) before his leader (8.3.15). He speculates that the response is such either because some of the onlookers had been ordered to do so, or else because they were so overawed by the leader's splendid appearance (8.3.14[53]). The author seems to be offering alternative explanations for the Persians' response to their leader's appearance, but it can also be argued that he implicitly points to the assimilation of the drama to an act of will, for the apparatus of theatre now has the same effect as command. The custom of prostration identifies power with the degradation of one's inferiors. Arrian characterizes *proskunesis* as a barbarian act of self-humiliation and degradation which emphatically stands in contrast to the Greek ideal of freedom. In the *Anabasis* he observes that Cyrus was the first person to be honoured in this fashion and that this custom remained amongst the Persians and Medians until the Scythians, who are significantly described as a poor but free (αὐτόνομοι) people in his narrative, brought them to their senses (*Anabasis* 4.11.8–9).

In the final book of the *Cyropaedia* the Assyrian eunuch Gadatas, the Persian leader's captive and subject, is someone who bows down for his first time before Cyrus according to the fashion of his people (5.3.18).[54] Gadatas is a significant figure because he draws attention to the way in which Cyrus subverts and redefines the traditional roles of authority in the pedagogical state. Like Gobryas, the Assyrian captive who has lost his son (4.6.5), the Assyrian is also childless, if for quite different reasons.[55] After grovelling before Cyrus, Gadatas offers the Persian leader gifts from his estate and livestock and proceeds to make the Persian leader his son and heir (5.4.30). This act is poignantly inappropriate. For one thing, as Gera notes, both Gadatas and Cyrus are roughly the same age and therefore should be figured as contemporaries rather than as father and son (5.3.19). For another thing, and more importantly, the conquered subject Gadatas becomes a paternal figure.[56] Gadatas turns on its head the ideal of a πατῆρ as the locus of political authority, transforming the father instead into a figure of abasement. This recognition of what 'father' might also signify reveals the extent to which Persia has departed from the pedagogical ideal when Xenophon observes that Cyrus later takes his castrated 'father' as a paradigm for the loyal *subject* of imperial Persia. The ruler surrounds himself with a bodyguard composed of eunuchs (7.5.65), and he appoints the archetypal eunuch, Gadatas, to be the commander of his bodyguard and the head of the royal οἶκος (8.4.2ff.).[57] The Persian leader declares that, because eunuchs possess no familial ties, having neither wives nor children on whom they can bestow their love, they are inclined to respect and revere their masters as the individuals who can most enrich and support them (7.5.60–61). Later at 8.2.9 he identifies the eunuch as the individual who can best exemplify a loyalty which surpasses even kinship ties. The three eunuchs who kill themselves following Abradatas' death in battle and the suicide of the latter's wife Pantheia provide evidence of the fidelity of the castrated servant (7.3.15).

At 8.2.9 Xenophon observes that through the magnitude of his gifts the Persian king, that is, Cyrus, makes his subjects prefer their leader to their own brothers, fathers and sons. It is in the light of this statement that the eunuch is to be regarded less as the faithful servant than as an individual who emblematizes the alienation of familial relationships and affections, which are the basis of Cyrus' authority. This alienation calls into question the identity of Cyrus' Persia as an ideal pedagogical state on the terms set out at the beginning of the work. The eunuch and the eunuch's creator resemble a figure presented to the reader earlier in the work as a *bad* teacher. In Book 3, Xenophon recounts the case of a sophist, who was known to both the Persian king and his friend Tigranes, and who had since been executed by the Armenian king for corrupting (διαφθέρειν) his son. The familiar charge against professional teachers and sometimes against philosophers (as in the case of Socrates) is specifically inflected so that this instance of didactic corruption has to do with the teacher's claim on an obedience that rightly belongs to the student's parents.[58] The sophist is other than, and so in competition with, the *Cyropaedia*'s ideal of the didactic father. To justify the execution of the pedagogue, the Armenian king draws an analogy between this individual and adulterers, who destroy the φιλία between husbands and wives (3.1.39[59]). Like sophists and adulterers, eunuchs corrupt the pedagogical state because they bring the process of political filiation to an end. Eunuchs, whether they are understood as being desexualized or, for the Greeks, as being feminized by the loss of their sexual organs,[60] cannot have sons or in turn become fathers to their sons. Cyrus' household of eunuchs is the demise of the father-teacher-king configuration precisely as the household (οἶκος) is a microcosm of the state (1.1.1; cf. 8.1.9).[61] The Persian pedagogical ideal is one which can only tolerate the masculine figure as pupil and teacher.

By denying to pedagogy the possibility of reproduction, both literally and metaphorically, Cyrus has not only displaced the role and figure of the father-teacher-ruler; he has also radically redefined it. The figure of the eunuch rearticulates the degradation emblematized by the Persians' *proskunesis* in the final book. As Luccioni observes, Xenophon's Greek audience would have seen castration as a barbaric custom, which would have contradicted even the Persian ideal of physical prowess presented in an earlier part of the work.[62] But the author does not rely on his reader's anthropological sensitivity in making the indignity of castration incontrovertible. He reports Cyrus' belief that men deprived of their sexual organs are no less courageous than others, a belief based on the analogy of gelded animals, which are not deprived of their strength and ability to work (7.5.62–3). Although Xenophon has valorized the comparison of political subjects to animals when he proposes that a herd of beasts is easier to control than men at 1.1.2–3, this subsequent analogy begins from quite a different assumption. Unlike the author, the Persian leader regards beasts as creatures to be exploited and mishandled by those who own and control them: they are the wretched beasts of burden (ὑποζύγια) to whom Xenophon poignantly compares the unfortunate slaves on Cyrus' military campaign (8.1.44). Indeed, Herodotus mentions eunuchs, along with pack-animals, as part of the auxiliary of Xerxes' campaign at *Histories* 7.187. Castration is a trope for the grotesque disfigurement of an implied body politic at the hands of Cyrus.[63]

The reappearance of Cyrus' father, Cambyses, in the narrative presents a subtle but nevertheless powerful critique of the prince's relationship with his subjects. At 8.5.22–6 Cambyses offers his final speech in which he warns Cyrus against using his political position to take advantage of his subjects (8.5.24). Tatum regards Cambyses' advice as a merely symbolic nod to the topos of warnings about the danger of tyranny and as one which has no bearing on a virtuous leader like Cyrus.⁶⁴ I prefer to regard this interaction as suggesting how far the Persian prince has departed from the ideal of pedagogical 'rule of the father', such that Cambyses has to reassert his identity as father and king of the state (8.5.26) and Cyrus' as his son ('you, Cyrus, are my child (παῖς)', 8.5.22. Cambyses' reappearance makes the reader aware that in the preceding narrative Cyrus has claimed leadership without the due reverence and deference due to his father-teacher, apart from the brief exchange with him in the first book. Xenophon points out to his reader in the final book that now nobles (οἱ ἄριστοι) and slaves alike call Cyrus 'father (πατέρα)' (cf. 8.1.44) so that the word παῖς now denotes the Persian subject as both, and simultaneously, as 'son' and 'slave'. The characterization of the Persian king as 'father' always figures that citizen as a παῖς, as a child, and then inevitably, in the case of a corrupt leader, as a slave. Cyrus reconstructs the Persian 'father' as a figure who not only rules but also dominates, such that any possibility of an Oedipal struggle between father and son is abrogated.⁶⁵

VI

Scholars have conventionally articulated what they perceive to be Cyrus' fulfilment of the ideals set out at the beginning of the work in terms of his Socratic qualities. Cyrus displays self-control, moderation, physical stamina, engages in dialogue and elenchus: in short, he is what Socrates would have been if he were the philosopher-king of the ideal state.⁶⁶ Yet it is doubtful whether Socratic pedagogy can be transferred in this manner into Xenophon's Persia. The *Cyropaedia* is a narrative about the failure of Cyrus' Persia to live up to the ideal of a pedagogical state, as has been noted, for instance, by two very different scholars. Christopher Nadon observes that Cyrus' education is defective and quite different from the one that Xenophon intended for the ruler, although claiming for the most part that Cyrus is a leader to be emulated.⁶⁷ For him, it is an account of the inadequate education of a future leader. P. Carlier notes that there is nothing supernatural about Cyrus' birth, something that the reader might expect of a remarkable and able leader.⁶⁸ This is extremely telling and indicative of the leader-to-be. He is responsible not for the aggrandizement of Persia but for the vitiation and perversion of the political structure, particularly as regards the relationship of the ruler to those he rules. The Persian leader achieves the complete and utter enslavement of his subjects and in doing so he can only call into question his authority as the state's father-teacher. He is responsible for turning Persia as a republic into Persia, an empire, even if Gray improbably thinks that Cyrus keeps the republic and empire separate in his rule.[69]

In depicting the disintegration of one ideal of the pedagogical state, the *Cyropaedia* perhaps implicitly provides the opportunity for a re-inscription with a more familiar literal and metaphorical pedagogical *topos*, namely Athens. Indeed, at the moment that the work's epilogue discloses the collapse of Persia as a state in which knowledge and virtue have failed to construct power, Xenophon significantly steps into the narrative to recast himself, the Athenian author, as the text's privileged teacher. He now portrays himself as offering in the final chapters of the work his lesson about the consequences of pursuing political power without knowledge, 'To speak in truth, I shall begin to teach (διδασκεῖν) … ' (8.8.2); in turn, the work's reader is characterized as Xenophon's pupil by the verb 'to learn (καταμαθεῖν)' (8.1.40) and 'we learned (κατεμάθομεν)' (8.2.10). The author designates himself as teacher and his audience as his pupils, as it would appear, in order to affirm a particular mode of questioning and unsettling pedagogy represented in the Socratic dialogues, the *Memorabilia* and the *Oeconomicus*, and invoked only by default in the *Cyropaedia*. In this model, the Greek πόλις, above all Athens, is the realized pedagogical state, while the philosopher, most obviously Socrates – perhaps together with the philosopher's biographer, Xenophon – is an ideal citizen and leader. Pedagogy is thus the trope which articulates the political and cultural superiority of the Attic democratic state by inviting the replacement of Persia by Athens and of Cyrus by Socrates.

12

Coming Home? The *Anabasis* as Community

I begin with the conventional observation that the *Anabasis* is regarded as one of Xenophon's historical works,[1] although P. J. Bradley observes that there is no announcement of genre or content in this work.[2] The *Anabasis* is certainly historical in dealing with events – military campaigns, politics and the long trek of fighting men returning from Persia to Greece from spring 401 to spring 399[3] – and personalities in the Greek world that help to tell a story of what happened and who did what at that time. John Marincola observes that, like the *Hellenica*, the text does not state the reason as to why Xenophon composed the work and in this the author differs from Herodotus and Thucydides, who each in their own way and distinctly preface their works as seeking to preserve memory and glory and to offer learning and understanding of the human condition.[4]

But I observe that Xenophon is generally not in the habit of announcing his intentions or his goals in writing a work – note also the marked lack of preface in the *Hellenica*. Rather he engages in irony as a way of selectively communicating to *some* of his reading public – for not everyone can perceive the irony – what he wishes them to understand about the world around them. And so, I suggest that the *Anabasis* is a work with some interesting surprises where the author in particular is concerned, and it is in these surprises that the irony lies. I propose that the *Anabasis* offers a very gentle, and perhaps for this reason, a rather sophisticated irony. Events take various turns which are unexpected and therefore, defeat common perceptions of what might otherwise have occurred. Perhaps most surprising to the reader of the corpus is how Xenophon turns out to be a prominent actor in his own narrative, proving himself an able leader of his men on a military campaign. It is a work in which I suggest the author's attitude to war changes somewhat, from being perhaps rather more nonchalant about it to being more obviously opposed to militaristic ventures. Accordingly, the *Anabasis* does support my claim that Xenophon is indeed an ironic author in the way in which he shows the world to the reader.

But if differing levels of knowledge between different individuals are responsible for irony, the *Anabasis* must overall be an ironic text. It was probably composed by the author Xenophon some thirty years after the narrated return to Greece by the army and so with the wisdom of hindsight[5] as far as the actions of the character Xenophon, who was involved in the matters being narrated only at the time, are concerned. The narrator knows after the event the outcome of decisions and actions taken in the story whereas Xenophon the character and actor does not have this larger perspective. If irony relies most essentially on a different knowledge between actors, then irony may be assumed in light of the double presence of Xenophon as actor and as experienced narrator to underlie the whole narrative of the *Anabasis*. And I suggest that the irony being proposed has to do with the realization that Greek unity is much more important than relying on a foreign, i.e. Persian, power so that the *Anabasis* becomes an assertion of the significance of Hellenism for the ancient world.

I

The premise of the *Anabasis* sets the reader up for a major disappointment. The reader finds himself amidst political turmoil in Persia. The work begins and carries on for several chapters with the struggle over succession as Darius is weak and expects to die. The two sons of Darius, Artaxerxes and Cyrus the Younger (the Elder is the subject of the *Cyropaedia*), are summoned to their father with the former already present and the latter being recalled with Tissaphernes and three hundred Greek hoplites from his satrapy (1.1.1–2). Darius dies and Artaxerxes is established as king (1.1.3). It is at this point that Tissaphernes engages in treachery. He accuses Cyrus of plotting against his brother to the latter and believing Tissaphernes, Artaxerxes has Cyrus arrested with the intention of killing him. Their mother Parysatis intervenes and Cyrus returns to his province. Artaxerxes' arrest of Cyrus is the cause for a struggle for supremacy between the brothers, for Cyrus has the support of his mother and seeks the kingship. He searches for capable soldiers, is good to them, and collects a Greece force in secret so that he may catch his brother unprepared (1.1.5).

Cyrus gathers Peloponnesian soldiers by telling them that Tisserphernes has designs on the cities in Ionia, which were garrisoned by Peloponnesian mercenaries (1.1.6). These cities had initially belonged to Tisserphernes but had revolted, going over to Cyrus. Tisserphernes puts a number of Milesians to death and Cyrus collects an army of exiles (1.1.7). Cyrus also asks his brother to place several Ionian cities under his charge rather than that of Tisserphernes and he has his mother's support in this matter (1.1.8). As a consequence, Artaxerxes does not perceive that Cyrus is preparing to go to war with him and thinks that money being spent on troops is for the end of war with Tisserphernes. Furthermore, the Greeks in the Chersonese collect an army for Cyrus under Clearchus, the Spartan exile, who is also aided by cities in the Hellespont in that they send money for troops (1.1.9). Cyrus continues to collect support in the Greek world. He induces Proxenus the Boeotian to gather as many men as possible on a supposed mission against the Pisidians. And he also approaches Sophaenetus the Stymphalian and Socrates the Achaean with the same request to collect as many men as they can for a war against Tissaphernes (1.1.11). Cyrus begins his upward march on the pretence that he wants to drive the Pisidians out of his land (1.2.1). His men are gradually amassed and he makes progress on his travels through the Greek lands. The march of Cyrus from Sardis, through Lydia and Phrygia is recounted at 1.2.5. He remains thirty days at Celaenae in Phrygia. (1.2.7 and 1.2.9) while the Spartan exile, Clearchus, arrives with a thousand strong force, eight hundred Thracian peltasts and two hundred Cretan bowmen assemble. Syracusans and Arcadians also gather (1.2.9). The expedition continues with Cyrus and his army proceeding through Cappadocia (1.2.20) to Cilicia (1.2.21), arriving in Tarsus (1.2.23) where he remains for twenty days (1.3.1).

It is at Tarsus that the Greek armies oppose the Spartan Clearchus and Cyrus, suspecting quite correctly that they will go against the Persian king Artaxerxes, something that they had not been hired for (1.3.1). At 1.3.3–6 Clearchus tries to force his men to go on with the march and he offers his men a speech of self-defence, saying that he will go with his men and rather abandon Cyrus (1.3.9). Clearchus expresses his fear that Cyrus will punish him for abandoning the latter. He finishes by saying at 1.3.12 that Cyrus can be a valuable friend when he decides to be a friend and a most dangerous enemy when he is a foe since he now has a cavalry, infantry and a fleet. Following Clearchus' speech various individuals debate how they are to return to Greece, Clearchus declares that he is not the man to lead them back (1.3.15). The speakers decide to ask Cyrus to persuade them to follow him on what might be a dangerous and exhausting venture as friends or else to permit them to return home (1.3.19). Cyrus then agrees to give the Greeks half as much more in pay to continue marching with him, not saying that he is marching against the King but against Abrocomos, an enemy of his (1.3.20–1).

The armed force continues its march beyond the Psarus river, the Pyramus river and to Issus in Cilicia (1.4.1). Cyrus sends for the fleet at 1.4.5 and various naval contingents, commanded by Greeks and the Egyptian Tamos, who had earlier besieged Miletus when he was friendly to Tissaphernes, and hoplites arrive to meet the Persian leader (1.4.2–4). Cyrus' actual intention now is to engage the King as the Greeks had feared (1.4.7). There are a couple of desertions as Xenias and Pasion leave Cyrus' forces (1.4.8). It is then that Cyrus marches on to the Chalus river (1.4.9), to the Daradas river (1.4.10), to the Euphrates river and to a city named Thapascus (1.4.11). At this point, Cyrus reveals his true intention, namely to go to Babylon to confront the Great King, Artaxerxes (1.4.11). Cyrus has to persuade his men to follow him and does so by giving them more money (1.4.13). He continues through Syria, which provides the army with many provisions (1.4.19).

The fifth chapter of Book 1 sees Cyrus and his force march through Arabia (1.5.1). The contingent then proceeds through the desert to a city named Corsote (1.5.4) and because there is nothing for the animals to eat, they die of hunger (5.5) while the soldiers subsist by eating meat rather than grain, which is extremely expensive in the markets (1.5.6). His army, however, manages to provision itself at a city called Charmande (1.5.10). In 1.7 Cyrus and his army march through Babylonia. Cyrus anticipates doing war with his brother here and appoints Clearchus and Menon as commanders of the left and right wings (1.7.2). Cyrus then proceeds to praise the Greek men in his army, stating that they are there not because he does not have enough barbarians but because the Greeks are better and stronger than the barbarians and because they represent freedom (1.7.3). The leader offers as an incentive the satrapies ruled by his brother's friends to his own friends and wreaths of gold to the Greek soldiers (1.7.6–7).

The men on each side are counted up and Artaxerxes' army is reported by deserters to be immense, outnumbering Cyrus' army of less than four hundred thousand by one million two hundred thousand men, in addition to scythe bearing chariots and horsemen (1.7.11–12). The sides do not engage for some ten days (1.7.17–20), although Cyrus prepares his men and himself takes the centre of his army with six hundred horsemen (1.8.6). Significantly and consequentially, he does not wear a helmet, unlike his men (1.8.6). In the afternoon, the enemy is sighted advancing evenly (cf. 1.8.14). The Greeks strike up a paean at 1.8.17 and have success in pursuing the Persian enemy without any of the Greeks being injured (cf. 1.8.20). So successful are the Greeks in this first foray that they begin to hail Cyrus the 'King' (1.8.21). Cyrus seeks then to encircle the enemy and while pursuing the enemy, catches sight of the king, Artaxerxes, and strikes him on the breast (1.8.26). As he attacks the King, someone hits Cyrus under the eye with a javelin and the King and Cyrus fight each other with their supporting attendants (1.8.27).

Cyrus is killed in this encounter, παρ' ἐκείνῳ γὰρ ἦν Κῦρος δὲ αὐτός τε ἀπέθανε. Michael Flower finds the death an ironic one, observing that it comes about because Cyrus the Younger is the only leader portrayed by Xenophon as unable to profit from divine favour and assistance. He does not know how to receive or interpret divine signs, and he engages in an act of impiety when he plots fratricide against his brother Artaxerxes. The gods had no regard for Cyrus because he did not deserve their regard.[6]

II

The unexpected death of Cyrus in September 401 is the major disappointment for the men on the expedition. In terms of the narrative, it is presented as the unexpected turn of events that has occurred in the first part of the *Anabasis* after the long march and build-up to the battle, although the readers of the *Anabasis* would have been well aware of this event.[7] The fight between Cyrus and Artaxerxes is over far too soon, even before it properly begins. The Greek forces do not get to engage the Persian forces of Artaxerxes in any prolonged or meaningful way, and Cyrus does not manage to exercise a longer leadership over the Hellenic and barbarian soldiers. I suggest that the reader does not anticipate the killing of Cyrus at this point, if only because the narrative has been focalized from his point of view. The narrator, who is at this point in the work a barely present and disembodied but apparently omniscient presence, has not given any attention to Artaxerxes or Tisserphernes, their intentions, or their actions at this time and his attention to Cyrus and his preparations for battle have perhaps induced the reader rather to sympathize with the latter and to expect better for him. It would appear that the author engages in what Gerard Genette terms an 'internal' focalization with the narrator knowing at least as much as his character.[8] Xenophon follows with a eulogy of Cyrus. He states that the leader was most kingly and he was the most worthy to rule of all the Persians since Cyrus the Great (9.1). This last statement is telling. The narrator has a broader perspective and a wider knowledge than his character in this part of the *Anabasis*, and this knowledge may after all explain the downfall and death of Cyrus.

As we have seen, the author's chief work on Persia and its ruling family is the *Cyropaedia* and this work ends with a condemnation of Cyrus' descendants, of which the Cyrus of the *Anabasis* would have been one, as a consequence of their ancestor's shortcomings. The *Cyropaedia* raises serious questions because we know from this text that Cyrus the Great was not a leader that one might look up to. He manifested faults such as lack of discipline and a shortage of self-control and consequently, he was a far from perfect ruler. In fact, we learn that the behaviour and failed education of Cyrus the Great resulted in the bad education of his offspring and it is tempting to read of Cyrus the Younger's self-control, modesty and obedience, which he supposedly learned at the King's court, with some cynicism. Indeed, at *Cyropaedia* 8.8.2 Xenophon observes that upon Cyrus the Great's death, his children fight with one another – indeed Artaxerxes and Cyrus are engaged in a struggle for power in the *Anabasis*, cities and nations revolt and everything takes a turn for the worse. I suggest that the infrastructure the King has established in Persia in the *Cyropaedia* is deeply problematic and faulty, with the consequence that the state collapses upon his passing. It is at this point that the narrator takes over the role of teacher from Cyrus, instructing his audience in what the Persian religion should have been, ὡς δ'ἀληθῆ λέγω ἄρχομαι διδάσκων ἐκ τῶν θείων ... (*Cyropaedia* 8.8.2).

If Cyrus is like his ancestor, he is a problematic and a hardly faultless character. Cyrus the Younger is presented as being the most skilled in equestrian arts and in other military accomplishments (1.9.5), but his death thrusts that into some question. He is too readily and easily killed to be an accomplished soldier. Cyrus is commended for his generosity in offering half of the wine that he has enjoyed (1.9.25–6), yet one might ask if this is actually as kind and as generous as it seems. The Persian leader has himself consumed half of the food he is giving away so that his subjects receive partly eaten scraps. It would be far more generous if Cyrus had given uneaten food to his benefactees, as he indeed could. If many go over to Cyrus' camp after he splits with the King, it is only because they believe that they will get better rewards from Cyrus than from the King (1.9.29). It is not because he is more noble or virtuous. Finally, we are told that when Cyrus fell, all his men died fighting in his defence, except Ariaeus, who fled with the cavalry that he commanded (1.9.31). But it is also the case that only a few of his six hundred strong entourage remained with him to the end (cf. 1.8.25). Ariaeus will later go over to fight with Tissaphernes (3.2.5), and he is an important figure in this respect because he casts loyalty to Cyrus into some doubt.

III

Cyrus' death comes quite suddenly after the buildup of events during the march in the prior part of the book. The march up to this point has been narrated in some detail. Cyrus is gone, and the reader wonders what the material of the rest of the work could be without the presence of Cyrus. But this is only one's view if the *Anabasis* is viewed wholly as the march of Cyrus. It is not and cannot be that. And that perhaps is one of the great and obvious ironies of the *Anabasis*, the expectation that this would be a work completely about Cyrus and the more aware reader's realization is that it is not. It is in fact an account of how the Greek army works its way back home to Greece and in doing so, how it organizes itself even while on the march into a community of sorts and how the Greeks, and especially Xenophon, are able to lead this community.

After the death of Cyrus, the Persian presence in the narrative is considerably diminished and the remaining seven books of *Anabasis* become only concerned with Greeks. This is because Xenophon takes the Greeks as the new focalization point for the narrative so that Persian affairs and personalities appear to be increasingly inconsequential in the narrative and diminished in importance. In fact, the reader only hears of the Persians occasionally organizing attacks against the army. The text of Xenophon becomes a long account of the Greeks' march back to their homeland, with this march possessing a much more prominent role than the one under Cyrus, which took them to this point.

Cyrus has taken his army as far as Cunaxa, along the Euphrates in Babylonia (cf. 1.7.15) before he is killed. At the beginning of Book 3, the story of the *Anabasis* comes into its own as an account of how the Ten Thousand, that is, the Greeks who joined Cyrus' venture as mercenaries – actually, some 12,900 at the beginning of the return to Greece and 6,000 when they ended in Thrace, according to Robert Bonner[9] – attempt to return to Greece. The Greeks find themselves surrounded by hostile tribes and cities and without any markets. They are 10,000 stadia from Greece without a guide, cut off by impassable rivers and betrayed by the barbarians, who had initially marched with them (3.1.1–2).

In Book 2 the Greeks are found to be in some disarray as many are still not aware that Cyrus has died (2.1.3–4). The majority of the Greeks experience perplexity upon learning this news: they do not eat, they do not light fires, and they have trouble sleeping (cf. 3.1.2–3). Ariaeus flees (2.1.3) but is told that he will be made king if he returns (2.1.5). The Greeks have no food and the Spartan exile Clearchus enters into relations with the Persian Tissaphernes, having dinner with him and beginning to trust a notably treacherous figure,[10] Clearchus returns to his camp and organizes a larger meeting of the Greeks with Tissaphernes. The Greeks go to Tissaphernes' door and are killed by the Persian leader (2.5.32). It emerges that Clearchus was plotting against the Persians (2.5.41) and he is judged to have been a warmonger (2.6.1, 2.6.6). People recollect that he fought on the side of the

Spartans when they were at war with the Athenians and then sought to make war on the Thracians (2.6.2). Clearchus is judged to have been severe and rough (2.6.12) so that he did not inspire friendship or goodwill from his men (2.6.13). The author ends the book, offering other obituaries of the other Greek generals: of Proxenus, a general who was though worthy to rule and who nurtured friendships (2.6.16–20), and of Menon, a man who wanted great wealth and is very treacherous (2.6.21–8). Agias the Arcadian and Socrates the Achaean are also killed by Tissaphernes and are commended by the author for being brave and trustworthy friends (2.6.30). This clears the way for Xenophon, not yet a commander of any Greek forces, to become prominent in the narrative.

The narrator mentions himself several times in Book 2. At 2.4.15 Xenophon is walking with Proxenus after dinner when they are accosted by someone who tells them to be on the lookout for attacks from barbarians (cf. 2.4.16). At 2.5.37 he is mentioned again as 'Xenophon the Athenian' (Ξενοφῶν Ἀθηναῖος), who wishes to learn the fate of Proxenus. Slightly later at 2.5.40 the author Xenophon gives his younger self a more assertive role as he states that Clearchus should perish if he violates his oaths, while Proxenus and Menon are the benefactors of the Persians who supported Cyrus and will therefore offer them good advice (cf. 2.5.41). But it is in Book 3 that Xenophon is more fully reintroduced to the reader. At 3.1.4 the narrator states that in the army was a man named Xenophon, an Athenian, who was neither general, captain or a common soldier, ἦν δέ τις ἐν τῇ στρατιῇ Ξενοφῶν Ἀθηναῖος, ὃς οὔτε στρατηγὸς οὔτε λοχαγὸς οὔτε στρατιώτης ὤν. The narrator tells us why Xenophon is on the expedition. He has been invited by Proxenus, an old friend, to go along with the promise that he would become a friend to Cyrus, for whom the former has great regard. Xenophon consults the philosopher Socrates, who tells him in turn to consult the oracle at Delphi for the reason that going on an expedition to help Cyrus would bring him blame because Cyrus was thought to have helped the Spartans in their war against the Athenians (3.1.5). Unfortunately, in Socrates' view, Xenophon does not ask the correct question. He requests the god to tell him what the best way is to go rather than whether he should go or stay (3.1.7). (In fact, Xenophon is misled as to the reasons for the expedition. When he meets Cyrus, he is told by the leader that the campaign is against the Pisidians (3.1.10) and not the king and his brother, Artaxerxes, for the throne of Persia.)

Notable in all this is the fact that the expedition is *not* presented as a military venture so much as an opportunity to make the acquaintance of the Persian leader, whom Xenophon in any case at that point in time admires. Xenophon thus goes on the march out of curiosity and out of a desire for friendship.

IV

In fact, I want to suggest that Xenophon is present on the march of the Ten Thousand as an individual who seeks to form and maintain a community, one which is better than the actual political communities of Athens and Sparta. In a speech he makes to the generals and captains of the Greek army, Xenophon declares his vision for the forces. He requests that the leaders of the army appoint generals and captains as soon as they possibly can to replace those who have died. The reason is that nothing fine or good can be accomplished without leaders (ἄνευ γὰρ ἀρχόντων) in any discipline and certainly not in warfare, and it is the case, as Marincola well observes, that Xenophon was particularly interested in the issue of leadership.[11] Discipline (εὐταξία) keeps the men safe, while poor and ill-discipline (ἀταξία) has destroyed many (3.1.38).[12] Discipline involves obedience to one's leaders (τὸ πείθεσθαι τοῖς ἄρχουσιν, *Hellenica* 7.1.8), which will ensure the superiority of one's army or naval forces.[13] Xenophon expresses sentiments which are characteristic of an Athenian aristocrat who seeks the maintenance of the status quo, but these thoughts are perhaps also made after what John Dillery notes as confusion and major disorder after the Battle of Mantinea (cf. *Hellenica* 7.5.27).[14] Order is extremely desirable for a community or society to function properly, as is also apparent from the discussion between Pericles and Socrates in the *Memorabilia* (cf. *Mem.* 3.5–7).[15] In contrast, war tends to promote disorder and chaos at large, but disorder and chaos must also be avoided within the community, whether this is the army itself or the city-state which supports the army. Furthermore, the men must come to realize that death is the common fate of everyone and therefore they should attempt to meet death nobly rather than seek to save their own lives (3.1.43). His comments on bravery are also characteristic of Spartan ideology and it is no accident that the Lacedaimonian leader Cheirisophorus praises him for his words and actions as being a 'common good' (cf. 3.1.45).

The story of the *Anabasis* is in part the story of the character Xenophon's development into becoming a leader.[16] And he turns out to be a good leader of the Athenian men as he comes to the fore as a prominent character in the *Anabasis*. For one thing, he appears to be a motivated and humane leader. When he is summoned with the peltasts by Cheirisophus to the front of the army, he comes forward alone without his men to converse with the Greek leader (3.4.38–9). The author suggests that the Greeks should aim for the mountain top where the Persians are and himself chooses to go because he is the younger of the leaders (3.4.41–2). Xenophon's kindness emerges when he urges the men to climb the mountain as if they were racing for Greece (3.4.46) and he is confronted by Soteridas the Sicyonian, who comments that while Xenophon is on horseback, he has become tired of carrying his shield (3.4.47). Xenophon's response is to leap down from his horse, push Soteridas out of line and to march as quickly as he can with the latter's shield (3.4.48). The men, however, take issue with Soteridas and force him to march onwards with his shield so that Xenophon remounts and rides as long as it is possible for him to do so (3.4.49). When the Greeks are victorious in gaining the mountain, Xenophon rides with the Greeks of the rescuing party to offer encouragement to the men (3.5.4–5).

Book 5 reveals Xenophon to be a man who is concerned for the welfare of his fellows and who is concerned to do the right thing with regard to the gods. At the beginning of this book the author says to the Greek army what is appropriate for him to say, ὅσα μοι οὖν δοκεῖ καιρὸς εἶναι ποιεῖν ἐν τῇ μονῇ, ταῦτα ἐρῶ (5.1.5). He tells that army that they must obtain provisions where they are, as there is no market and they have no money, so they must have groups that will forage for food (5.1.6–7). Those who forage must tell those who stay behind in case they need help in the process of foraging (5.1.8). The Greek army is also to look for ships in case Cheirosophorus does not bring back enough ships (5.1.10). But if they do not get enough ships the Greek army is to go by land (5.1.13). The army approves all of Xenophon's proposals except the last, but he does not put the last to a vote, knowing the foolishness of the army (5.1.14).

Xenophon is the responsible leader, caring for his men. About two thousand of the Greeks had gone out to the villages to gather provisions, but when they were ready to plunder they were attacked by the horsemen of Pharnabazus, who killed five hundred of them (6.4.24). When Xenophon hears about the events from one of the men, he offers a sacrifice and readies himself to go after the men (6.4.25). His group picks up the survivors and returns to the camp (6.4.26). Nonetheless, the Greeks manage to come back at Pharnabazus' men. Xenophon encourages the army, stating that he never willingly introduced them to a danger, seeking not a reputation for bravery but their safe return (6.5.14–15). He urges them to attack rather than to retreat, for this is more fitting for men of honour (6.5.16–18). Furthermore, he notes that the omens were favourable (6.5.22) and indeed, the Greeks have success that day, routing the cavalry of Pharnabazus (6.5.31).

Xenophon's character continues to be positively delineated in Book 4. Here he presents himself as recovering the Greek dead through the intervention of an interpreter (4.2.18). Recovery of the dead is one of the most important acts in Greek ethics and it marks Xenophon as pious. The Persians attempt to rush the Greeks while these negotiations are in progress, but Xenophon, together with

Cheirisophus, manages to broker a deal and receive back the dead, paying honours to their deceased comrades as best they can (4.2.23). Xenophon, furthermore, casts himself as an eminently approachable leader. While at breakfast, he is approached by two young men, who, he says, know they might come up to him no matter what he is doing, eating or sleeping (καὶ ἀριστῶντι τῷ Ξενοφῶντι προσέτρεχον δύο νεανίσκω· ᾔδεσαν γὰρ πάντες ὅτι ἐξείη αὐτῷ καὶ ἀριστῶντι καὶ δειπνοῦντι προσελθεῖν καὶ εἰ καθεύδοι ἐπεγείραντα εἰπεῖν, εἴ τίς τι ἔχοι τῶν πρὸς τὸν πόλεμον, 4.3.10). Xenophon's availability to his men has some very good consequences. The men inform him that while they were gathering sticks for a fire, they notice an old man, a woman and some little girls putting clothes in a cavernous rock along the edge of the river on the other side (4.3.11). This helped them to decide that it was safe to cross and they went across, discovering that the water was so shallow that they did not wet themselves above the middle (4.3.12). The news brought to the approachable Xenophon allows the Greeks to cross the river to defeat the enemy.

Xenophon is a figure who shows initiative. He relates that the Greek army was snowed upon during the night and the men did not move because the snow kept them warm (4.4.11). But Xenophon takes the courage to get up and split wood for a fire and is followed by the soldiers. He thereby provides his men with the incentive to build fires and to anoint themselves (4.4.12–13). On another occasion he comes upon his men falling in the snow and discovers that they are ailing from lack of food (4.5.7–8). He solves the problem by going to the pack animals and finding food for the sick men. They eat and are able to continue the march (4.5.9). Xenophon is practical and readily able to solve problems by interacting easily with the men. He has the qualities of the good cavalry commander, who is to show a concern for the provisioning of his men as far as fodder, tents, water, firewood and all supplies are concerned (cf. *On the Cavalry Commander* 6.3). But he is also such with the non-Greeks whom he meets on the march. For instance, he makes the chief man of a village his guest at dinner and promises him food (4.5.28). He gives this individual the privilege of taking whatever he wants, although the latter declines it (4.5.32). The village chief later serves as a guide to Cheirisophus but is mistreated by the latter (4.6.2). The author shows up the difference between his own treatment of the natives and that of Cheirisophus in this manner. The accessibility of Xenophon is further illustrated as one of the peltasts, a former slave at Athens, comes up to him and states that he knows the language of the Macronians (4.8.4–5). With this exchange the Macronians help the Greeks to arrive at the boundary of the Colchians with whom they engage in battle.

Xenophon is, as we know from other works, pious and he does what is right by the gods. At Socrates' behest he had consulted the oracle at Delphi about the appropriateness of the whole expedition but had asked the wrong question of the goddess (cf. 3.1.5-7). At 5.3.5ff. he makes out a votive offering to Apollo, dedicating it to Delphi and inscribing his name with 'Proxenus', meaning 'patron' or 'guardian'. He also leaves behind an offering to Artemis of the Ephesians (5.3.6). The author's piety is further established as we learn that he purchased land for Artemis in a location indicated by Apollo's oracle at his estate in Scillus (5.3.7). He offered tithes of his produce and all the surrounding citizens would take part in the devotional banquet (5.3.9). Xenophon offers sacrifices to the gods on three occasions in Book 6. At 6.4.9 he makes an offering for the naval expedition back to Greece. He also undertakes the necessary rite of burial of the dead Arcadians. The realization is that he and the men must travel by land, for they have no ship and no more provisions where they currently are (6.4.12). He sacrifices again for provisions at 6.4.19-20 and he keeps on making sacrifices until they turn out to be favourable. At 6.5.2 he sacrifices for a third time after a ship arrives from Heracleia with barley meal, sacrificial victims and wine (6.5.1). This time the omens are favourable and the soothsayer, Arexion the Parrhasian, sees in addition an eagle in an auspicious quarter, which is another good omen. This causes Xenophon to continue with his journey, which he had begun to do when he sailed to the boundaries separating Thrace and Heracleia at 6.2.19.

Xenophon shows his leadership qualities when he addresses the Greeks and tells them to remain heartened even though they have experienced a setback from the Mossynoecian enemy at 5.4.19. He encourages them, saying that they must show themselves better men than their barbarian allies. Xenophon speaks on behalf of the Greeks before the men of Sinope again at 5.5.13. Here he stresses the way in which the Greeks have provisioned themselves, buying supplies at Trapezus (5.5.14) and purchasing them from a market of the Macronians (5.5.18). The Cotyorites, who are allies of the Sinopeans, however, shut out the Greeks, as Xenophon observes (5.5.19-21). The result of the author's speech is that the Cotyorites now give them gifts of hospitality and the Greek generals entertain the Sinopean ambassadors (5.5.25). As a leader, Xenophon is also held to accountability by the Greeks and at 5.8.1ff. he has to answer charges that he had beaten certain of the men. He questions one of the men he is reputed to have struck and discovers that he was carrying a sick man (5.8.6). The man appears to have died and the accuser prepares to bury him. When he shows signs of life, Xenophon strikes the man he had questioned after he refuses to carry him (5.8.10). When they learn of these events, the men approve of Xenophon's actions, shouting that he should have given the man more blows (5.5.12).

At the beginning of the sixth book, Xenophon has shown himself to be such a good and effective leader that the captains of the army urge him to assume the command (6.1.19). The author reports that by some accounts he was inclined to accept this honour because it would increase his standing amongst his friends and at home and furthermore, he could thereby accomplish some good for the army (6.1.20). But he also has some doubts about this matter, for the reason that no person can see how the future will turn out and thereby he might lose the reputation he already has earned (6.1.21). Xenophon is unable to decide whether or not to become the commander and once again shows himself respectful of the gods and their will. He sacrifices two victims at the altar to Zeus, the god who he believes induced him to set out on the expedition (6.1.20). This time the god indicates that Xenophon should not seek the command of the army (6.1.24) and the latter gives a speech fending off the men (6.1.26–9), who nonetheless clamour for him to be their leader (6.1.30). In the end, Xenophon has to tell the army that the gods have steered him away from their leadership (6.1.31) and Cheirisophus is chosen commander (6.1.32). But that is not the end of it. Xenophon becomes in effect the leader of the Greeks because Cheirisophus dies from a medicine he has taken for a fever (6.4.11). We are told that Cheirisophus' command officially passes to Neon the Asinaean but it is the case that Xenophon continues to hold a major role in the army.

V

Xenophon endeavours to impose a sociological and political ideal upon the mercenary army. I suggest that the qualities of the good military leader are not distinct from those of the good and effective civic leader. Xenophon wants his men to be a well-ordered, functioning community, which is desirable where any city-state is concerned. Because the author has observed at the beginning of the *Poroi* that states resemble their leaders (cf. *Poroi* 1.1), it should be the case that the Greeks on campaign function well as an orderly community even if Dillery observes that the Ten Thousand are not a perfect community but are constantly evolving.[17] As this scholar notes, after the death of Cyrus they are in such a demoralized state as to be atomized individuals rather than a group of men with a unified purpose. But more than just being a disciplined body of soldiers, under

Xenophon they become a model society created on the basis of panhellenic ideal – after all, the Ten Thousand come from many different Greek states. Greek citizens tended to also be soldiers, and the author seeks now to remind the soldiers (and his audience) that they are also Greek citizens. In Book 1 Clearchus proposes seeing the Greek army as a society when he declares that he considers them his 'homeland, friends and allies' (cf. καὶ πατρίδα καὶ φίλους καὶ συμμάχους) without whom he is unable to help a friend or ward off a foe, activities which define relationships within the Greek state (1.3.6).[18] The most clearly pronounced vision of the army as a community comes at Book 5.6.15–19 where Xenophon regards the hoplites, peltasts, archers, slingers and cavalry in Pontus and ponders founding them as a city in order to gain additional land and power for Greece, which, articulated as a political entity by the author, confirms a panhellenic vision.[19] From this it would appear that militarism is warranted for Xenophon when the Greeks as a whole are united against a common, non-Greek enemy. If the author has become a quietist, he has become a qualified one, for war is still permitted if it is in the service of protecting the Hellenic entity.

I quote from the *Anabasis*:

> At this time, as Xenophon's eyes rested upon a great body of Greek hoplites, and likewise upon a great body of peltasts, bowmen, slingers, and horsemen also, all of them now exceedingly efficient through constant service and all there in Pontus, where so large a force could not have been gathered by any slight outlay of money, it seemed to him that it was a fine thing to gain additional territory and power for Greece by founding a city. It would become a great city, he thought, as he reckoned up their own numbers and the peoples who dwelt around the Euxine. And with a view to this project, before speaking about it to any of the soldiers, he offered sacrifices, summoning for that purpose Silanus the Ambraciot, who had been the soothsayer of Cyrus.
>
> 5.6.15–16; tr. Carleton Brownson

Xenophon does not see the forces as a fighting army, but rather envisages the well-trained and -disciplined army and cavalry as a great city given its potential size. He also does not view it any longer as a mercenary army, for a single expenditure of money could not buy this group of men, according to him (5.6.15). To him, it is no more a body of men motivated just by money but it conforms to a larger vision of itself as a panhellenic community settled in Asia.[20] If Dalby sees the army as behaving like a colonizing expedition,[21] Simon Hornblower suggests that the army in any case behaves up to a point – as can only be the case – like a political entity when it requires a decision to be made:[22]

the army resorts to a show of hands (cf. 3.2.9 and 3.2.33) to resolve issues under discussion, as one would expect in a democratic city-state, rather than relying on decisions made from above. With his ideal and idealized plan of founding a state enacted, Xenophon would become a founder of a city, rather than a soldier or general,[23] although Silanus fears this prospect coming to fruition, wishing the army to return to Greece instead (5.6.17).

Yet founding a city is something of a dream and not to be so easy a task in any case given objections from the men. In Book 6 chapter 4, the army ends up at Calpe Harbour in Thrace-in-Asia, near the Bithynian Thracians, who abuse Greeks (cf. 6.4.2). There is plenty of fresh water here (6.4.3), an abundance of wood for ship-building (6.4.4), and land which produces grains, beans, figs and grapes – only olives are missing (6.4.6). The men refuse to camp on the spot which might become a city (εἰς δὲ πόλισμα ἂν γενόμενον οὐκ ἐβούλοντο στρατοπεδεύεσθαι, 6.4.7) and they suspect that they have come there due to some of the men wanting to found a city there (βουλομένων τινῶν κατοικίσαι πόλιν, 6.4.7). The soldiers have no intention of settling down away from Greece because they only intended to help out Cyrus, who was supposed to have a good character and have rewarded his soldiers well, and because they have left family at home (6.4.8).

Founding a city-state where there is not one and away from Greece may be a wish of Xenophon's that has its basis in his own stateless condition. Xenophon did not have a city that he properly belonged to as he was an exile from Athens. Having gone over to Sparta, he was given by Agesilaus an estate at Scillus, which was a colony established by the Spartans near Olympia (cf. Pausanias 5.6.5), by the Lacedaemonians in 392 BCE but later lost by them.[24] The author recalls this home at 5.3.7–13, noting that he had dedicated a plot of land there to the goddess Diana. Jonas Grethlein suggests that the author's description of the estate as tranquil and bucolic suggests that this is the home the Greeks are longing for.[25]

But it is also the case that Xenophon seeks to transform a military society – the army and cavalry – into a civic community. The elite individual, who does not ostensibly or explicitly seek to go on the expedition to undertake war but rather to get to know Cyrus, seeks to found a society of men, who originally have their raison d'etre as soldiering, as a non-military community. Founding a colony of course runs counter to the directive for *nostos* or homecoming, which the men have, and counter to the plan of the seer Silanus, who stood to profit from the three thousand darics which Cyrus had given him (5.6.18 and 1.7.18).[26] And here lies the chief irony of the *Anabasis*, a military venture becomes the pretext for a peaceful venture: conflict must eventually give way to peace; men no longer wish to fight and kill one another having experienced war, as the cost of war takes much too high a toll (as is certainly the case in the *Hellenica*).

The irony in Xenophon's desire to create a non-military state is that his city becomes very different from both the existing communities created and sponsored by Athens and Sparta. It is perhaps the expression of an escapist fantasy for the author, who is becoming disengaged from militaristic concerns on the course of the march back to Greece and did not in any case go on the expedition on a military pretext. The two city-states, according to the author, in fact create war machines, so that apparently civic society has as its goal a (self-) destructive military society. As we have seen, the *Poroi* is a work that reveals silver to be the commodity underpinning Athens' identity as a military state. (The silver mines at Laurion had after all funded the ship-building programme under Themistocles, as one reads in Herodotus 7.144). It is only in a state of peace, Xenophon suggests, that Athens can fully enjoy the wealth produced by her mines and escape the vicious cycle of the city's wealth leading to war, which results in its impoverishment and therefore requiring more wealth production. In the case of Sparta, Xenophon commented at *Agesilaus* 1.25–6 that the Spartan leader Agesilaus had made Ephesus a city-state that has war as its goal when he settles his men there while on campaign. He establishes games where the men can show off their military skills. Cavalry squadrons compete to see who rides best, heavy infantry engage in display to determine who is most fit, while in the case of Persia Cyrus also mounts contests for the targeters and archers (1.25). But more than this the Persian leader turns the whole city into a military machine with arms and horses on sale, and the various craftsmen making weapons of war. The narrator comments that one might think Ephesus a 'war factory' (πολέμου ἐργαστήριον). At *Hellenica* 3.4.7 we learn that this is Agesilaus in a state of quiet and leisure on the assumption that actually going to war is activity. The author shows that the most powerful city-states in the Greek world at this time are thus flawed, for civic structures underlie military machines. Contrary to common expectations and therefore a point of irony, the community at war – that is the panhellenic army – is to be recreated and reformed so that it is after all better for Greece as a whole than the communities which are supposedly at peace.

VI

Bradley observes that Xenophon is prevented from returning home no less than five times in Books 6 and 7,[27] and this theme is pronounced in the final book of the *Anabasis* as it sees Xenophon wanting to go home to Athens at 7.1.5 and again at 7.8.57. Amidst this desire to return home, he is tempted by the soldiers with greatness. They rush to him while they are in Byzantium, saying that he has a city, triremes, money and men and that these things should make him great (7.1.21). His response is to quieten the men down and to address them, declaring that their wishes are good (7.1.22). He also speaks about the need for sensible action: the Greeks should not be at war with the Spartans (7.1.26) and they should declare peaceful intention to Anaxibius, whose city they are now at (7.1.31). Xenophon does not depict himself as consciously seeking greatness but as looking out for his men's best interests. Later in the book we find the author concerned with sacrificing to the gods and receiving favourable portents (7.2.16). His piety is apparent again at 7.6.44 when he hears that he is being betrayed and may be killed by the Spartans; he sacrifices two victims to Zeus to learn if he should stay with the Thracian king Seuthes or if he should leave. Once more the author engages in sacrifice near the end of the work, at 7.8.20, to see if the army should march through Lydia.

The character of Xenophon is faultless as a leader. At 7.2.23 the author meets Seuthes, with whom he has desired to meet (7.2.19). He recalls that through Medosades Seuthes had promised to treat him well if he brought the army across Asia (7.2.24). Xenophon has accomplished this without taking any pay, and Seuthes and he give and receive pledges from each other (7.3.1). At 7.4.8 the author relates an incident where Seuthes is about to kill a handsome youth and Xenophon begs him to spare the lad because Episthenes of Olynthus is a lover of boys (7.3.7). Seuthes then asks Episthenes if he would die for the youth and the latter holds out his neck for Seuthes to strike. Seuthes then asks the youth if he should kill Episthenes. The boy asks him to spare both and the matter is resolved. Xenophon is thus cast as a merciful individual.

Loyalty of the members of the army who are loyal to Xenophon is extremely high. Timasion, the Dardanian, who is one of the leaders of the Greek army although he was an exile (5.6.23), declares that he will undertake a campaign with only Xenophon even if he receives a partial pay (7.5.10). Clearly, Timasion's estimation of the author and his leadership skills is very high. Again later, Xenophon's friends in the army urge the author not to return home, which he is preparing to do when his desire to found a city at Calpe Harbour is disappointed, until he leads the army to Thibron, the Spartan (7.7.57). Xenophon is beloved by the men, having demonstrated the qualities of a superlative leader and he returns home triumphant and with much wealth. At 7.6.4 the Lacedaimonians inquire what sort of a man Xenophon is to gauge whether they can gain control of the army, and are told that he was not a bad fellow and was a friend of soldiers, with the result that things could go badly for him. Later in the same chapter at section 39, Charminus the Sparta recalls that Seuthes has said that he found no fault with him except that the author was too much a lover of the army (ἄγαν δὲ φιλοστρατῶν ἔφη αὐτον εἶναι) so that things went badly for him.

The plan to recreate the Ten Thousand as a civic and panhellenic community remains only a dream, but it is one that ironically shows up the city-states which currently exist and, as the *Hellenica* shows too well, continue to fight with one another for supremacy in the Greek world.

VII

To conclude, I suggest that in effect the *Anabasis* has recounted two marches: the first, brief march with Cyrus the Younger to fight his brother Artaxerxes and the second, longer march of the Greeks under various leaders including Xenophon to return home. Cyrus' march is a far less consequential one. It ends very abruptly with his death and the reader is perhaps at a loss, together with the Greek soldiers, as to where the work will go next. Persians barely figure in the remainder of the *Anabasis*, showing up only occasionally as a threat that the Greek army must fend off. The work is hardly 'the Persian expedition' and much more 'the Greek expedition'. The rest of the work continues with the struggles of the Ten Thousand to return home, but it is as much a narrative about the functioning of the army as a panhellenic community of their way home. And in it, the most consistently present and important figure is the author, Xenophon, who debuts quite notably in Book 3. Not formally a leader of the Greek army until after the death of Cyrus, when he becomes a general, his actions reveal him to be a very important player in events. The other prominent Greek leader is Cheirisophus, who goes off on various errands during the march and who dies of a medicine he has taken for a fever at 6.4.11.

Let me offer a further characterization of the work. The *Anabasis* begins with the Persians, namely Cyrus, as the leaders of the Greeks who accompany the Persian leader on his expedition against his brother. The work presents a Persian world that is divided and at odds with itself. The men who accompany Cyrus come from different Greek states but they are generally unified as Greeks, suggesting the unity of the race Xenophon presents us with the Persians dominating the work at first and then fading into pockets of opposition with the Greeks and their affairs taking precedence. This may suggest his view for the world as one in which the Persians pass into inconsequence while the Greeks assume dominance. Furthermore, Xenophon is specifically portrayed as an able and credible leader of the Greeks. He cares for his men and they for him. He casts himself as an Athenian and this suggests the supremacy of Athens in the Greek world.

Despite initial appearances, the *Anabasis* is not primarily a work about Persia or about the Persians. It is rather a text about the Greeks and their renewed ascendancy if they can come together in a peaceable state, and in particular about the ascendancy of the author Xenophon. One irony of the work comes early in Book 1 with the death of Cyrus, who is also subtly critiqued, and the growing presence of Xenophon.[28] What appears to be a text about the Persians is demonstrably Hellenic in its emphasis. But there is a second greater irony: the *Anabasis* is a justification of Xenophon as a military and political leader, who ultimately seeks to form a civic community, and for this reason, the work stands as a culmination in the author's corpus. It is contrary to expectations a text that, far more powerfully than a war narrative, demonstrates the superiority of the Greeks.

In addition to Greek supremacy, the *Anabasis* makes a point on the expedition, with a leadership that appears to be military but is actually also effective for a civic community. This is demonstrated by the record of Xenophon's actions on the march back to Greece and this perhaps suggests a role for the author in the city when he returns there. Going home is not about changing geographical position; rather going home is finding unity and peace with one's own race.

Concluding Thoughts

I

I hope to have established that Xenophon is an ironic author; that is, he uses gaps between what certain people assume to be the case and what others, the few including himself, know to be the actual reality, and I also hope to have demonstrated in what ways he is an ironic author. There is no sinister underlying agenda to irony, as some, namely Leo Strauss and his followers, have thought. Xenophon is no more a misogynist than anyone of his culture or era would be, and he is no more of a conservative than any other conservative of fourth-century Athens would be. Xenophon is not the keeper or bearer of any mystical revelations or understandings about human nature.[1] He is not denigrating anything that a fourth-century individual of means with conservative and oligarchical tendencies would not. Xenophon is representative of oligarchical thought in fourth-century BCE Athens, and that is all. And I am here strongly affirming a historicist frame, which Blau observes is so sorely lacking in Straussian treatments of Xenophon.[2]

Xenophon seems to be against war, which would by its nature imperil his wealth, and he is therefore critical of Athens' imperialist policies, especially as regards her finances (see esp. *Hellenica* and *Poroi*). Furthermore, Xenophon does not approve of the culture of public discourse, of the constant haranguing that occurs in the courtrooms, assembly and other public places of gathering, and is therefore more concerned with the discourse of the small gathering or one-to-one exchange, where one can speak and ideally be understood by others or by one another. This is ideally instantiated in the discourses that Socrates has with his interlocutors as represented in the *Memorabilia* and the *Symposium*, although the philosopher is generally not comprehended in the exchanges he has with his interlocutors. But the author foremost seeks refuge from the noisy world of oratory in the culture of the written word, where the recipient has time and opportunity to think and rationalize about what he has read or heard (as reading may have involved someone reading out a text to a group). The written word is also the ideal medium for irony as the audience has the opportunity to consider carefully, and revisit, what is actually being articulated in the text.

Xenophon's literary corpus demonstrates that irony has various forms, some more apparent and obvious than others. Where the Socratic works are concerned, irony is understated and simply present because the philosopher is in a scene where people are unknowing or mistaken about their lives. In the *Apology* the irony lies in the city's misunderstanding of Socrates' piety, while in the *Memorabilia* Xenophon rehearses the charges against Socrates in the *Apology* and proceeds with a fuller defence that shows up the misunderstanding of the city: the philosopher did not corrupt the youths in his care and is overall revealed to be a proponent of justice in the state. The ultimate irony that the *Memorabilia* presents us with has to do with the injustice of Socrates' execution at Athens. In the *Symposium* irony rests in juxtaposition of the city's desire for wealth and glory and Socrates' non-materialistic outlook. The interlocutors enjoy great wealth, food and drink, which Socrates shows to be insignificant in comparison to understanding of the truth and reality and to no avail as his audience is not ready to learn. The *Oeconomicus* is perhaps where the irony is most apparent, with Socrates engaging with his unknowing and unseeing interlocutor, the husband Ischomachus. The husband thinks that he is teaching his young wife the art of household management, but he does so in a rather inefficient manner and in a way that ignores any previous knowledge she may have had. The interlocutor fails to take any of Socrates' suggestions about how to reform his wifely instruction, and indeed, his view of his wife so that she is valued as a producer and preserver rather than mistrusted as a consumer.

The presence of Socrates as the knowing philosopher amongst the ignorant citizens of Athens necessarily constitutes irony in the texts of Xenophon, as Socrates embodies the difference in levels of knowledge that constitute the rhetorical device. In contrast, the non-Socratic works require that the author constructs irony by showing himself to be more cognizant of the way things are, that is, of reality, than others in the scenario, including the reader, who enters the scenario by engaging with the text. And, as we have seen, Xenophon introduces his ironies into the text in various ways. It can be present throughout the whole work, as in the case of the Socratic texts and the works on equine culture, *On Horsemanship* and the *Cavalry Commander*, where the overriding irony of Athens and Sparta engaging in military activities through the cultivation of horses and equine culture is in any case set against the background of Xenophon's non-militarism. In the *Cyropaedia* there are moments throughout the text where

Cyrus' actions seem to go against the Persian ideal of the young royal and it is in the last few chapters, where the decline of the empire and internecine conflict occur after the death of Cyrus, that irony is most apparent. In the case of the longer historiographical works, the *Hellenica* and the *Anabasis*, there is gradual realization on the part of the audience that the work is not really about what it seems to be. War between the Greek states turns out to be pointless and futile so that the overall message of the *Hellenica* must be that peace is to be preferred, while the *Anabasis*, concerning the march of the ten thousand Greek soldiers back home, explores the army as a potential community that is not focussed on military activity.

II

I am arguing that irony is a feature of Xenophontic discourse and this definitively and decisively explains why the *Constitution of Athens*, which Glen Bowersock dates to 440/39 and 437/6 BCE due to a reference to a legal ban on comedy (cf. 2.18),[3] is Pseudo-Xenophontic and not by Xenophon.[4] The work is an open rant against contemporary Athens. The author makes his position about the city clear and apparent already at the very beginning of the work. Athens has decided to allow the worst sorts of people to be better off than the good people and it is for this reason that the author has a bad opinion of the constitution (1.1). The worst sort of people are the poorer, lower class individuals in the city, while the good people are the well-born with the privilege of wealth and education. The reader is aware that the author's stance towards Athens is a negative one so that there is no gap of knowledge between what the latter thinks and feels and what the former realizes to be the case. Yet he acknowledges that the poor are the strength of the city in that they man the ships, unlike the hoplites or the aristocrats (1.2). It becomes very apparent that the author of the *Constitution of Athens* is strongly opposed to popular democracy as something that is disorderly and wanton (cf. 1.5). And the lower the class of the person the worse he is for the state: accordingly, slaves are the most wanton (1.10) and they live the most luxurious of lives (1.11).

The common people of Athens hate athletic and musical activities because they are no good at them and because they are controlled by the wealthy, upper classes (1.13). The Athenians also hate the aristocrats in other cities and kill them (1.14) and they ensure that allies come to the city for trials so that they can collect the pay for being dicasts (1.16).

Athens is a city built for the poor to enjoy themselves and to benefit from. In chapter 2 the author observes that the people benefit from the sacrifices which the city provides, participating in the feasts which result from the religious observances (2.9). The mob also avails itself of the wrestling quarters, dressing rooms and public baths far more than the rich upper classes do (2.10). Furthermore, Athens supports a culture of slander. There are laws to prevent people being spoken of badly in comedy; however, Athens allows one to attack another, generally an individual of the upper classes, in private, presumably through the lawcourts (2.18). The author is attacking the phonocentric Athens of the fourth century, where the lawcourts and Assembly offered demagogic orators the opportunity to sway and to control the city's crowds, who would come to these places for their entertainment and excitement. The author concludes his second chapter by observing that while the city knows who is actually good and who is actually bad, it cultivates those who are useful to itself, often the bad, and ends up hating the good (2.19). It is easier for someone to do wrong in a democratic city than in an oligarchical city, where he will be found out (2.20).

Athens is currently a city which advocates the side of the lower classes, and in cases of civil strife it will support this faction. It is in any case the reality that the upper classes are not well-disposed towards the lower classes (3.10). Similar classes and groups advocate for similar classes and groups, and as the author observes, when Athens has supported the upper classes in other states, it has gone rather badly for their decision, with the preferred side attacking and defeating the other side.

The *Constitution of Athens* may well articulate the views of Xenophon as an oligarchical elite who favoured the rule of the few, but the work does not express these views in a way that Xenophon wishes. What one sees in the *Constitution of Athens* is an unabated negative criticism of the democracy of the time. The city supports the common people at the expense of the upper classes; it enriches and indulges the common people with the result that good order and justice go by the wayside in fifth- and fourth-century Athens. The *Constitution of Athens* is not at all Xenophontic in its tone or approach to social criticism. Nowhere in Xenophon's writings do we see such a strongly outspoken position. Social criticism – of contemporary Athens, of historical and contemporary Sparta, of historical Persia, of war and so on – is only gently hinted at to the point that it is easily missed or not noticed as being criticism of the status quo.

What this means is that Xenophon has a double voice and accordingly, produces a double text, one which may be read at face value as describing affairs in a positive and affirmative light *and* another in quite another voice, as faulting the situation and individuals being depicted. Irony requires a degree of reading between the lines.⁵ This entails that the author is able to bridge two worlds at the same time, to feign belonging in the world which goes to war in military fervour, which has greedy and self-indulgent leaders, which favours the popular rabble over those who have the abilities to rule and to lead, and over the elite sphere, which is critical of the more popular world. Xenophontic irony may be characterized as being negative but it is, in my view, rather and foremost, enlightened. What I mean is that those involved in the ironic scenario fail to understand or to see what reality is, and Xenophon makes this point by having several of his works, e.g. the Socratic texts, the *Hiero*, *On Hunting*, *On Horsemanship* and the *Cyropaedia*, present the reader with a failed pedagogy – that is the essence of irony – while the author and the audience that understands perceive the greater truth. And the insight which they have is optimistic, for it enables an alternative perspective from the way things are; it permits the possibility of a reality that is better than the current one.

Irony is a mode of subtle but damning criticism in Xenophon's hands, and it is one which does not play the author's hand so very openly. Because of this, in political terms irony is very clever and dextrous, enabling the author to play both sides of an issue with the less aware ignorant of this double play. If one realizes that Xenophon lived a rather precarious existence in the Greek world, not comfortably belonging in the communities he lived in, then irony makes complete sense. He was a somewhat disaffected Athenian. After being convinced by Proxenus, he allied himself with the younger Cyrus of Persia and joined the Persian expedition and long march narrated in the *Anabasis* and travelled through much of the Hellenic landscape, covering territory near Mesopotamia, then along to the Tigris to the Black Sea until returning to Greece on a westward trajectory by way of Chrysopolis (cf. *Anabasis* 6.3.1). Sympathizing with Spartan ideology and interests up to the point of fighting under King Agesilaus II at the Battle of Coronea in 394 BCE, he was exiled from Athens and fled to Sparta, settling at Scillus near Olympus, where the Spartans had given him an estate. Possibly in his lifetime, his banishment was revoked and he moved either to Corinth or back to Sparta, where he died in the mid 350s. Accordingly, Xenophon's life seems to have been of constant dislocation, of finding home in a new and foreign place, even when that place was an Athens fundamentally changed and transformed by politics.

Irony was the strategy which enabled Xenophon to exist in these very different communities; it was a means of self-preservation. He could make his voice heard in his various communities and throughout Greece without letting everyone know what he really thought. He could criticize Athens and Sparta and their military programmes and denigrate historical Persia in his other, ironic voice, while appearing to approve of and even praise them. Xenophon could thus exist simultaneously in very different spheres in the Greek world in a manner that would be acceptable to different constituencies. Irony had the effect of producing a double voice that in turn generated a double existence for the author. Individuals who did not read, or perhaps did not wish to read, the other, critical voice in the text – the rabble which was more intent on oratorical displays in the Assembly and court rooms, and Vivienne Gray, for instance, who admittedly generally rejects irony in the text because she is quite rightly rejecting Straussian irony – assume only the naïvely positive view of the worlds which Xenophon portrayed. These readers miss out on what the author was really and actually saying. The author becomes slightly boring, even anodyne perhaps, as he has been for decades of schoolboys reading the *Hellenica*. The critical perspective which irony provides certainly allows for a more complex and nuanced text that takes different directions at various points from those that it initially seems to be taking. Xenophon was having to negotiate other people – indeed, as a public figure, a lot of them and from different cultures – and irony enabled him to do so.

Irony is definitely historicist; it engages and criticizes people and places at particular times in history, with the result that Xenophon is an author of the fourth century BCE with very particular views peculiar to that time. He can only be criticizing an Athens which surrenders itself to orators and to the rabble, as was the case in the fourth century BCE. Accordingly, irony here is not of the Straussian kind, which A. Blau observes to be completely anti-historicist and which uses this anti-historicism to impose contemporary ideologies, such as an anachronistic misogyny and intellectual elitism, upon the text.[6] Xenophontic irony is less uniform in its subject matter; it criticizes particular and individual things and persons *in* society at a particular moment in time.

Irony appeals to the elite in offering a reading of the text that not everyone can comprehend. It is thus implicit in that superiority which Søren Kierkegaard and Wayne Booth, whom I cited in the Introduction to this study, attribute to it, in ignoring the discourse that the (common) people understand simply and at face value.[7] And irony appeals to the elite because it conveys an ideology of those who are privileged in terms of wealth and education. But irony also defines the elite. It may be the case that those who are privileged through wealth and their upbringing are more inclined to comprehend the double text that Xenophon offers because they are by nature more sympathetic to the message that the author conveys. Yet it is also the case that others who are able to see and understand the ironic text due to intellectual dexterity belong to the elite that Xenophon above all wishes to nurture and cultivate. The ability to read texts carefully and with discernment is perhaps the ultimate mark of distinction that the author above all seeks for his community. In common with the Socratic project but also distinct from it, elitism is being redefined by Xenophon so that its basis is no longer material but rather intellectual. And that perhaps is Xenophon's legacy to subsequent times such as ours.

Notes

Introduction

1. Patterson, A., *Reading Between the Lines*. Madison, WI: Routledge, 1993, 24.
2. See, for instance: Tuplin, C. (ed.), *Xenophon and His World: Papers from a Conference held in Liverpool in 1999*. Historia Heft 172. Stuttgart: F. Steiner, 2004; Azoulay, V., 'The Medo-Persian Ceremonial: Xenophon's Cyrus and the King's Piety', in Tuplin (2004) ; Dillery, J., *Xenophon and the History of His Times*. London: Routledge, 1995; Tatum, J., *Xenophon's Imperial Fiction: On the Education of Cyrus*. Princeton: Princeton University Press, 1989; Morrison, D., 'On Professor Vlastos' Xenophon', *AP* 7 (1987), 9–22, esp. p. 10.
3. 'Finally, with respect to irony, there is not one trace of it in Xenophon's Socrates' – Kierkegaard, S., *The Concept of Irony with Continual Reference to Socrates*. Eds. and trans. Hong, H. V. and Hong, E. H., Princeton: Princeton University Press, 1989, 25.
4. Vlastos refers to Kierkegaard's work in Vlastos, G., 'Socratic Irony', *Classical Quarterly* 37.1 (1987), 79–96.
5. Gray, V., *Xenophon's Mirror of Princes: Reading the Reflections*. Oxford: Oxford University Press, 2011, 100–14. Johnson, D., 'Strauss on Xenophon' in Hobden, F. and Tuplin, C. (eds), *Xenophon: Ethical Principles and Historical Enquiry*. Leiden and Boston: Brill, 2012, 123 notes that Gray finds irony in Xenophon 'almost painfully explicit' at one point.
6. Kierkegaard in Hong and Hong (1989), 12.
7. Kierkegaard in Hong and Hong (1989), 269.
8. Kierkegaard in Hong and Hong (1989), 24.
9. Gray, V., *Xenophon on Government*. Cambridge: Cambridge University Press, 2007, 142. For criticism of Gray's reading of irony in Xenophon, see Johnson, D., 'Review of *Xenophon's Mirror of Princes: Reading the Reflections* by Gray', *Classical Philology* 108.1 (2013), 86.
10. Gray (2007), 142–3.
11. Gray, *Xenophon*. Oxford: Oxford University Press, 2010, 5.
12. Flower, M., *The Cambridge Companion to Xenophon*. Cambridge: Cambridge University Press, 2017.
13. Cawkwell, G., *Xenophon: The Persian Expedition*. Harmondsworth: Penguin Classics, 1951, 26 and *Xenophon: A History of My Times*. Harmondsworth: Penguin Classics, 1966, 8.

14 See Bandini, M. and Dorion, L-A., *Xénophon Mémorables*. Paris: Les Belles Lettres, 2000, xlii and cxxxi.
15 See Connor, R., *The New Politicians of Fifth-Century Athens*. Princeton: Princeton University Press, 1972.
16 On the dangers of oratory and the mob to democracy, see Ober, J., *Mass and Elite in Democratic Athens*. Princeton: Princeton University Press, 1989, 166 and 169.
17 See: Ehrenberg, V., *From Solon to Socrates: Greek History and Civilization During the Sixth and Fifth Centuries B. C.*. London: Methuen, 1968, 46–67; Adkins, W. H., *Moral Values and Political Behaviour in Ancient Greece: From Homer to the End of the Fifth Century*. London: W. W. Norton and Co., 1976, 301–27; Allison, J., 'Thucydides and ΠΟΛΥΠΡΑΓΜΟΣΥΝΗ', *American Journal of Ancient History* 4 (1979), 10–22; Campbell, B., 'Thought and Political Action in Athenian Tradition: The Emergence of the "Alienated" Individual', *History of Political Thought* 5.1 (1984), 17–59.
18 On *isêgoria* see Griffith, G., 'Isegoria in the Assembly at Athens' in Badian, E, (ed.), A. *Athenian Society and Institutions: Studies Presented to Victor Ehrenberg on his 75th Birthday*. Oxford: Blackwell, 1966, 115–38 and Woodhead, A. G., 'ΙΣΗΓΟΡΙΑ and the Council of 500', *Historia* 16 (1967), 129–40.
19 See Pontier, P., 'Isocrate et Xénophon, de l'éloge de Gryllos à l'éloge du roi: échos, concordances et discordances,' *Ktema* 41 (2016), 43–58 for a discussion of links between the rhetorician and Xenophon, who was the former's student.
20 See Rhodes, P. J., 'Civic Ideology and Citizenship', in Balot, R., *A Companion to Greek and Roman Political Thought*. Malden, MA and Oxford: Wiley-Blackwell, 2013), 66.
21 Harris, W. observes that most Athenians were in fact illiterate and suggests that it was unlikely for literacy to reach above ten per cent. Harris, W. V., *Ancient Literacy*. Cambridge, MA and London: Harvard University Press, 1989, 8–10 and 24. Also see F. Pownall, 'From Orality to Literacy: the Moral Education of the Elite in in Fourth-Century Athens' in Cooper, C. (ed.), *Politics of Orality (Orality and Literacy in Ancient Greece, Vol. 6)*. Leiden and Boston: Brill, 2007, 235–50, esp. p. 235.
22 See Raaflaub, K., 'Early Greek Thought in its Mediterranean Context' in Balot (2013), 42: 'To fix laws in writing and to publish them by inscription on stone or bronze was in Greece an unprecedented and, given the still very limited use of writing and restricted literacy (W. Harris 1989; Whitley 1989), far from obvious innovation.' Raaflaub goes on to suggest that public writing perhaps had a religious connotation, cf. p. 44.
23 There is an enormous scholarly discussion of Socratic irony. I cite here some of the more recent work: Vlastos, G., chapter 1 of *Socrates, Ironist and Moral Philosopher*. Cambridge: Cambridge University Press, 1991, 21–44; Gottlieb, P., 'The Complexity of Socratic Irony: A Note on Professor Vlastos' Account', *Classical Quarterly* 42.1 (1992), 278–9; Layne, D., 'From Irony to Enigma: Discovering Double Ignorance and Socrates' Divine Knowledge', *Methexis* 23 (2010), 73–90; Vasiliou, I., 'Conditional

Irony in the Socratic Dialogues', *Classical Quarterly* 49.2 (1999), 456–72; Destrée, P., 'Platon et l'ironie dramatique', *Métaphysique et de Morale* 4 (2013), 543–556; Edmunds, L., 'The Practical Irony of the Historical Socrates', *Phoenix* 58.3/4 (2004), 193–207; Wolfsdorf, D., 'The Irony of Socrates', *Journal of Aesthetics and Art Criticism* 65.2 (2007), 175–87 are just a few examples.

24 See Burnyeat, M. F., 'Sphinx Without a Secret', *New York Review of Books* 32.9 (1985), 30–6 (1985), reprinted as essay 15 in part 2 of *Explorations in Ancient and Modern Philosophy, vol. 1.* Cambridge: Cambridge University Press, 1991.

25 See irony in Fowler, H. W., *A Dictionary of Modern English Usage.* Oxford: Oxford University Press, 1926.

26 See Goldhill, S., *Sophocles and the Language of Tragedy: Onassis Series in Hellenic Culture.* Oxford, New York: Oxford University Press, 2012, 25 and Wohl, V., *Law's Cosmos: Juridical Discourse in Athenian Forensic Oratory.* Cambridge: Cambridge University Press, 2010 193: 'Irony results when a speaker's words seem to imply more than he literally intends: it is a joke at one's own expense, a sort of collusion with the audience against oneself'.

27 See Gottlieb (1992), 278.

28 See Booth, W. (1974), p. 29, citing Kierkegaard as translated by Lee M. Capel in Kierkegaard (1966), 265.

29 Strauss, L., *The City and Man.* Chicago: University of Chicago Press, 1964, 51.

30 Vlastos (1987) suggests that the ironist deceives (p. 80) or is disingenuous (p. 84).

31 de Romilly, J., *A Short History of Greek Literature.* Chicago: University of Chicago Press, 1985, 137–9.

32 See Buxton, R. F., who writes 'Although Xenophon wrote in a dizzying array of genres ...' as he recognizes that Xenophon's works were not confined to only one type of literary category, at p. 1 of his Preface to *Aspects of Leadership in Xenophon. Histos* Supplement 5. Newcastle-Upon-Tyne: Histos, 2016.

33 Depew, M. and Obbink, D. (eds), *Matrices of Genre: Authors, Canons and Society.* Cambridge, MA: Harvard University Press, 2000, 2.

34 Nightingale, A., *Genres in Dialogue: Plato and the Construct of Philosophy.* Cambridge: Cambridge University Press, 1995; Waterfield, R. A. H., 'Xenophon's Socratic Mission' in Tuplin, *Xenophon and His World: Papers from a Conference Held in Liverpool in July 1999.* Stuttgart: F. Steiner, 2004, 85.

35 Most, G., 'Generating Genres: The Idea of the Tragic' inDepew and Obbink (2000), 25.

36 Too, Y. L., *The Rhetoric of Identity in Isocrates: Text, Power, Pedagogy.* Cambridge: Cambridge University Press, 1995, 10–35.

37 Higgins, W. E., *Xenophon the Athenian: The Problem of the World and the Society of the Athenian Polis.* Albany: State University of New York Press, 1977 xi and Dillery, J., 'Xenophon's "Poroi" and Athenian Imperialism', *Historia* 42.1 (1993), 7–8.

38 Flower, M. A. observes that antiquity generally thought of Xenophon as a philosopher: Flower, M. A., *The Cambridge Companion to Xenophon*. Cambridge: Cambridge University Press, 2017, 28.
39 Tuplin, C., 'The Failings of Empire: A Reading of Xenophon', *Hellenica* 2.3.11–7.5.27. Historia Einzelschriften, Heft 76. Stuttgart: Franz Steiner, 1993; *Xenophon and His World: Papers from a Conference held in Liverpool in 1999. Historia Heft 172.* Stuttgart: F. Steiner, 2004.
40 Fox, R. L., *The Long March. Xenophon and the Ten Thousand*. New Haven and London: Yale University Press, 2004.
41 Higgins, W. E., *Xenophon the Athenian: The Problem of the World and the Society of the Athenian Polis*. Albany: State University of New York Press, 1977.
42 Hirsch, S. W., *The Friendship of the Barbarians: Xenophon and the Persian Empire*. Hanover, NH: University Press of New England, 1985.
43 Waterfield, R. A. H., *Xenophon's Retreat: Greece, Persia, and the End of the Golden Age*. Cambridge, MA: Harvard University Press, 2008.
44 Dillery, *Xenophon and the History of His Times*. London: Routledge, 1995, 8.
45 Dillery (1995), 7.
46 Immerwahr, H. R. and Connor, W. R., 'Historiography', and Sandbach, F. H., 'Plato and the Socratic Work of Xenophon', in Easterling, P. E., and Knox, B. M. W. (eds), *The Cambridge History of Classical Literature*. Cambridge: Cambridge University Press, 1985, 426–471 and 478–497 respectively.
47 Dorion, L.-A., 'The Straussian Exegesis of Xenophon: The Paradigmatic Case of *Memorabilia* IV.4' in Gray, V. (ed.), *Xenophon*. Oxford: Oxford University Press, 2010, 282–323.
48 Morrison, D., 'On Professor Vlastos' Xenophon', *Ancient Philosophy* 7 (1987), 9–22 and Danzig, G., Johnson, D., and Morrison, D., *Plato and Xenophon. Comparative Studies*. Leiden, Boston: Brill, 2018.
49 Danzig, G., 'Apologizing for Socrates: Plato and Xenophon on Socrates' Behavior in Court', *Transactions of the American Philological Association* 133 (2003), 281–321; *Apologizing for Socrates. How Plato and Xenophon Created our Socrates*. Lanham: Lexington Books, 2010; 'The Best Way to Die: Wisdom, Boasting and Strength of Spirit in Xenophon's *Apology*', *Classica and Mediaevalia* 65 (2014b), 155–89; Danzig, G., Johnson, D., and Morrison, D., *Plato and Xenophon. Comparative Studies*. Leiden, Boston: Brill, 2018.
50 Van der Waerdt, P. (ed.), *The Socratic Movement*. Ithaca: Cornell University Press, 1994.
51 Strauss, L., *On Tyranny*, Eds. Gourevitch, V. and Roth, M. S. Chicago: University of Chicago Press, 1961, 1992, 2000; *Xenophon's Socratic Dialogue: An Interpretation of the Oeconomicus*. Ithaca: Cornell University Press, 1970.
52 Most recently, Pangle, T., 'Socratic Political Philosophy in Xenophon's Symposium', *American Journal of Political Science* 54.1 (2010), 140–52.

53 Anderson, J. K., *Xenophon*. London: Bloomsbury Publishing PLC, 1974.
54 Tatum, J., *Xenophon's Imperial Fiction: On the Education of Cyrus*. Princeton: Princeton University Press, 1989.
55 Due, B., *The Cyropaedia*. Aarhus: Aarhus University Press, 1989.
56 Gera, D., *Xenophon's Cyropaedia: Style, Genre and Literary Technique*. Oxford: Oxford University Press, 1993.
57 Gray (2010), 1.
58 Gray (2010), 1.
59 Nadon, C., *Xenophon's Prince: Republic and Empire in the Cyropaedia*. Berkeley: California University Press, 2001.
60 See Patterson (1993),11–35, esp. p. 22.
61 See Higgins, W. E., *Xenophon the Athenian: The Problem of the World and the Society of the Athenian Polis*. Albany: State University of New York Press, 1977.
62 Tell, H., 'Wisdom for Sale? The Sophists and Money', *Classical Philology* 104.1 (2009), 13.

Chapter 1

1 Danzig (2003), 289.
2 Danzig (2003), 281–321.
3 Shero, L. R., 'Plato's *Apology* and Xenophon's *Apology*', *Classical Weekly* 20.14 (1927), 107.
4 Danzig (2003), 287.
5 Danzig (2003), 288 and 300.
6 Danzig, 'The Best Way to Die: Wisdom, Boasting and Strength of Spirit in Xenophon's Apology', *Classica and Mediaevalia* 65 (2014b), p. 156.
7 Kierkegard (1989), 15.
8 Ralkowski, M. A., *Plato's Trial of Athens*. London and New York: Bloomsbury Academic, 2019.
9 Cf. Shero (1927), 107.
10 Danzig (2003), 307, 309 and 314.
11 Pucci, P., *Xenophon: Socrates' Defense: Introduction and Commentary*. Amsterdam: Adolf M. Hakkert Editore, 2002, 12.
12 Shero (1927), 110.
13 Adam, J (ed.), *Platonis Apologia Socratis*. Cambridge: Cambridge University Press, 1916 xxvi.
14 Danzig (2003), 314.
15 Baker, W. W., 'An Apologetic for Xenophon's *Memorabilia*', *Classical Journal* 12.5 (1917), 307–8.
16 Kierkegaard (1989), 25.

Chapter 2

1. Ralkowski, M. A., *Plato's Trial of Athens*. London and New York: Bloomsbury Academic, 2019, *passim*.
2. Straussians are concerned with ἐγκράτεια as a means to achieve strength and as a component of good leadership, e.g. Higgins (1977), 25, Pangle, T.L., *The Socratic Way of Life: Xenophon's "Memorabilia"*. Chicago: University of Chicago Press, 2018 55–65, and Buzzetti, E., *Xenophon the Socratic Prince: The Argument of the Anabasis of Cyrus*. New York: Palgrave Macmillan, 2014, 68, who observes that Cyrus' death is caused by 'lack of self-control'. Buzzetti declares himself a Straussian; see p. 8.
3. See e.g. Pangle (2018), 50–5 and 65.

Chapter 3

1. Freeman, K., 'Portrait of a Millionaire – Callias Son of Hipponicus', *Greece & Rome* 8.22 (1938), 20–35.
2. Also see Eucken, C., *Isokrates. Seine Positionen in der Auseinandersetzung mit den zeitgenössischen Philosophen*. Berlin and New York: De Gruyter, 1983.
3. Too, Y. L., *The Rhetoric of Identity in Isocrates: Text, Power, Pedagogy*. Cambridge: Cambridge University Press, 1995, 157–9.
4. Pucci (2002), 12.
5. Thesleff, H., 'The Interrelation and Date of the 'Symposia' of Plato and Xenophon', *Bulletin of the Institute of Classical Studies* 25 (1978), 168.
6. Sidwell, K., *Aristophanes the Democrat: The Politics of Satirical Comedy During the Peloponesian War*. Cambridge and New York: Cambridge University Press, 2009, 220.
7. Bromberg, J., 'A Sage on the Stage: Socrates and Athenian Old Comedy', in Stavru, A. and Scafuro, A. (eds), *Socrates and the Socratic Dialogue*. Leiden: Brill, 2018, 42.
8. Hindley, C., 'Xenophon on Male Love' in Gray (2010), 110.
9. Cohen, D., 'Law, Society and Homosexuality in Classical Athens', *Past and Present* 117 (1987), 3–21 and Hindley, C., 'Debate: Law, Society and Homosexuality in Classical Athens', *Past and Present* 133.1 (1991), esp. 179–80.
10. Hindley (1991), 167.
11. See Cohen, D., 'Law, Society and Homosexuality in Classical Athens: Reply', *Past and Present* 133 (1991), 186.
12. Hindley (2010), 110.
13. Hindley (2010), 105.
14. The fact that Xenophon arrives at the court of Seuthes with only a boy and some money for travelling expenses at *Anabasis* 7.3.20, as Hindley observes at (2010) p. 84,

suggests that Socrates' views on homosexual desire were somewhat distinct from Xenophon's.

15 The represented scene of love between Dionysius and Ariadne confirms Michel Foucault's point that homosexual and heterosexual desire were not opposed to one another in Ancient Greece. Cf. Foucault, M. and Hurley, R., 'Erotics', *October* 33 (1985), 3–30, 4–5.

16 See Bowen, A. J., *Xenophon Symposium*. Warminster: Aris & Phillips Classical Texts, 1998, 11.

Chapter 4

1 A version of this paper was initially published in *Proceedings of the Cambridge Philological Society* 47 (2001), 65–80.

2 Murnaghan, S., 'How a Woman Can Be More Like a Man: The Dialogue Between Ischomachus and His Wife in Xenophon's *Oeconomicus*', *Helios* 15 (1988), 9–22; see also Scaife, R., 'Ritual and Persuasion in the House of Ischomachus', *The Classical Journal* 90 (1995), 225–32, esp. 226; Cohen, D., 'Seclusion, Separation, and the Status of Women in Classical Athens,' *Greece & Rome* 36.1 (1989), 6 and Foxhall, L., 'Household, Gender and Property in Classical Athens', *Classical Quarterly* 39.1 (1989), 30, the latter of which argues that husband and wife may be partners, although their reciprocity ultimately gives way to a status hierarchy.

3 See Pomeroy, S. B., 'Slavery in the Greek Domestic Economy in the Light of Xenophon's <<Oeconomicus>>', *Index* 17 (1989), which proposes that Xenophon's text is more 'an idealistic vision than a description of reality' (p. 12) in which natural hierarchies, including those of gender, race and class are abolished (p. 16).

4 Pomeroy, S. B., *Xenophon, Oeconomicus. A Social and Historical Commentary*. Oxford: Clarendon Press, 1994, 33–40.

5 Cantarella, E., *Pandora's Daughters: The Role and Status of Women in Greek and Roman Antiquity*, tr. Fant, M. B., Baltimore and London: Johns Hopkins University Press, 1987, 53–5.

6 Blundell, S., *Women in Ancient Greece*. London: British Museum Press, 1995, 140ff.

7 Pomeroy (1994), 28.

8 Yet Pomeroy observes that this dialogue does not simply propose a 'debate between opposing views', and she makes this point in order to establish that the *Oeconomicus* distinguishes itself from the Platonic dialogue form. Pomeroy (1994), 19–20.

9 See Too, Y. L., 'The Pedagogical State and the Disfigurement of Power in Xenophon's *Cyropaedia*', in Too, Y. L. and Livingstone, N. (eds), *Pedagogy and Power: Rhetorics of Classical Learning*. Cambridge: Cambridge University Press, 1998, 282–302.

10 For this approach, see, for instance, Higgins, W. E., *Xenophon the Athenian: The Problem of the World and the Society of the Athenian Polis*. Albany: State University of New York Press, 1977.
11 Purves wants to see the arrangement of speeches as parallel to the structure of the house. See Purves, A., *Space and Time in Ancient Greek Narrative*. Cambridge: Cambridge University Press, 2010 197.
12 Nehamas, A., *The Art of Living: Socratic Reflections from Plato to Foucault*. Berkeley, Los Angeles, London: University of California Press, 1998, 103–7.
13 See also Book 3 of Ps.-Aristotle *Oeconomica*, which survives only in Latin and which probably borrows heavily from Xenophon's *Oeconomicus*.
14 See Vernant, J.-P., *Myth and Thought among the Greeks*. London: Routledge & Kegan Paul, 1983, 139 and Redfield, J., 'Homo Domesticus' in Vernant, J.-P. (ed.), *The Greeks*, tr. Lambert, C. and Fagan, T. L. Chicago and London: University of Chicago Press, 1991, 157; also cf. Foxhall, L., 'Household, Gender and Property in Classical Athens', *Classical Quarterly* 39.1 (1989) 39.
15 The implication is that economic production is gendered as ideally and exclusively male, and possibly also hints at androcentric reproduction as enacted, for instance, in Aphrodite's extraordinary birth from Ouranos' blood falling into the sea in the *Theogony* (vv. 195ff.). See Bergren, A., 'Language and the Female in Early Greek Thought', *Arethusa* 16 (1983), 74, which observes that for Hesiod the fundamental struggle in the *Theogony* is over control of reproduction.
16 Loraux, N., *The Children of Athena: Athenian Ideas About Citizenship and the Division Between the Sexes*, tr. Levine, C. Princeton: Princeton University Press, 1993 [= *Les enfants d' Athena: Idées athéniennes sur la citoyenneté et la division des sexes* (Paris: 1984)], 89.
17 See also the complementary discussions in Loraux (1993), 89–98 and Zeitlin, F., *Playing the Other: Gender and Society in Classical Greek Literature*. Chicago and London: University of Chicago Press, 1996 56–72, who sets the negative image of woman against that of woman as (re)producer.
18 Vilatte argues that the household of the καλὸς καγαθός, e.g. the slave, wife, dog, horse, mirrors the καλὸς καγαθός; see Vilatte, S., 'La femme, l'esclave, le cheval et le chien: les emblèmes du KALOS KAGATHOS Ischomaque', *Dialogues d' histoire ancienne* 12 (1986),esp. 287–8.
19 P. 38 does not contain the line, while Aristotle appears to be aware of it (*Pol.* 1252b; *Oec.* 1343a20f.), although Timaeus 566F157 Jac. acknowledges its existence.
20 See Pomeroy (1994), 284.
21 Murnaghan (1988).
22 Nails, D., *The People of Plato: A Prosopography of Plato and Other Socratics*. Indianapolis: Hackett Publishing Co., Inc., 2002, 95.

23 See Cartledge, P., 'Xenophon's Women: A Touch of the Other', *Tria Lustra. Liverpool Classical Papers* 3 (1993), 9–10; also Harvey, D., 'The Wicked Wife of Ischomachos', *Echos du monde Classique: Classical Views* 3 (1984), Stevens, J., 'Friendship and Profit in Xenophon's *Oeconomicus*', in Van der Waerdt, P. (ed.), *The Socratic Movement*. Ithaca: Cornell University Press, 1994, 223, and Goldhill, S., *Foucault's Virginity*. Cambridge: Cambridge University Press, 1995, 140. Pomeroy (1994), 261–4 is disinclined to accept the identification of Ischomachus' otherwise nameless wife as Chrysilla for the reason that this would undermine the dialogue's purpose.
24 See Danzig (2010), 258 and Dorion, L.-A., 'Fundamental Parallels between Socrates and Ischomachus', Positions in the *Oeconomicus*', in Stavru, A. and Moore, C., *Socrates and the Socratic Dialogue*. Leiden: F. Steiner, 537.
25 See Dorion (2018), 537.
26 Gini, A., 'The Manly Intellect of His Wife: Xenophon *Oec.* Ch. 7', *The Classical World* 96 (1992/3), 483.
27 See Gini (1992/3), 485 for the wife's use of the adjective γέλοιος in a 'logical' and 'philosophical' sense at 7.39 only to be echoed by her husband at 7.40 and Blundell (1995), 140 for the view that the husband comes over as an 'insufferably pompous and patronising character'.
28 Gray, V., 'Dialogue in Xenophon's *Hellenica*', *Classical Quarterly* 31.2 (1981), 331–2.
29 See Gray (2011), 100–3 for Xenophon's opposition between individuals *seeming* to be something and actually *being* quite different from what they appear to be.
30 Pomeroy (1994), 259.
31 See e.g. de Ste. Croix, G., *The Origins of the Peloponnesian War*. London: Bloomsbury, 1972, 371–6; also Strauss, L., *The City and Man*. Chicago: University of Chicago Press, 1964, 42.
32 See Vilatte (1986), 278 and 288.
33 Stevens (1994), 210.
34 See Pomeroy (1994), 265–6; also Gabrielsen, V., 'The *Antidosis* Procedure in Classical Athens', *Classica et Mediaevalia* 38 (1987), and Christ, M., 'Liturgy Avoidance and *Antidosis* in Classical Athens', *Transactions of the American Philological Association* 120 (1990).
35 Pomeroy (1994), 313 and Gini (1992/3), 484. Vilatte writes: 'Image inversée de la cité: le procès public est devenu procès privé au creux de la maison, le juge est la femme, le coupable le mari'. For her, this parody of civic process within the household literally 'mirrors' and therefore reinforces the husband's authority; see Vilatte (1986), 280.
36 Chaintraine, P., *Xenophon. Economique*. Paris: Les Belles Lettres, 1949, 9.
37 See Wellman, R., 'Socratic Method in Xenophon', *Journal of the History of Ideas* 37.2 (1976).
38 See Just, R., *Women in Athenian Law and Life*. London: Routledge, 1991, 144.

39 See Stevens (1994), 210–11 for the view that Ischomachus is like Critobulus, following Strauss (1970), 90.
40 Pomeroy (1994), 197 and St. Augustine *De Magistro* 12.40.
41 Stevens (1994), 232–3.
42 See Cantarella (1987), 53–5.
43 Murnaghan (1988), esp. 15–16, while Goldhill takes the comment as marking the wife's potential for moral disorder; see Goldhill (1995), 141.
44 Against the conventional classical background of misogyny, contemporary feminist writing has insisted upon the resource of woman/the female: e.g. Irigaray, L., *This Sex Which is Not One*, tr. Porter, C. Ithaca: 1985 = *Ce sexe qui n'en est pas un*. Paris: Cornell University Press, 23–4; Le Doeuff, M., *Hipparchia's Choice: An Essay Concerning Women, Philosophy, Etc.*, tr. Selous, T. Oxford and Cambridge, MA: Columbia University Press, 1991. [= *L'Etude et le rouet*. Paris: 1989, and Kofman, S., 'Beyond Aporia?' in Benjamin, A. (ed.), *Post-Structuralist Classics*. New York and London: Routledge, 1988, 25–30.
45 Stevens (1994), p. 210.
46 See Miller, A., *For Your Own Good: The Roots of Violence in Child-rearing*, tr. Hannum, H. and H. London: Virago, 1987.

Chapter 5

1 Gray, V., 'Xenophon's "Cynegeticus"', *Hermes* 113.2 (1985), 156.
2 Gray (1985), 157.
3 Radermacher, L., 'Uber den Cynegeticus des Xenophon', *RhM* 51 (1856), 591–627.
4 Norden, E., *Die Antike Kunstprosa*. Leipzig: B. G. Teubner, 1895, 431–4.
5 Nickel, R., *Xenophon*. Darmstadt: Wissenschaftliche Buchgesellschaft, 1979.
6 Jaeger, W., *Paideia* III. Oxford: Oxford University Press, 1947, 177–84.
7 Johnstone, S., 'Virtuous Toil, Vicious Work: Xenophon on Aristocratic Style', *Classical Philology* 89.3 (1994), pp. 228–9.
8 Johnstone (1994), 229.
9 See Blank, D., 'Socratics Versus Sophists for Payment on Teaching', *Classical Antiquity* 4.1 (1985), 1–49.
10 See Guthrie, W. K., *The Sophists*. Cambridge: Cambridge University Press, 1971 313.
11 Gray (1985), 159.
12 Gray (1985), 163 and 172.
13 Sanders, H. N., *The Cynegeticus*, PhD thesis. Baltimore: The Friedenwald Company, 1903, 13 notes that the authenticity of the final chapter of the work has been doubted.
14 Hesk, J., 'Xenophon and Arrian, On Hunting', *Bryn Mawr Classical Review* 2000.11.19, 196.
15 Taylor, A. E., *Plato: The Man and His Work*. London: Methuen, 1937, 379.

16. Blank (1985).
17. Morgan, K. A., *Myth and Philosophy from the pre-Socratics to Plato*. Cambridge: Cambridge University Press, 2009, 22–3.
18. Morgan (2009), 22.
19. Sanders (1903), on p. 19 expresses the view that the *Cynegeticus* is influenced by Platonic doctrine.
20. See e.g. Fredal, J., 'Why Shouldn't the Sophist Charge Fees?', *Rhetoric Society Quarterly* 38.2 (2008), 153; Tell (2009), 15 and C. Zuckert, 'Who's A Philosopher? Who's a Sophist? The Stranger v. Socrates', *Review of Metaphysics* 54.1 (2000), who observes that the sophist is a hunter on p. 71.

Chapter 6

1. See Too, Y. L., 'Introduction: Writing the History of Ancient Education' in *Education in Greek and Roman Antiquity*. Leiden: Brill, 2001, 11–16.
2. See Christensen, P., 'Xenophon's "Cyropaedia" and Military Reform in Sparta', *Journal of Hellenic Studies* 126 (2006), 54. Christensen sees the Spartan cavalry as being weak and in need of reform.
3. Johnson, D., 'Persians as Centaurs in Xenophon's "Cyropaedia"', *Transactions of the American Philological Association* 135.1 (2005), 174 and 181.

Chapter 7

1. See Dillery, J., 'Xenophon's "Poroi" and Athenian Imperialism', *Historia* 42.1 (1993), 1 and 'Xenophon: the Small Works' in Flower, M. A., *The Cambridge Companion to Xenophon*. Cambridge: Cambridge University Press, 2017 216.
2. Cf. Gauthier, P., 'Le Programme de Xenophon dans le Poroi (Xenophon's Programme de Poroi) in Gray, V. (ed.), *Xenophon* (2010), 115.
3. Dillery also regards Xenophon as a hesychist; see (1993), 7.
4. Dillery (1995), 2 and Polanyi, K., *The Livelihood of Man*. New York: Academic Press Inc., 1977. 196.
5. Dillery (1995) p. 2.
6. Gauthier, in Gray (2010), 113–36, esp. 118.
7. See Pritchard, D., 'War, Democracy and Culture in Classical Athens', *Australasian Society for Classical Studies* 31 (2010), 4.
8. Pritchard (2010), 7 and Roisman, H., *The Rhetoric of Manhood: Masculinity and the Attic Orators*. Berkeley, CA: University of California Press, 2005, 105.
9. On the figure of the quietist, see Too, Y. L., *The Rhetoric of Identity in Isocrates: Text, Power, Pedagogy*. Cambridge: Cambridge University Press, 1995, 90–112.

10 See North, H., *Sophrosyne: Self-Knowledge and Self-Restraint in Greek Literature*. New York: Cornell University Press, 1966, 102–4.
11 Zenker, F., *The Rural Basis of the Ancient Greek City*. Honors dissertation, Wesleyan University: 2009, 40.
12 Dillery (1993), 3.
13 Also see Flament, C., 'Le Laurion et la cité d'Athènes à la fin de l'époque archaïque', *L'Antiquité Classique* 80 (2011), 73-94, 73.
14 Cartledge, P., 'Xenophon's Women: A Touch of the Other', *Tria Lustra*. Liverpool Classical Papers 3 (1993), 181.
15 Redway, J. W., 'The Silver Mines of Athens', *The Journal of Education* 61.15 (1905), 412.
16 Polanyi (1977), 196.
17 Dillery (2017), 218.
18 Dillery (1995), 10.
19 Schorn, S., 'The Philosophical Background of Xenophon's *Poroi*' in Hobden, F. and Tuplin, C., *Xenophon: Ethical Principles and Historical Enquiry*. Leiden and Boston: Brill, 2012, 702.
20 Dillery (2017), 217.

Chapter 8

1 See Alders, G. J. D., 'Date and Intention of Xenophon's "Hiero"', *Mnemosyne* 6.3 (1957), 208–15, 208.
2 Strauss, L., *On Tyranny*, Eds. Gourevitch, V. and Roth, M. S. Chicago: University of Chicago Press, 1961, 1992, 2000, 5.
3 Gray, V., 'Xenophon's *Hiero* and the Meeting of the Wise Man and Tyrant in Greek Literature', *Classical Quarterly* 36 (1986), 115 and 117.
4 Tymura, D., 'The Bitter Life of a Tyrant – Remarks on Xenophon's *Hiero*', in Reid, H.., Tanasi, D., Kimbell, S., *Politics and Performance in Western Greece: Essays on the Hellenic Heritage of Sicily and Southern Italy*. Sioux City, IA: 2017, 98–9.
5 Gray (1986), 123.
6 Tymura (2017), 99.
7 Gray, V., 'Xenophon's Symposion: The Display of Wisdom', *Hermes* 120.1 (1992), 58–75, 60.
8 Gray (1986), 115.
9 Gray (1992), 66.
10 Nagy, G., 'Early Views of Poets and Poetry', in Kennedy, G. (ed.), *The Cambridge History of Literary Criticism*. Cambridge: Cambridge University Press, 1989, 24.
11 Robb, K., *Literacy and Paideia in Ancient Greece*. New York: Oxford University Press, 1994, 30.

12 Robb (1994), 77.
13 Robb (1994), 164.
14 Gray (2007), 110.
15 See also Fertik, H., 'The Absent Landscape in Xenophon's *Hiero*', *Mnemosyne* 70 (2017), 5.
16 Gray (2007), 124.
17 Too (2001), 77.
18 Gray (1986), 119–2; see also Gray (2007), 32.
19 Gray (1986), 118.
20 Strauss (1961, 1991, 2000), 29.
21 Long, A. and Sedley, D., *The Hellenistic Philosophers. Vol. 1. Translations of the Principal Sources, with Philosophical Commentary*. Cambridge, 1987, 349–50. Cosmopolitanism is also evident in later Stoic writers, namely Epictetus (*Diatribe* 2.10.3), Seneca (*De vita beata* 5) and Marcus Aurelius (4.4 and 6.44).
22 Sevieri (2004), 278–9.
23 Gray (1986), 116.
24 See Cicero, *D.O.* 2.351–4; Quintilian *IO* 11.2.11–16; Phaedrus 4.26 and Aelian *VH* 4.1; also see Takakjy, L. C., 'Xenophon the Literary Critic: The Poetics and Politics of Praise in *Hiero*', *Greek, Roman and Byzantine Studies* 57 (2017), 50.
25 Anderson, G., 'Before *Turannoi* Were Tyrants: Rethinking a Chapter of Early Greek History', *Classical Antiquity* 24.2 (2005), 192–4.
26 See Strauss (1961), 66.

Chapter 9

1 Humble, N., 'Sparta in Xenophon and Plato', in Danzig, G., Johnson, D., and Morrison, D. (eds), *Plato and Xenophon: Comparative Studies*. Leiden, Boston: Brill, 2018, 552 observes that Xenophon, like Plato, may have admired Sparta but found much to criticize; both were strongly Athenian.
2 Christensen, P., 'Xenophon's Views on Sparta' in Flower (2017), pp. 37–8.
3 Christensen (2017), 379. Also see Strauss, L. 'The Spirit of Sparta, or the Taste of Xenophon', *Social Research* 6 (1939), 502–36, esp. 522–3; Higgins, W. E., *Xenophon the Athenian: The Problem of the World and the Society of the Athenian Polis*. Albany: State University of New York Press, 1977, 60–75; Humble, N., 'The Author, Date and Purpose of Chapter 14 of *Lacedaimonia Politeia*', in Tuplin, C. (ed.), *Xenophon and His World. Papers from a Conference held in Liverpool in 1999*. Historia Heft 172. Stuttgart: F. Steiner, 2004, 215–28 and Proietti, G., *Xenophon's Sparta*. Leiden: Brill, 1987, 44–79.
4 See Strauss (1939), 528.

5 Cawkwell, G., 'The Decline of Sparta', *Classical Quarterly* 33.2 (1983), 396.
6 Humble (2004), 225.
7 Bury, J. B., *The Ancient Greek Historians*. New York: The Macmillan Company, 1909, 153.
8 Momigliano, A., *The Development of Greek Biography*. Cambridge, MA: Harvard University Press, 1993, 50.
9 See Tamiolaki, M., 'Virtue and Leadership in Xenophon: Ideal Leader or Ideal Losers?', in Hobden, F. and Tuplin, C. (eds), *Xenophon: Ethical Principles and Historical Enquiry*. Leiden and Boston: Brill, 2012, 569.
10 Wheeler, E. L., review of 'C. D. Hamilton, *Agesilaus and the Failure of Spartan Hegemony*', *American Journal of Philology* 114 (1993), 457.
11 Also see Hamilton, C. D., *Agesilaus and the Failure of Spartan Hegemony*. Ithaca and London: Cornell University Press, 1991, 13.
12 Frost, F. J., 'The "Ominous" Birth of Peisistratos' in Titchener, F. B., Morton, R. F. and Green, P. (eds), *The Eye Expanded: Life and the Arts in Greco-Roman Antiquity*. Berkeley: California University Press, 1999, 11.
13 See Frost (1999), 10 and 12.
14 Hamilton (1991), 10.
15 Hamilton (1991), 59.
16 Harman (2012), 444.
17 Harman (2012), 449.
18 Hamilton (1991), 256.
19 Kovacs, D., 'Two Notes on Xenophon *Hellenica* 1.4.20 and *Agesilaus* 2.26', *Classical Quarterly* 61.2 (2011), 253.
20 See Dillery (1995), 228–30.
21 Cawkwell, G. L., 'Agesilaus and Sparta', *Classical Quarterly* 26.1 (1976), 70.
22 Dillery (1995), 236.
23 Trego, K. M., 'Agesilaus the Puppet? The Effects of Thematic Development on Plutarch's Story of the Accession', *Illinois Classical Studies* 39 (2014), 45.
24 See e.g. Cawkwell (1951), p. 14; Cawkwell (1966), p. 12, and Rice, D. G., *Agesilaus, Agesipolis, and Spartan Politics, 386–379 B.C.* Historia: Zeitschrift fur Alte Geschichte (2nd Qtr.), 1974, 164.
25 See Marincola in Flower (2017), 116 and Tuplin (1993), 164; also Hau, L. I., *Moral History from Herodotus to Diodorus Siculus*. Edinburgh: Edinburgh University Press, 2016, 231, n. 49, which cites Krentz, P., *Xenophon: Hellenika II.3.11–IV.2.8*. Warminster: Aris & Phillips, 1995 and Harman (2013) as sharing this view.

Chapter 10

1 Marincola (2017), 104.
2 Marincola (2017), 105 and Hau (2016), 217.

3. See MacLaren, M., 'On the Composition of Xenophon's *Hellenica*', *American Journal of Philology* 55.3 (1934a), 228. He cites, for instance, Defosse, P., 'A propos du début insolite des Hélleniques', *Revue Belge de Philologie Et D'Histoire* 46 (1968), 5–24, esp. 14–19.
4. See Pelling, C., 'Xenophon's Authorial Voice', in Flower (2017), 254 with note 25.
5. See Strauss, L., 'Greek Historians', *The Review of Metaphysics* 21.4 (1968), 663.
6. Cf. Pelling in Flower (2017), 254.
7. Gray, 'Continuous History and Xenophon *Hellenica* 1–2.3.10', *American Journal of Philology* 112.2 (1991), 227.
8. Tamiolaki declares that Xenophon was not at all an imperialist; see Tamiolaki, M., 'Xenophon's Conception of Friendship in *Memorabilia* 2.6 (with Reference to Plato's *Lysis*)', in Danzig, G., Johnson, D., and Morrison, D. (eds), *Plato and Xenophon: Comparative Studies*. Leiden, Boston: Brill, 2018, 456.
9. MacLaren (1934a), 122.
10. MacLaren (1934b), 262.
11. Dillery (1995), 241.
12. MacLaren (1934a), 133 and 137.
13. Cf. Dillery (1995), 148.
14. Dillery (1995), 162.
15. Cf. Dillery (1995), 151.
16. Hau (2016), 216.
17. Rahn, P. J., 'Xenophon's Developing Historiography', *Transactions of the American Philological Association* 102 (1971) 502; also Rochi, E. D., 'Hégémonie et Autonome: La Petites Poleis dans les 'Helléniques' de Xénophon', *Ancient Society* 38 (2008), 17.
18. Simonton, M., *Classical Greek Oligarchy: A Political History*. Princeton: Princeton University Press, 2017, 232.
19. Shrimpton, G. 'The Theban Supremacy in Fourth-Century Literature', *Phoenix* 25.4 (1971), 311–2 and 318.
20. Also see Gray (1991), 201–28 on 'continuous history'.
21. Pelling in Flower (2017), 258.
22. Pelling in Flower (2017), 256.
23. Cf. Pelling in Flower (2017), 257.
24. On the importance of the small state in the *Hellenica*, see Rochi (2008), 1–21.
25. Cf. Pelling in Flower (2017), 258.
26. Luraghi, N., 'Xenophon's Place in Fourth-Century Greek Historiography', in Flower (2017), 98. Also see MacLaren (1934a), 122–39.

Chapter 11

1. An earlier version of this chapter was published in Too, Y. L. and Livingstone, N. (eds), *Pedagogy and Power: Rhetorics of Classical Learning*. Cambridge: Cambridge University Press, 1998 282–302.

2 For the work's influence on historical kingship, see Farber, J. J., 'The *Cyropaedia* and Hellenistic Kingship', *American Journal of Philology* 100 (1979), 497–514.
3 Tatum, J., *Xenophon's Imperial Fiction: On the Education of Cyrus*. Princeton: Princeton University Press,, xiii.
4 Also e.g. Breebart, A. B., 'From Victory to Peace: Some Aspects of Cyrus' State in Xenophon's Cyropaedia', *Mnemosyne* 36.1/2 (1983), 117–34.
5 Cf. Aristotle, *Politics* 1277a25-9, who says that it is the virtue of the respectable (δοκίμοι) to rule and to be ruled.
6 In the *Constitution of the Laecedaimonians* Xenophon tells his reader that the παιδονόμοι is referred to as an ἄρχων (.2.10.11; cf. Plato *Republic* 479d).
7 Due, B., *The Cyropaedia*. Aarhus: Aarhus University Press, 1989, 71.
8 Καὶ βασιλεὺς ὥσπερ καὶ ἐν πολέμῳ ἡγεμών ἐστιν αὐτοῖς, 1.2.10.
9 Carlier in Gray (2010), 339.
10 Nickel (1979); Higgins (1977), 54; Due (1989), 15; Tatum (1989), 90. On the understanding that the Persian teacher has a limited function and that Persian education has this preparatory status, R. Breitenbach regards the work's title, 'The Education of Cyrus' as being appropriate as a description only for Book 1, which relates the strict training and regimen of the Persian youth: Breitenbach, R., *Realencyclopädie der classischen Altertumswissenschaft* IX, A 2 col. 1707a. Also see H. Arendt, 'What Was Authority?' in Friendrich, C. J. (ed.) *Authority (Nomos 1)*. Cambridge, MA: Harvard University Press, 1958, 96–7. Arendt insists on a distinction between political and pedagogical authorities, assuming that in antiquity once the pupil took up his position as a full subject in the state, he ceases to have to answer to pedagogical authority.
11 ἐπαιδεύσθη γε μὲν εἰν Πέρσων νομοῖς
12 e.g. διδάσκειν, 2.1.20, 2.2.6, διδασκέτω, 6.2.24 ἐδίδαξε, 8.1.15; διδάσκω . . . αὕτη γὰρ ἀρίστη διδασκαλία, 8.7.24.
13 Discussion of the analogy between the οἶκος and the πόλις may be found in Strauss, B. S., '*Oikos/Polis*: Towards a Theory of Athenian Paternal Ideology 450–399 BC' in Connor, W. R., Hansen, M. H., Raaflaub, K. A., Strauss, B. S. (eds), with a preface by J. R. Fears, *Aspects of Athenian Democracy*, Classica et Mediaevalia Dissertationes XI. Copenhagen: Museum Tusculanum Press, 1990, 101–27 at p. 108 and Strauss, B., *Fathers and Sons in Athens: Ideology and Society in the Era of the Peloponnesian War*. London: Routledge, 1993 32ff.
14 See Due (1989), 17, for other comparisons of a political leader to a 'father' in Greek literature.
15 Tatum (1989), 87.
16 See Tatum (1989), 139 on the characterization of Tigranes as a 'bright young man armed with a little learning from study with a sophist'.

17 Tatum (1989), 234. Also see Gera, D., *Xenophon's Cyropaedia: Style, Genre and Literary Technique*. Oxford: Oxford University Press, 1993, 12.
18 Field, L, '*Cyropaedia*: Educating Our Political Hopes', *The Journal of Politics* 74 (2012), 734.
19 Note that Herodotus blames the introduction of luxury into Persia on the influence of the conquered Lydians (*Histories* 1.71.2).
20 See Carlier, P., 'L'idée de monarchie imperial dans la Cyropédue de Xenophon', *Ktema* 3 (1978), 133–68 and Breebart (1983), 133.
21 Tatum (1989), 220ff. The 'decline' motif perhaps begs a question as to whether, and how, it should be seen in relation to the Greeks' perceptions of themselves and of the decline of their own institutions (see, for instance, the nostalgia of Isocrates' *On the Peace* and the *Areopagiticus*). Also see Field (2012), 723–5.
22 Cf. Bizos, M., *Xenophon. Cyropédie* I. Paris: Les Belles Lettres, 1971), xxviff., and Hirsch (1985), 92f. and 181.
23 Tatum (1989), 220ff.
24 W. Weathers has proposed that the account of the decline of the Persian empire after the death of Cyrus affirms the greatness of Cyrus in that it suggests it is the force of the king's personality which holds together his kingdom. See Weathers, W., 'Xenophon's Political Idealism', *Classical Journal* 49 (1954), 317.
25 Delebecque, E., 'Xénophon, Athenes et Lacédémonie', *Revue des Études Grecques* 59–60 (1946–7), pp. 10f.
26 Due (1989), 18–9.
27 Due (1989), 25 and Wood, N., 'Xenophon's Theory of Leadership', *Classica et Mediaevalia* 25 (1964), 33–66, esp. 55ff.
28 Tatum (1989), 237.
29 Gera, (1993), 299–300.
30 Field (2012), 737.
31 See Cizek, A., 'From the Historical Truth to the Literary Convention: the Life of Cyrus the Great viewed by Herodotus, Ctesias and Xenophon', *L'Antiquité Classique* 44 (1975) 531–52; Hirsch (1985), 61–74; and more recently, S. B. Pomeroy (1994), 248–50.
32 For 'reading between the lines' as a strategy for reclaiming an esoteric and subversive text intended for an elite as distinct from the face value message intended for the generality, seePatterson, A., *Reading Between the Lines*. Madison, WI: Routledge, 1993, 11–35, esp. 22.
33 Higgins (1977), 12 and 44.
34 Due (1989), 152.
35 Tatum must invest in such a reading because he regards the *Cyropaedia* as a precursor of the *Bildungsroman*, or narrative which relates the development of an

adolescent into maturity; in this case, of the uninhibited child Cyrus into restrained leader at e.g. 1.4.11–12. Tatum (1989), 97–8; also see pp. 37 (for the comparison of the *Cyropaedia* to a *Bildungsroman*) and 107.

36 Due regards Cyrus' interaction with his grandfather's favourite, Sakas, as evidence for a development of the youth's character for the better. Due (1989), 154 and Erasmus, S., 'Die Gedanke der Entwicklung eines Menschen in Xenophons Kyroupaedie', in Zucker, F. and *Müller*, W. (eds), *Festschrift für Fr. Zucker*. Berlin: Akademie-Verl., 1954, 111–125, esp. p. 115.

37 Αὐτὸς ἤδη Σάκας ἑαυτῷ, 1.4.6.

38 'First of all, you yourselves were doing what you did not allow us [your] children to do' (πρῶτον μὲν γὰρ ἃ οὐκ ἐᾶτε ἡμᾶς τοὺς παῖδας ποιεῖν, ταῦτα αὐτοὶ ἐποιεῖτε, 1.3.10) and 'You had completely forgotten that you were the king, the others, that you were their ruler' (ἐπελέλησθε δὲ παντάπασι σύ τε ὅτι βασιλεὺς ἦσθαι, οἵ τε ἄλλοι ὅτι σὺ ἄρχων, 1.3.10).

39 Gera (1993), 26, deems self-control to be one of Cyrus' Socratic qualities.

40 Due (1989), 44–5.

41 Stadter, P., 'Fictional Narrative in the Cyropaedia', *American Journal of Philology* 112.4 (1991), 488.

42 Καὶ τῇ μὲν πρώτῃ ἡμέρᾳ ἐξεστρατοπεδεύσατο ὡς δυνατὸν ἐγγύτατα, ὡς δυνατὸν ἐγγύγατα, ὅπως εἴ τίς τι ἐπιλελησμένος εἴη, μετέλθοι ... 6.3.1.

43 Tatum (1989), 88.

44 See Gill, C., 'The Question of Character-Development: Plutarch and Tacitus', *Classical Quarterly* 33 (1983), 469–87, esp. 469 and n. 2.

45 We could say that the institution of the linguistic sign is a contractual act (at the level of entire community and of history), while the institution of the Fashion sign is a tyrannical act: there are *mistakes* in language and *faults* in Fashion'; see Barthes, R., *The Fashion System*, tr. Ward, M. and Howard, R. Berkeley and Los Angeles: University of California Press, 1990, 216 (=*Systeme de la mode* (Paris, 1967)).

46 Due (1989), 59.

47 Carlier in Gray (2010), 363.

48 Wood (1964), 64–5. Gera (1993), 291, notes that most editors delete 8.1.40–2.

49 For the association between magic and persuasion, see de Romilly, J., *Magic and Rhetoric in Ancient Greece*. Cambridge, MA and London: Harvard University Press, 1975, 13ff, 28–35 and passim.

50 Cf, καὶ τότε πρῶτον Πέρσαι Μηδικὴν στολὴν ἐνέδυσαν.

51 Wood (1964), 63.

52 See Foucault, M., 'The Eye of Power' in *Power/Knowledge: Selected Interviews and Other Writings 1972–77*, Ed. Gordon, C. New York: Random House USA Inc., 1980, 145–65.

53 τῷ δόξαι μέγαν τε καὶ καλὸν φανῆναι τὸν Κῦρον, 8.3.14.

54 Others prostrate to Cyrus also at 4.4.13 and 7.5.32. Nadon criticizes me for seeing Gadatas as the first person to prostrate to Cyrus; rather I argue, in fact, that Gadatas is himself prostrating for the first time to Cyrus (2001), 134 n. 48.
55 Due (1989), 87.
56 Gera, *Xenophon's Cyropaedia*, p. 255.
57 The majority of critics deny that Cyrus actually castrated his servants, believing that he merely selected eunuchs for his households. This is a crucial move for those who wish to maintain that the Persian leader is an ideal monarch. See Gera, *Xenophon's Cyropaedia*, p. 287, n. 32.
58 See Gera (1993), 92, who cites Xen. *Apol.* 19–20; *Mem.* 1.2.49.
59 Cf. νομίζοντες ἀφαιρεῖσθαι αὐτους τὴν πρὸς αὐτοὺς φιλίαν, διὰ τοῦτο ὡς πολεμίοις αὐτοις χρῶνται, 3.1.39.
60 Hall, E., *Inventing the Barbarian: Greek Self-Definition through Tragedy*. Oxford: Oxford University Press, 1989, 209, observes that eunuchs present Eastern effeminacy in Greek tragedy. Also see Guyot, P., *Eunuchen als Sklaven und Friegelassene in der griechisch-römischen Antike*. Stuttgart: Klett-Cotta, 1980 77–81, and Hopkins, K. and Hopkins, M. K., 'Eunuchs in Politics in the Later Roman Empire', *Proceedings of the Cambridge Philological Society* 9.189 (1963), 72–80.
61 Tatum (1989), 59–60; also see Wood (1964), 57, and Strauss (1990).
62 See Luccioni, J., *Les idées politiques et socials de Xénophon*. Athens: Ophrys, 1948, 238.
63 Carlier, (1978), 133–65, esp. 155ff. suggests that Cyrus' eunuchs signify the ruler's aspirations to complete domination over his subjects.
64 Tatum (1989),78.
65 Note that in classical Athens the individual is only properly a citizen once he ceases to be a child and is formally recognized as an adult male, in a public ceremony called the *dokimasia*. See Goldhill, S., 'The Great Dionysia and Civic Ideology' in Winkler, J. and Zeitlin, F., *Nothing to Do with Dionysos? Athenian Drama in its Social Context*. Princeton: Princeton University Press, 1990, 113; on the *dokimasia*, the ceremony of adult initiation, see D. Whitehead, *The Demes of Attica* (Princeton, 1986), pp. 97–109.
66 E.g. Gera (1993), 26ff.
67 Nadon (2001), 179.
68 Carlier in Gray (2010), 336.
69 Gray (2011), 264.

Chapter 12

1 Gray (2010), 1.
2 Bradley in Gray (2010), 532.

3 Fox, R. L., *The Long March: Xenophon and the Ten Thousand*. New Haven and London: Yale University Press, 2004, 21.
4 Marincola (2017), 105.
5 See Stylianou in Fox (2004), 78.
6 Flower, 'Piety in Xenophon's Theory of Leadership' in Buxton, R. F., *Aspects of Leadership in Xenophon. Histos* Supplement 5. Newcastle-Upon-Tyne: Histos, 2016, 104.
7 For the date of Cyrus' death, see Fox (2004), 1.
8 Genette, G., *Narrative Discourse: An Essay in Method*. Oxford: Cornell University Press, 1980 (1972), 188–9.
9 Bonner, R. J., 'The Name Ten Thousand', *Classical Philology* 5 (1910) 97.
10 See Marincola in Flower (2017), 110.
11 Marincola in Flower (2017), 108; also see Hau, L. I., *Moral History from Herodotus to Diodorus Siculus*. Edinburgh: Edinburgh University Press, 2016, 223, in which Hau sees the good leader represented in the *Hellenica*, although she mistakenly views Agesilaus as an ideal leader of his people.
12 Dillery, J., *Xenophon and the History of His Times*. London: Routledge, 1995, 28.
13 Cf. Marincola in Flower (2017), 111.
14 Dillery (1995), 27 and 38.
15 Cf. Dillery (1995), 33.
16 Marincola in Flower (2017), 108.
17 Dillery (1995), 64.
18 See Dillery (1995), 66.
19 See Dillery (1995), 41 and 85.
20 Cf. Cawkwell in Lane Fox (2004), 64. Cawkwell argues that panhellenism became a powerful vision after 401.
21 Cf. Dalby, A., 'Greeks abroad. Social organization and food among the Ten Thousand', *Journal of Hellenic Studies* 112 (1992), 16–30.
22 See Hornblower, S., 'This Was Decided (*edoxe tauta*): The Army as Polis in Xenophon's *Anabasis* – and Elsewhere' in Lane Fox (2004), 245.
23 Dillery (1995), 86.
24 See Cawkwell in Lane Fox (2004), 47.
25 Grethlein (2012), 30.
26 Cf. Grethlein (2012), 26.
27 Bradley in Gray (2010), 541.
28 Flower (2012), 95 prefers to downplay the inconsistencies and 'slips' in Xenophon, choosing to characterize the author as vague and inconsistent instead of seeing irony in the text.

Concluding Thoughts

1 See Blau, A., 'Anti-Strauss', *The Journal of Politics* 74.1 (2012), 142–55, esp. 147.
2 Blau (2012), p. 143; also Smith, G. B., 'Who was Leo Strauss?', *The American Scholar* 66.1 (1997), 99.
3 Bowersock, G. W., 'Pseudo-Xenophon', *Harvard Studies in Classical Philology* 71 (1967), 35.
4 Also see Humble (2004), 217.
5 Here I cite Patterson (1993).
6 Blau (2012), 43.
7 Again, see Booth, W., *A Rhetoric of Irony*. Chicago: University of Chicago Press, 1974, 29, citing Kierkegaard as translated by Capel, L. M., in *The Concept of Irony, with Constant Reference to Socrates*. London: Indiana University Press, 1966, 265.

Bibliography

Adam, J (ed.), *Platonis Apologia Socratis*. Cambridge: Cambridge University Press, 1916.
Adkins, W. H., *Moral Values and Political Behaviour in Ancient Greece: From Homer to the End of the Fifth Century*. London: W. W. Norton and Co., 1976.
Alders, G. J. D., 'Date and Intention of Xenophon's "Hiero"', *Mnemosyne* 6.3 (1957), 208–15.
Allison, J., 'Thucydides and ΠΟΛΥΠΡΑΓΜΟΣΥΝΗ', *American Journal of Ancient History* 4 (1979), 10–22.
Anderson, G., 'Before *Turannoi* Were Tyrants: Rethinking a Chapter of Early Greek History', *Classical Antiquity* 24.2 (2005), 173–222.
Anderson, J. K., *Xenophon*. London: Bloomsbury Publishing PLC, 1974.
Andrisano, A. M., 'Les performances du symposium de Xenophon', *Pallas* 61 *Symposium: Banquets et Représentations en Grèce et à Rome* (2003), 287–302.
Arendt, H., 'What Was Authority?', in Friedrich, C. J. (ed.) *Authority (Nomos 1)*. Cambridge, MA: Harvard University Press, 1958.
Azoulay, V., 'The Medo-Persian Ceremonial: Xenophon's Cyrus and the King's Piety' in Tuplin, C. (ed.), *Xenophon and His World: Papers from a Conference held in Liverpool in 1999*. Historia Heft 172. Stuttgart: F. Steiner, 2004, 147–73.
Badian, E, (ed.), *Athenian Society and Institutions: Studies Presented to Victor Ehrenberg on his 75th Birthday*. Oxford: Blackwell, 1966.
Baker, W. W., 'An Apologetic for Xenophon's *Memorabilia*', *Classical Journal* 12.5 (1917), 293–309.
Balot, R., *A Companion to Greek and Roman Political Thought*. Malden, MA and Oxford: Wiley-Blackwell, 2013.
Bandini, M. and Dorion, L-A., *Xénophon Mémorables*. Paris: Les Belles Lettres, 2000.
Barthes, R., *The Fashion System*, tr. Ward, M. and Howard, R. Berkeley and Los Angeles: University of California Press, 1990 (=*Systeme de la mode* (Paris, 1967)).
Benjamin, A. (ed.), *Post-Structuralist Classics*. New York and London: Routledge, 1988.
Bergren, A., 'Language and the Female in Early Greek Thought', *Arethusa* 16 (1983), 69–96.
Bizos, M., *Xenophon. Cyropédie* I. Paris: Les Belles Lettres, 1971.
Blank, D., 'Socratics Versus Sophists for Payment on Teaching', *Classical Antiquity* 4.1 (1985), 1–49.
Blau, A., 'Anti-Strauss', *The Journal of Politics* 74.1 (2012), 142–55.
Bloom, A., 'Leo Strauss: September 20, 1899–October 18, 1973', *Political Theory* 2.4 (1974), 372–92.

Blundell, S., *Women in Ancient Greece*. London: British Museum Press, 1995.
Bonner, R. J., 'The Name Ten Thousand', *Classical Philology* 5 (1910), 97–9.
Booth, W., *A Rhetoric of Irony*. Chicago: University of Chicago Press, 1974.
Bowen, A. J., *Xenophon Symposium*. Warminster: Aris & Phillips Classical Texts, 1998.
Bowersock, G. W., 'Pseudo-Xenophon', *Harvard Studies in Classical Philology* 71 (1967), 33–55.
Breebart, A. B., 'From Victory to Peace: Some Aspects of Cyrus' State in Xenophon's Cyropaedia', *Mnemosyne* 36.1/2 (1983), 117–34.
Breitenbach, R., *Realencyclopädie der classischen Altertumswissenschaft* IX, A 2 col. 1707a.
Bromberg, J., 'A Sage on the Stage: Socrates and Athenian Old Comedy', in Stavru, A. and Scafuro, A. (eds), *Socrates and the Socratic Dialogue*. Leiden: Brill, 2018, 31–63.
Burnyeat, M. F., 'Sphinx Without a Secret', *New York Review of Books* 32.9 (1985), 30–6.
Burnyeat, M. F., *Explorations in Ancient and Modern Philosophy, vol. 1*. Cambridge: Cambridge University Press, 1991.
Bury, J. B., *The Ancient Greek Historians*. New York: The Macmillan Company, 1909.
Buxton, R. F., *Aspects of Leadership in Xenophon*. Histos Supplement 5. Newcastle-Upon-Tyne: Histos, 2016.
Buzzetti, E., *Xenophon the Socratic Prince: The Argument of the Anabasis of Cyrus*. New York: Palgrave Macmillan, 2014.
Campbell, B., 'Thought and Political Action in Athenian Tradition: The Emergence of the "Alienated" Individual', *History of Political Thought* 5.1 (1984), 17–59.
Cantarella, E., *Pandora's Daughters: The Role and Status of Women in Greek and Roman Antiquity*, tr. Fant, M. B., Baltimore and London: Johns Hopkins University Press, 1987 [=*L'ambiguo malanno.*, Rome: 1981].
Capel, L. M., *The Concept of Irony, with Constant Reference to Socrates*. London: Indiana University Press, 1966.
Carlier, P., 'L'idée de monarchie imperial dans la Cyropédue de Xenophon', *Ktema* 3 (1978), 133–68.
Cartledge, P., 'Xenophon's Women: A Touch of the Other', *Tria Lustra. Liverpool Classical Papers* 3 (1993), 5–14.
Cawkwell, G., *Xenophon: The Persian Expedition*. Harmondsworth: Penguin Classics, 1951.
Cawkwell, G., *Xenophon: A History of My Times*. Harmondsworth: Penguin Classics, 1966.
Cawkwell, G., 'Agesilaus and Sparta', *Classical Quarterly* 26.1 (1976), 62–84.
Cawkwell, G., 'The Decline of Sparta', *Classical Quarterly* 33.2 (1983), 385–400.
Cawkwell, G., 'When, How and Why Did Xenophon Write the *Anabasis*?' in Fox, R. L. (ed.), *The Long March: Xenophon and the Ten Thousand*. New Haven and London: Yale University Press, 2004, 46–67.
Chaintraine, P., *Xenophon. Economique*. Paris: Les Belles Lettres, 1949.
Christ, M., 'Liturgy Avoidance and *Antidosis* in Classical Athens', *Transactions of the American Philological Association* 120 (1990), 147–69.

Christensen, P., 'Xenophon's "Cyropaedia" and Military Reform in Sparta', *Journal of Hellenic Studies* 126 (2006), 47–65.
Christensen, P., 'Xenophon's Views on Sparta' in Flower, M. A. (ed.), *The Cambridge Companion to Xenophon*. Cambridge: Cambridge University Press, 2017.
Cizek, A., 'From the Historical Truth to the Literary Convention: the Life of Cyrus the Great viewed by Herodotus, Ctesias and Xenophon', *L'Antiquité Classique* 44 (1975) 531–52.
Cohen, D., 'Law, Society and Homosexuality in Classical Athens', *Past and Present* 117 (1987), 3–21.
Cohen, D., 'Seclusion, Separation, and the Status of Women in Classical Athens', *Greece & Rome* 36.1 (1989), 3–15.
Cohen, D., 'Law, Society and Homosexuality in Classical Athens: Reply', *Past and Present* 133 (1991), 184–94.
Connor, R., *The New Politicians of Fifth-Century Athens*. Princeton: Princeton University Press, 1972.
Connor, W. R., Hansen, M. H., Raaflaub, K. A., Strauss, B. S. (eds), *Aspects of Athenian Democracy*, Classica et Mediaevalia Dissertationes XI. Copenhagen: Museum Tusculanum Press, 1990.
Cooper, C. (ed.), *Politics of Orality (Orality and Literacy in Ancient Greece, Vol. 6)*. Leiden and Boston: Brill, 2007,
Dalby, A., 'Greeks abroad. Social organization and food among the Ten Thousand', *Journal of Hellenic Studies* 112 (1992), 16–30.
Danzig, G., 'Apologizing for Socrates: Plato and Xenophon on Socrates' Behavior in Court', *Transactions of the American Philological Association* 133 (2003), 281–321.
Danzig, G., 'Why Socrates was Not a Farmer: Xenophon's *Oeconomicus* as a Philosophical Dialogue', *GR* 50 (2003), 57–76.
Danzig, G., *Apologizing for Socrates. How Plato and Xenophon Created our Socrates*. Lanham: Lexington Books, 2010.
Danzig, G., 'The Best Way to Die: Wisdom, Boasting and Strength of Spirit in Xenophon's *Apology*', *Classica and Mediaevalia* 65 (2014b), 155–89.
Danzig, G., Johnson, D., and Morrison, D. (eds), *Plato and Xenophon: Comparative Studies*. Leiden, Boston: Brill, 2018.
de Romilly, J., *Magic and Rhetoric in Ancient Greece*. Cambridge, MA and London: Harvard University Press, 1975.
de Romilly, J., *A Short History of Greek Literature*. Chicago: University of Chicago Press, 1985.
de Ste. Croix, G., *The Origins of the Peloponnesian War*. London: Bloomsbury, 1972.
Defosse, P., 'A propos du début insolite des Hélleniques', *Revue Belge de Philologie Et D'Histoire* 46 (1968), 5–24.
Delebecque, E., 'Xénophon, Athenes et Lacédémonie', *Revue des Études Grecques* 59–60 (1946–7), 71–138.
Depew, M. and Obbink, D. (eds), *Matrices of Genre: Authors, Canons and Society*. Cambridge, MA: Harvard University Press, 2000.

Destrée, P., 'Platon et l'ironie dramatique', *Métaphysique et de Morale* 4 (2013), 543–556.
Dillery, J., 'Xenophon's "Poroi" and Athenian Imperialism', *Historia* 42.1 (1993), 1–11.
Dillery, J., *Xenophon and the History of His Times*. London: Routledge, 1995.
Dillery, J., 'Xenophon: the Small Works', in Flower, M.A. (ed.), *The Cambridge Companion to Xenophon*. Cambridge: Cambridge University Press, 2017, 195–219.
Dorion, L.-A., 'The Straussian Exegesis of Xenophon: The Paradigmatic Case of *Memorabilia* IV.4' in Gray, V. (ed.), *Xenophon*. Oxford: Oxford University Press, 2010, 282–323.
Dorion, L.-A., *L'Autre Socrates. Études sur les écrits Socratiques de Xénophon*. Paris: Les Belles Lettres, 2013.
Dorion, L.-A., 'Fundamental Parallels between Socrates and Ischomachus' Positions in the *Oeconomicus*', in Stavru, A. and Moore, C. (eds), *Socrates and the Socratic Dialogue*. Leiden and Boston: Brill, 2018, 521–43.
Due, B., *The Cyropaedia*. Aarhus: Aarhus University Press, 1989.
Easterling, P. E., and Knox, B. M. W. (eds), *The Cambridge History of Classical Literature*. Cambridge: Cambridge University Press, 1985.
Edmunds, L., 'The Practical Irony of the Historical Socrates', *Phoenix* 58.3/4 (2004), 193–207.
Ehrenberg, V., *From Solon to Socrates: Greek History and Civilization During the Sixth and Fifth Centuries B. C.*. London: Methuen, 1968.
Erasmus, S., 'Die Gedanke der Entwicklung eines Menschen in Xenophons Kyroupaedie, in Zucker, F. and Müller, W. (eds), *Festschrift für Fr. Zucker*. Berlin: Akademie-Verl., 1954, 111–125.
Eucken, C., *Isokrates. Seine Positionen in der Auseinandersetzung mit den zeitgenössischen Philosophen*. Berlin and New York: De Gruyter, 1983.
Farber, J. J., 'The *Cyropaedia* and Hellenistic Kingship', *American Journal of Philology* 100 (1979), 497–514.
Fertik, H. 'The Absent Landscape in Xenophon's *Hiero*', *Mnemosyne* 70 (2017), 1–10.
Ferrario, S. B., 'Historical Agency and Self-Awareness in Xenophon's *Hellenica* and *Anabasis*' in Hobden, F. and Tuplin, C. (eds), *Xenophon: Ethical Principles and Historical Enquiry*. Leiden and Boston: Brill, 2012, 342–76.
Field, L, '*Cyropaedia*: Educating Our Political Hopes', *The Journal of Politics* 74 (2012), 723–38.
Flament, C., 'Le Laurion et la cité d'Athènes à la fin de l'époque archaïque', *L'Antiquité Classique* 80 (2011), 73–94.
Flower, M. A., 'Agesilaus of Sparta and the Origins of the Ruler Cult', *CQ* 38.1 (1988), 123–34.
Flower, M. A., "Piety in Xenophon's Theory of Leadership' in Buxton, R. F. (ed.), *Aspects of Leadership in Xenophon*. *Histos* Supplement 5. Newcastle-Upon-Tyne: Histos, 2016, 85–119.
Flower, M. A., '*The Cambridge Companion to Xenophon*. Cambridge: Cambridge University Press, 2017.

Foucault, M., *Power/Knowledge: Selected Interviews and Other Writings 1972-77*, Ed. Gordon, C. New York: Random House USA Inc., 1980.
Foucault, M., *Histoire de la Sexualité 3. Le Souci de Soi*. Paris: Editions Gallimard, 1984.
Foucault, M. and Hurley, R., 'Erotics', *October* 33 (1985), 3-30.
Fowler, H. W., *A Dictionary of Modern English Usage*. Oxford: Oxford University Press, 1926.
Fox, R. L., *The Long March: Xenophon and the Ten Thousand*. New Haven and London: Yale University Press, 2004.
Foxhall, L., 'Household, Gender and Property in Classical Athens', *Classical Quarterly* 39.1 (1989), 22-44.
Fredal, J., 'Why Shouldn't the Sophist Charge Fees?', *Rhetoric Society Quarterly* 38.2 (2008), 148-70.
Freeman, K., 'Portrait of a Millionaire – Callias Son of Hipponicus', *Greece & Rome* 8.22 (1938), 20-35.
Friedrich, C. J. (ed.) *Authority (Nomos 1)*. Cambridge, MA: Harvard University Press, 1958.
Frost, F. J., 'The "Ominous" Birth of Peisistratos' in Titchener, F. B., Morton, R. F. and Green, P. (eds), *The Eye Expanded: Life and the Arts in Greco-Roman Antiquity*. Berkeley: California University Press, 1999, 9-18.
Gabrielsen, V., 'The *Antidosis* Procedure in Classical Athens', *Classica et Mediaevalia* 38 (1987), 7-38.
Gauthier, P., 'Un commentaire historique des Poroi de Xenophon' *CR* 29 (1979), 17-19.
Gauthier, P., 'Le Programme de Xenophon dans le *Poroi*', *RPh* 58 (1984), 181-99.
Genette, G., *Narrative Discourse: An Essay in Method*. Oxford: Cornell University Press, 1980 (1972).
Gera, D., *Xenophon's Cyropaedia: Style, Genre and Literary Technique*. Oxford: Oxford University Press, 1993.
Gill, C., 'The Question of Character-Development: Plutarch and Tacitus', *Classical Quarterly* 33 (1983), 469-87.
Gini, A., 'The Manly Intellect of His Wife: Xenophon *Oec*. Ch. 7', *The Classical World* 96 (1992/3), 483-6.
Goffman, E., *Behavior in Public Places: Notes on the Social Organization of Gatherings*. New York: Free Press, 1963.
Goldhill, S., 'The Great Dionysia and Civic Ideology', in Winkler, J. and Zeitlin, F., *Nothing to Do with Dionysos? Athenian Drama in its Social Context*. Princeton: Princeton University Press, 1990.
Goldhill, S., *Foucault's Virginity*. Cambridge: Cambridge University Press, 1995.
Goldhill, S., *Sophocles and the Language of Tragedy: Onassis Series in Hellenic Culture*. Oxford, New York: Oxford University Press, 2012.
Golfin, E., 'Essai sur la construction du temps dans la narration historique. L' exemple des Héllenique de Xénophon', *L' Antiquité Classique* 72 (2003), 75-94.
Gottlieb, P., 'The Complexity of Socratic Irony: A Note on Professor Vlastos' Account', *Classical Quarterly* 42.1 (1992), 278-9.

Gray, V., 'Dialogue in Xenophon's *Hellenica*', *Classical Quarterly* 31.2 (1981), 321–34.
Gray, V., 'Xenophon's "Cynegiticus"', *Hermes* 113.2 (1985), 156–72.
Gray, V., 'Xenophon's *Hiero* and the Meeting of the Wise Man and Tyrant in Greek Literature', *Classical Quarterly* 36.1 (1986), 115–123.
Gray, V., *The Character of Xenophon's Hellenica*. London: Johns Hopkins University Press, 1989.
Gray, V., 'Continuous History and Xenophon *Hellenica* 1–2.3.10', *American Journal of Philology* 112.2 (1991), 201–28.
Gray, V., 'Xenophon's Symposion: The Display of Wisdom', *Hermes* 120.1 (1992), 58–75.
Gray, V., 'Interventions and Citations in Xenophon, Hellenica and Anabasis', *CQ* 53 (2003), 111–23.
Gray, V., *Xenophon on Government*. Cambridge: Cambridge University Press, 2007.
Gray, V., *Xenophon*. Oxford: Oxford University Press, 2010.
Gray, V., *Xenophon's Mirror of Princes: Reading the Reflections*. Oxford: Oxford University Press, 2011.
Grethlein, J., 'Xenophon's *Anabasis* from Character to Narrator', *JHS* 132 (2012), 23–4.
Griffith, G., 'Isegoria in the Assembly at Athens' in Badian, E, (ed.), *Athenian Society and Institutions: Studies Presented to Victor Ehrenberg on his 75th Birthday*. Oxford: Blackwell, 1966, 115–38.
Guthrie, W. K., *The Sophists*. Cambridge: Cambridge University Press, 1971.
Guyot, P., *Eunuchen als Sklaven und Friegelassene in der griechisch-römischen Antike*. Stuttgart: Klett-Cotta, 1980.
Hadzits, G. P., 'Some Xenophon Problems and Recent Xenophon Literature', *CJ* 3.6 (1908), 211–12.
Hall, E., *Inventing the Barbarian: Greek Self-Definition through Tragedy*. Oxford: Oxford University Press, 1989.
Hamilton, C. D., *Agesilaus and the Failure of Spartan Hegemony*. Ithaca and London: Cornell University Press, 1991.
Harman, R., 'A Spectacle of Greekness: Panhellenism and the Visual in Xenophon's Agesilaus', in Hobden, F. and Tuplin, C. (eds), *Xenophon: Ethical Principles and Historical Enquiry*. Leiden and Boston: Brill, 2012, 427–53.
Harris, W. V., *Ancient Literacy*. Cambridge, MA and London: Harvard University Press, 1989.
Harvey, D., 'The Wicked Wife of Ischomachos', *Echos du monde Classique: Classical Views* 3 (1984), 68–70.
Hau, L. I., *Moral History from Herodotus to Diodorus Siculus*. Edinburgh: Edinburgh University Press, 2016.
Hesk, J., 'Xenophon and Arrian, On Hunting', *Bryn Mawr Classical Review* 2000.11.19, 196.
Higgins, W. E., *Xenophon the Athenian: The Problem of the World and the Society of the Athenian Polis*. Albany: State University of New York Press, 1977.
Hindley, C., 'Debate: Law, Society and Homosexuality in Classical Athens', *Past and Present* 133.1 (1991), 167–83.

Hindley, C., 'Eroas and Military Command in Xenophon', *CQ* 44.2 (1994), 347–66.
Hindley, C., 'Xenophon on Male Love' in Gray, V. (2010), 72–110.
Hirsch, S. W., *The Friendship of the Barbarians: Xenophon and the Persian Empire*. Hanover, NH: University Press of New England, 1985.
Hobden, F. and Tuplin, C., *Xenophon: Ethical Principles and Historical Enquiry*. Leiden and Boston: Brill, 2012.
Hodkinson, S. (ed.), *Sparta: Comparative Approaches*. Swansea: Classical Press of Wales, 2009.
Hopkins, K. and Hopkins, M. K., 'Eunuchs in Politics in the Later Roman Empire', *Proceedings of the Cambridge Philological Society* 9.189 (1963), 62–80.
Howland, J., 'Xenophon's Philosophic Odyssey: On the Anabasis and Plato's Republic', *The American Political Science Review* 94.4 (2000), 875–89.
Humble, N., 'The Author, Date and Purpose of Chapter 14 of *Lacedaimonia Politeia*', in Tuplin, C. (ed.), *Xenophon and His World. Papers from a Conference held in Liverpool in 1999*. Historia Heft 172. Stuttgart: F. Steiner, 2004, 215–28.
Humble, N., 'Treatises on Government by V. J. Gray', *Classical Review* 60.1 (2010), 43–4.
Humble, N., 'Sparta in Xenophon and Plato', in Danzig, G., Johnson, D., and Morrison, D. (eds), *Plato and Xenophon: Comparative Studies*. Leiden, Boston: Brill, 2018, 547–575.
Huss, B., 'The Dancing Socrates and the Laughing Xenophon, or the Other "Symposium"', *AJP* 120.3 (1999), 381–409.
Huss, B., *Xenophons Symposion. Ein Kommentar*. Stuttgart and Leipzig: B. G. Teubner, 1999.
Immerwahr, H. R. and Connor, W. R., 'Historiography', in Easterling, P. E., and Knox, B. M. W. (eds), *The Cambridge History of Classical Literature*. Cambridge: Cambridge University Press, 1985, 426–471.
Irigaray, L., *This Sex Which is Not One*, tr. Porter, C. Ithaca: 1985 = *Ce sexe qui n' en est pas un*. Paris: Cornell University Press, 1977.
Jaeger, W., *Paideia* III. Oxford: Oxford University Press, 1947.
Jansen, J. 'Strangers Incorporated: Outsider's in Xenophon's *Poroi*', in Hobden, F. and Tuplin, C. (eds.), *Xenophon: Ethical Principles and Historical Enquiry*. Leiden and Boston: Brill, 2012, 723–60.
Johnson, D., 'Persians as Centaurs in Xenophon's "Cyropaedia"', *Transactions of the American Philological Association* 135.1 (2005), 177–207.
Johnson, D., 'Strauss on Xenophon' in Hobden, F. and Tuplin, C. (eds), *Xenophon: Ethical Principles and Historical Enquiry*. Leiden and Boston: Brill, 2012, 123–59.
Johnson, D., 'Review of *Xenophon's Mirror of Princes: Reading the Reflections* by Gray', *Classical Philology* 108.1 (2013), 86.
Johnstone, S., 'Virtuous Toil, Vicious Work: Xenophon on Aristocratic Style', *Classical Philology* 89.3 (1994), 219–40.
Just, R., *Women in Athenian Law and Life*. London: Routledge, 1991.
Kennedy, G. (ed.), *The Cambridge History of Literary Criticism*. Cambridge: Cambridge University Press, 1989.

Kierkegaard, S., *The Concept of Irony with Continual Reference to Socrates*. Eds. and trans. Hong, H. V. and Hong, E. H., Princeton: Princeton University Press, 1989.

Kofman, S., 'Beyond Aporia?' in Benjamin, A. (ed.), *Post-Structuralist Classics*. New York and London: Routledge, 1988, 7–44.

Kovacs, D., 'Two Notes on Xenophon *Hellenica* 1.4.20 and *Agesilaus* 2.26', *Classical Quarterly* 61.2 (2011), 751–3.

Krentz, P., *Xenophon: Hellenika II.3.11–IV.2.8*. Warminster: Aris & Phillips, 1995.

Kronenberg, L., *Allegories of Farming from Greece and Rome. Philosophical Satire in Xenophon, Varro and Vergil*. Cambridge: Cambridge University Press, 2009.

Layne, D., 'From Irony to Enigma: Discovering Double Ignorance and Socrates' Divine Knowledge', *Methexis* 23 (2010), 73–90.

Le Doeuff, M., *Hipparchia's Choice: An Essay Concerning Women, Philosophy, Etc.*, tr. Selous, T. Oxford and Cambridge, MA: Columbia University Press, 1991. [= *L'Etude et le rouet*. Paris: 1989.]

Long, A. and Sedley, D., *The Hellenistic Philosophers. Vol. 1. Translations of the Principal Sources, with Philosophical Commentary*. Cambridge: Cambridge University Press, 1987.

Loraux, N., *The Children of Athena: Athenian Ideas About Citizenship and the Division Between the Sexes*, tr. Levine, C. Princeton: Princeton University Press, 1993. [= *Les enfants d'Athena: Idées athéniennes sur la citoyenneté et la division des sexes*. Paris: 1984.]

Luccioni, J., *Les idées politiques et socials de Xénophon*. Athens: Ophrys, 1948.

Luraghi, N., 'Xenophon's Place in Fourth-Century Greek Historiography' in Flower, M. A. (ed.), *The Cambridge Companion to Xenophon*. Cambridge: Cambridge University Press, 2017, 84–100.

MacLaren, M., 'On the Composition of Xenophon's *Hellenica*', *American Journal of Philology* 55.3 (1934a), 121–39.

MacLaren, M., 'Xenophon and Themistogenes', *TAPA* 65 (1934b), 240–7.

MacLaren, M., 'A Supposed Lacuna at the Beginning of Xenophon's Hellenica', *AJP* 100 (1979), 228–38.

Marincola, J., 'Xenophon's *Anabasis* and *Hellenica*', in Flower, M. (ed.), *The Cambridge Companion to Xenophon*. Cambridge: Cambridge University Press, 2017, 103–18.

Marr, J. L. and Rhodes, P. J. (eds), *The 'Old Oligarch': The Constitution of the Athenians Attributed to Xenophon*. Oxford: Aris and Phillips Classical Texts, 2008.

Millender, E., 'The Spartan Dyarchy: A Comparative Perspective' in Hodkinson, S. (ed.), *Sparta: Comparative Approaches*. Swansea: Classical Press of Wales, 2009, 1–68.

Miller, A., *For Your Own Good: The Roots of Violence in Child-rearing*, tr. Hannum, H. and H. London: Virago, 1987.

Molyneux, J. H., *Simonides: A Historical Study*. Wauconda, Ill.: Bolchazy-Carducci Publishers, 1992.

Momigliano, A., *The Development of Greek Biography*. Cambridge, MA: Harvard University Press, 1993.

Morgan, K. A., *Myth and Philosophy from the Presocratics to Plato*. Cambridge: Cambridge University Press, 2009.
Morrison, D., 'On Professor Vlastos' Xenophon', *Ancient Philosophy* 7 (1987), 9–22.
Most, G., 'Generating Genres: The Idea of the Tragic' in M. Depew and D. Obbink (eds), *Matrices of Genre: Authors, Canons and Society*. Cambridge, MA: Harvard University Press, 2000, 15–36.
Murnaghan, S., 'How a Woman Can Be More Like a Man: The Dialogue Between Ischomachus and His Wife in Xenophon's *Oeconomicus*', *Helios* 15 (1988), 9–22.
Nadon, C., *Xenophon's Prince: Republic and Empire in the Cyropaedia*. Berkeley: California University Press, 2001.
Nagy, G., 'Early Views of Poets and Poetry', in Kennedy, G. (ed.), *The Cambridge History of Literary Criticism*. Cambridge: Cambridge University Press, 1989, 1–78.
Nails, D., *The People of Plato: A Prosopography of Plato and Other Socratics*. Indianapolis: Hackett Publishing Co., Inc., 2002.
Nehamas, A., *The Art of Living: Socratic Reflections from Plato to Foucault*. Berkeley, Los Angeles, London: University of California Press, 1998.
Nickel, R., *Xenophon*. Darmstadt: Wissenschaftliche Buchgesellschaft, 1979.
Nightingale, A., *Genres in Dialogue: Plato and the Construct of Philosophy*. Cambridge: Cambridge University Press, 1995.
Norden, E., *Die Antike Kunstprosa*. Leipzig: B. G. Teubner, 1895.
North, H., *Sophrosyne: Self-Knowledge and Self-Restraint in Greek Literature*. New York: Cornell University Press, 1966.
Nussbaum, G. B., *The Ten Thousand: A Study in Social Organization and Action in Xenophon's Anabasis*. Leiden: Brill, 1967.
Ober, J., *Mass and Elite in Democratic Athens*. Princeton: Princeton University Press, 1989.
Ostwald, M., *From Popular Sovereignty to the Sovereignty of Law*. Berkeley, CA: University of California Press, 1987.
Pangle, T., 'The Political Defence of Socratic Philosophy: A Study of Xenophon's "Apology of Socrates to the Jury"', *Polity* 18.1 (1985), 98–114.
Pangle, T., 'Socratic Political Philosophy in Xenophon's Symposium', *American Journal of Political Science* 54.1 (2010), 140–52.
Pangle, T., *The Socratic Way of Life: Xenophon's "Memorabilia"*. Chicago: University of Chicago Press, 2018.
Patterson, A., *Reading Between the Lines*. Madison, WI: Routledge, 1993.
Pelling, C., 'Xenophon's Authorial Voice', in Flower, M. (ed.), *The Cambridge Companion to Xenophon*. Cambridge: Cambridge University Press, 2017, 241–262.
Phillips, J., 'Xenophon's "Memorabilia" 4.2', *Hermes* 117 (1989), 366–70.
Polanyi, K., *The Livelihood of Man*. New York: Academic Press Inc., 1977.
Pomeroy, S. B., 'Slavery in the Greek Domestic Economy in the Light of Xenophon's <<Oeconomicus'>>', *Index* 17 (1989), 11–18.
Pomeroy, S. B., *Xenophon, Oeconomicus. A Social and Historical Commentary*. Oxford: Clarendon Press, 1994.

Pontier, P., 'Isocrate et Xénophon, de l'éloge de Gryllos à l'éloge du roi: échos, concordances et discordances,' *Ktema* 41 (2016), 43–58.

Pownall, F. S., 'Condemnation of the Impious in Xenophon's "Hellenica"', *Harvard Theological Review* 91.3 (1998), 251–77.

Pownall, F. S., 'From Orality to Literacy: The Moral Education of the Elite in Fourth-Century Athens' in Cooper, C. (ed.), *Politics of Orality (Orality and Literacy in Ancient Greece, Vol. 6)*. Leiden and Boston: Brill, 2007, 235–50.

Pownall, F. S., 'Critias in Xenophon's Hellenica' *Scripta Classica Israelica* 31 (2012), 1–17.

Pritchard, D., 'War, Democracy and Culture in Classical Athens', *Australasian Society for Classical Studies* 31 (2010).

Proietti, G., *Xenophon's Sparta*. Leiden: Brill, 1987.

Pucci, P., *Xenophon: Socrates' Defense: Introduction and Commentary*. Amsterdam: Adolf M. Hakkert Editore, 2002.

Purves, A., *Space and Time in Ancient Greek Narrative*. Cambridge: Cambridge University Press, 2010.

Raaflaub, K., 'Early Greek Thought in its Mediterranean Context' in Balot, R., *A Companion to Greek and Roman Political Thought*. Malden, MA and Oxford: Wiley-Blackwell, 2013, 66.

Radermacher, L., 'Uber den Cynegeticus des Xenophon', *RhM* 51 (1856), 591–627.

Radin, M., 'Xenophon's Ten Thousand', *CJ* 7.2 (1911), 51–60.

Rahn, P. J., 'Xenophon's Developing Historiography', *Transactions of the American Philological Association* 102 (1971), 497–508.

Ralkowski, M. A., *Plato's Trial of Athens*. London and New York: Bloomsbury Academic, 2019.

Redway, J. W., 'The Silver Mines of Athens', *The Journal of Education* 61.15 (1905), 412.

Redfield, J., 'Homo Domesticus' in Vernant, J.-P. (ed.), *The Greeks*, tr. Lambert, C. and Fagan, T. L. Chicago and London: University of Chicago Press, 1991, 154–83.

Reid, H.., Tanasi, D., Kimbell, S. (eds), *Politics and Performance in Western Greece: Essays on the Hellenic Heritage of Sicily and Southern Italy*. Sioux City, IA: 2017.

Rhodes, P. J., 'Civic Ideology and Citizenship', in Balot, R., *A Companion to Greek and Roman Political Thought*. Malden, MA and Oxford: Wiley-Blackwell, 2013), 66.

Rice, D. G., *Agesilaus, Agesipolis, and Spartan Politics, 386–379 B.C.* Historia: Zeitschrift fur Alte Geschichte (2nd Qtr.), 1974.

Robb, K., *Literacy and Paideia in Ancient Greece*. New York: Oxford University Press, 1994.

Rochi, E. D., 'Hégémonie et Autonome: La Petites Poleis dans les 'Helleniques' de Xénophon', *Ancient Society* 38 (2008), 1–21.

Roisman, H., *The Rhetoric of Manhood: Masculinity and the Attic Orators*. Berkeley, CA: University of California Press, 2005.

Rood, T., 'Panhellenism and Self-Presentation: Xenophon's Speeches' in Fox, R. L., *The Long March: Xenophon and the Ten Thousand*. New Haven and London: Yale University Press, 2004, 305–29.

Rood, T., 'Xenophon's Parasangs', *JHS* 130 (2010), 51–66.
Sage, P. W., 'Dying in Style: Xenophon's Ideal Leader and the End of the "Cyropaedia"', *CJ* 90.2 (1975), 161–74.
Sandbach, F. H., 'Plato and the Socratic Work of Xenophon', in Easterling, P. E., and Knox, B. M. W. (eds), *The Cambridge History of Classical Literature*. Cambridge: Cambridge University Press, 1985, 478–497.
Sanders, H. N., *The Cynegeticus*, PhD thesis. Baltimore: The Friedenwald Company, 1903.
Scaife, R., 'Ritual and Persuasion in the House of Ischomachus', *The Classical Journal* 90 (1995), 225–32.
Schaps, D. M., 'Socrates and the Socratics: When Wealth Became a Problem', *CW* 96.2 (2003), 131–57.
Schorn, S., 'The Philosophical Background of Xenophon's *Poroi*' in Hobden, F. and Tuplin, C., *Xenophon: Ethical Principles and Historical Enquiry*. Leiden and Boston: Brill, 2012, 689–723.
Seager, R., 'Xenophon and Athenian Democratic Ideology', *CQ* 51 (2001), 385–97.
Sevieri, R., 'The Imperfect Hero: Xenophon's *Hiero* and the (self)-Taming of the Tyrant' in Tuplin, C. (ed.), *Xenophon and His World. Papers from a Conference held in Liverpool in 1999*. Historia Heft 172. Stuttgart: F. Steiner, 2004, 277–87.
Shero, L. R., 'Plato's *Apology* and Xenophon's *Apology*', *Classical Weekly* 20.14 (1927), 107–11.
Shrimpton, G. 'The Theban Supremacy in Fourth-Century Literature', *Phoenix* 25.4 (1971), 310–8.
Sidwell, K., *Aristophanes the Democrat: The Politics of Satirical Comedy During the Peloponesian War*. Cambridge and New York: Cambridge University Press, 2009.
Simonton, M., *Classical Greek Oligarchy: A Political History*. Princeton: Princeton University Press, 2017.
Smith, G. B., 'Who Was Leo Strauss?', *The American Scholar* 66.1 (1997), 95–104.
Spence, I. G., *The Cavalry of Classical Greece: A Social and Military History with Particular Reference to Athens*. Oxford: Clarendon Press, 1993.
Stadter, P., 'Fictional Narrative in the Cyropaedia', *American Journal of Philology* 112.4 (1991), 461–91.
Stavru, A. and Moore, C. (eds), *Socrates and the Socratic Dialogue*. Leiden and Boston: Brill, 2018.
Stevens, J., 'Friendship and Profit in Xenophon's *Oeconomicus*' in Van der Waerdt, P. (ed.), *The Socratic Movement*. Ithaca: Cornell University Press, 1994, 209–37.
Strauss, B. S., '*Oikos/Polis*: Towards a Theory of Athenian Paternal Ideology 450–399 BC' in Connor, W. R., Hansen, M. H., Raaflaub, K. A., Strauss, B. S. (eds), *Aspects of Athenian Democracy*, Classica et Mediaevalia Dissertationes XI. Copenhagen: Museum Tusculanum Press, 1990, 101–27.
Strauss, B. S., *Fathers and Sons in Athens: Ideology and Society in the Era of the Peloponnesian War*. London: Routledge, 1993.
Strauss, L., 'The Spirit of Sparta or the Taste of Xenophon', *Social Research* 6 (1939), 502–36.

Strauss, L., *On Tyranny*, Eds. Gourevitch, V. and Roth, M. S. Chicago: University of Chicago Press, 1961, 1992, 2000.
Strauss, L., *The City and Man*. Chicago: University of Chicago Press, 1964.
Strauss, L., 'Greek Historians', *The Review of Metaphysics* 21.4 (1968), 656–666.
Strauss, L., *Xenophon's Socratic Dialogue: An Interpretation of the Oeconomicus*. Ithaca: Cornell University Press, 1970.
Takakjy, L. C., 'Xenophon the Literary Critic: The Poetics and Politics of Praise in *Hiero*', *Greek, Roman and Byzantine Studies* 57 (2017), 49–73.
Tamiolaki, M., 'Virtue and Leadership in Xenophon: Ideal Leader or Ideal Losers?', in Hobden, F. and Tuplin, C. (eds), *Xenophon: Ethical Principles and Historical Enquiry*. Leiden and Boston: Brill, 2012, 563–89.
Tamiolaki, M., 'Xenophon's Conception of Friendship in *Memorabilia* 2.6 (with Reference to Plato's *Lysis*)', in Danzig, G., Johnson, D., and Morrison, D. (eds), *Plato and Xenophon: Comparative Studies*. Leiden, Boston: Brill, 2018.
Tarkan, H., 'Wisdom for Sale? The Sophist and Money', *CP* 104 (2009), 13–33.
Tatum, J., *Xenophon's Imperial Fiction: On the Education of Cyrus*. Princeton: Princeton University Press, 1989.
Taylor, A. E., *Plato: The Man and His Work*. London: Methuen, 1937.
Tell, H., 'Wisdom for Sale? The Sophists and Money', *Classical Philology* 104.1 (2009), 13–33.
Thesleff, H., 'The Interrelation and Date of the 'Symposia' of Plato and Xenophon', *Bulletin of the Institute of Classical Studies* 25 (1978), 157–70.
Titchener, F. B., Morton, R. F. and Green, P. (eds), *The Eye Expanded: Life and the Arts in Greco-Roman Antiquity*. Berkeley: California University Press, 1999.
Too, Y. L., *The Rhetoric of Identity in Isocrates: Text, Power, Pedagogy*. Cambridge: Cambridge University Press, 1995.
Too, Y. L., 'The Pedagogical State and the Disfiguration of Power in Xenophon's *Cyropaedia*' in Too, Y. L. and Livingstone, N. (eds), *Pedagogy and Power: Rhetorics of Classical Learning*. Cambridge: Cambridge University Press, 1998, 282–302.
Too, Y. L., 'The Economies of Pedagogy: Xenophon's Wifely Didactics', *Proceedings of the Cambridge Philological Society* 47 (2001), 65–80.
Too, Y. L., (ed.), *Education in Greek and Roman Antiquity*. Leiden: Brill, 2001.
Too, Y. L. and Livingstone, N. (eds), *Pedagogy and Power: Rhetorics of Classical Learning*. Cambridge: Cambridge University Press, 1998.
Trego, K. M., 'Agesilaus the Puppet? The Effects of Thematic Development on Plutarch's Story of the Accession', *Illinois Classical Studies* 39 (2014), 39–62.
Tuplin, C., 'The Failings of Empire: A Reading of Xenophon', *Hellenica* 2.3.11–7.5.27. Historia Einzelschriften, Heft 76. Stuttgart: Franz Steiner, 1993.
Tuplin, C., (ed.), *Xenophon and His World: Papers from a Conference held in Liverpool in 1999*. Historia Heft 172. Stuttgart: F. Steiner, 2004.
Tymura, D., 'The Bitter Life of a Tyrant – Remarks on Xenophon's *Hiero*', in Reid, H.., Tanasi, D., Kimbell, S. (eds), *Politics and Performance in Western Greece: Essays on the Hellenic Heritage of Sicily and Southern Italy*. Sioux City, IA: 2017, 97–108.

Van der Waerdt, P. (ed.), *The Socratic Movement*. Ithaca: Cornell University Press, 1994.
Vasiliou, I., 'Conditional Irony in the Socratic Dialogues', *Classical Quarterly* 49.2 (1999), 456–72.
Vernant, J.-P., *Myth and Thought among the Greeks*. London: Routledge & Kegan Paul, 1983 [= *Mythe et pensée chez les Grecs*. Paris: 1965, 271–94.]
Vernant, J.-P., (ed.), *The Greeks*, tr. Lambert, C. and Fagan, T. L. Chicago and London: University of Chicago Press, 1991.
Vilatte, S., 'La femme, l'esclave, le cheval et le chien: les emblèmes du KALOS KAGATHOS Ischomaque', *Dialogues d' histoire ancienne* 12 (1986), 271–294.
Vlastos, G., 'Socratic Irony', *Classical Quarterly* 37.1 (1987), 79–96.
Vlastos, G., *Socrates, Ironist and Moral Philosopher*. Cambridge: Cambridge University Press, 1991.
Waterfield, R. A. H., 'Xenophon's Socratic Mission' in Tuplin, *Xenophon and His World: Papers from a Conference Held in Liverpool in July 1999*. Stuttgart: F. Steiner, 2004, 85.
Waterfield, R. A. H., *Xenophon's Retreat: Greece, Persia, and the End of the Golden Age*. Cambridge, MA: Harvard University Press, 2008.
Weathers, W., 'Xenophon's Political Idealism', *Classical Journal* 49 (1954), 317–21 and 330.
Wellman, R., 'Socratic Method in Xenophon', *Journal of the History of Ideas* 37.2 (1976), 307–18.
Wencis, L., 'Hypopsia and the Structure of Xenophon's Anabasis', *CJ* 73.1 (1977), 44–9.
Wheeler, E. L., review of 'C. D. Hamilton, *Agesilaus and the Failure of Spartan Hegemony*', *American Journal of Philology* 114 (1993), 456–9.
Whidden, C., 'The Account of Persia and Cyrus' Persian Education in Xenophon's *Cyropaedia*', *The Review of Politics* 69.4 (2007), 539–67.
Winkler, J. and Zeitlin, F., *Nothing to Do with Dionysos? Athenian Drama in its Social Context*. Princeton: Princeton University Press, 1990.
Wohl, V., *Law's Cosmos: Juridical Discourse in Athenian Forensic Oratory*. Cambridge: Cambridge University Press, 2010.
Wolfsdorf, D., 'The Irony of Socrates', *Journal of Aesthetics and Art Criticism* 65.2 (2007), 175–87.
Wood, N., 'Xenophon's Theory of Leadership', *Classica et Mediaevalia* 25 (1964), 33–66.
Woodhead, A. G., 'ΙΣΗΓΟΡΙΑ and the Council of 500', *Historia* 16 (1967), 129–40.
Zeitlin, F., *Playing the Other: Gender and Society in Classical Greek Literature*. Chicago and London: University of Chicago Press, 1996.
Zenker, F., *The Rural Basis of the Ancient Greek City*. Honors dissertation, Wesleyan University: 2009.
Zucker, F. and *Müller*, W. (eds), *Festschrift für Fr. Zucker*. Berlin: Akademie-Verl., 1954.
Zuckert, C., 'Who's A Philosopher? Who's a Sophist? The Stranger v. Socrates', *Review of Metaphysics* 54.1 (2000), 65–97.

Greek Index

ἀλαζών 5
ἀπραγμοσύνη 99
ἀράγμων 4, 106

βωμολόχος 5

διδάσκειν 92, 95–7 passim, 171, 230 n.12

εἰρών 5, 48
εἰρωνεία 3, 8, 74
ἔρως 52
ἐγκράτεια 35

ἰδιώτης 120–2

καλὸς κἀγαθός 45, 49, 62
καλοκαγαθία 49

μεγαληγορία 23
μικροφωνία 4

οἶκος 61, 65, 69, 70, 73

παῖς 185
πλεονεξία 107
πολυπράγμων 107, 112
πολυπραγμοσύνη 4

σοφροσύνη 67

τάξις 67–8
τὸ δαιμονίον 28

Index

Agesilaus 6, 17, 131, 137–49, 151, 156, 202, 228
Alcibiades 33–4, 36, 153–4
Alders, G. P. D. 119
Anderson, G. 127
Antisthenes 87
Anytus 25–6
appearance 179–81
Aristophanes 55, 96
Aristotle 5, 10, 69
Arrian 81, 182
Aspaia 76

Bacchylides 121
Biography 139–40
Blank, D. 89
Blau, A. 145, 207, 212
Bonner, R. 193
Booth, W. 7–8, 212
Bowersock, G. 209
Bradley, P. J. 187, 202
Bury, J. 139

Callias 45–59 passim, 70, 75, 91
Callimachus 3
Cantarella, E. 77
Carlier, P. 170, 172, 185
Cartledge, P. 110, 140
cavalry 98–104 passim
Cawkwell, G. 3, 136
Chaeronea, battle of 131
Chantraine, P. 75
Cheiron 82–3, 86, 87, 89, 91
Christensen, P. 131
Chrysilla 69, 71
class 114
classics 1
Cleon 3
Cohen, D. 56
community 195–202
Coronea, battle of 146, 211
Critias 33–4, 36, 156

Cyrus the Great 42, 70, 169–86, 188, 192, 209
Cyrus the younger 169, 173, 188–94, 201, 202, 204–5

Danzig, G. 12, 21–2, 27
Delebecque, E. 173, 231, 239
De Pew, M. 10
De Romilly, J. 9
Demosthenes 120
desire 52–5
didactic 66–7, 71, 92, 99, 104, 115
Dillery, J. 2, 11, 12, 105, 107, 114, 115, 148, 156, 194, 195, 199
Diogenes Laertius 172
Dorion, L.-A. 3, 12
Due, B. 12, 170, 173, 178

economics 63–78, 105–15
education 92, 132, 134, 142, 169–86
elitism 4, 8, 13, 26, 84
eunuch 182–4
Euthydemus 38–9, 41
exotericism 1

fees 47
feminism 61
Field, L. 173
Flower, M. 2, 191
Foucault, M. 181
Frost, F. J. 141
Funeral Oration 4, 14

Gauthier, P. 106
genre 10–11
Gera, D. 12, 173
Gini, A. 71
Gorgias 46, 87
Gray, V. 2, 12, 81, 88, 119, 120, 122, 124–6, 129, 152, 186, 212
Grethlein, J. 201

Hamilton, C. D. 140, 142

Harman, R, 144
Harris, W. 4
Hau, L. I. 157
Hellenism 25, 188, 236, 242
Hermogenes 23–4
Herodotus 11, 184, 187, 202
Hesiod 63, 64, 76
   Theogony 63, 121
   Works and Days 64–6, 75
Hiero 56, 119–30, 139
Hierocles 126
Higgins, W. E. 11–13
Hindley, C. 55–6
Hippias 51
Hirsch, S. 12
Hobden, F. 12
Homer 49
   Iliad 49, 65
   Odyssey 49
Hornblower, S. 200
horses 93–104, 143, 166
hunting 81–92, 178

ignorance 21, 48
irony 1–3, 5–7, 12, 16, 21, 27–8, 38, 61, 69,
   112, 138, 145, 151, 152, 163, 169,
   173, 187, 191, 202, 208, 211–12,
   217 n.26
   Socratic 21–9, 31, 39, 58–78 passim, 87,
   216–17 n.23
Ischomachus 29
Isocrates vii, 3, 4, 11, 14, 15, 47, 84, 87, 90,
   107, 120, 128
   Letter to Alexander 128–9
   To Nicocles 128

Jaeger, W. 81
Johnson, D. 102
Johnstone, S. 87
justice 127

Kierkegaard, S. 2, 8, 22, 212
knowledge 6, 14, 39, 46, 49, 170, 186
Kovacs, D. 145

Lane Fox, R. 12
Laurion 109–12, 114–15, 202
lawcourts 3
leisure 120

Leuctra, battle of 131
literacy 4
Loraux, N. 64, 65
Luccioni, J. 184, 233
Lycurgus 17, 132, 137–9, 149
Lysias 57, 75
Lysimachus 3
Lysistratus 108

MacLaren, M. 156, 229
Mantinea, battle of 17, 109, 156, 162, 194,
   195
Marincola, J. 148, 151, 187, 195
mercenary 103
metics 108
Miller, A. 78, 173
misogyny 61–2, 78
Morgan, K. 89
Morrison, D. 1, 12
Most, G. 10
Murnaghan, S. 68, 77

Nadon, C. 12, 185
Nagy, G. 121
Nehemas, A. 63
new politician 3
Nickel, R. 81
Nightingale, A. 10
Norden, E. 81

Obbink, D. 10
Old Comedy 5
oligarchy 131, 156, 160, 174
orators 3
oratory 3

Pandora 64
Pangle, T. 12, 59
panopticism 182
Patterson, A. 1
peace 113
pedagogue 170
pedagogy 27, 34, 91, 94, 96, 169–86
pederasty 133
Peisistratos 141
Pelling, C. 163
Peloponnesian War 17
Pericles 13–15, 76, 129, 194, 195
Persia 58, 169–86, 187–205 passim

Persian Wars 106
Philips, A. A. 89
philosopher 88
philosopher-king 185
'piety' 25, 27, 42
Pindar 121
Plato 2, 4, 6–7, 11, 27, 46, 120, 171, 172
   Protagoras 121
   Republic 46, 120, 127
   Sophist 90
   Symposium 53
Plutarch 140
poet 130
Polanyi, K. 105
Pomeroy, S. 61, 74, 75
Pritchard, K. 106
Prodicus 46, 51, 87, 91
Prometheus 64
prostration 184
Protagoras 46, 91
Pucci, P. 23, 51

quietist/m 4, 99, 105, 107, 112, 166
Quintilian 5

Radermacher, L. 81
Rahn, P. J. 157, 229
Ralkowski, M. 22
'reading between the lines' 13, 62, 173
rhapsodes 49
rhetoric 83
Robb, K. 121
Russell, D. M. A. vii

Sappho 73
Scillus 211
Scopas 127
Semonides of Armorgos 64, 66
Sevieri, R. 126
Shero, L. R. 22, 24
Simonides 56, 70, 119–30 passim, 139
social criticism 3
Social War 105, 109
Socrates 3, 5, 6, 10, 45–78, 96, 127, 154, 171, 194, 195, 208
   corrupting youth 25, 33
   and old age 24, 39
   trial of 23–9, 31
   worshipping new gods 24–5, 32, 35
sophists 3, 14, 15–16, 46–9, 59, 81, 87–92, 183–4
Sparta 132–49,
Spartans 55, 151–66, 194, 203
Stadter, P. 177
Strauss, B. 171
Strauss, L. 1, 9, 12, 69, 76, 119, 125, 136, 152, 208
superiority 9

Tamiolaki, E-M. vii, 140
Tatum, J. 2, 12, 170, 172, 173, 187
Taylor, A. E. 89
teacher 15, 78, 83, 184
Ten Thousand 16, 23, 199–200, 204
theatricality 181
Themistocles 55
Theophrastus
   Characters 71, 77
Thirty, the 156
Thucydides 4, 11, 14, 15, 152–3, 164, 187
Tuplin, C. 2, 11, 12
Tymura, D. 119

Van der Waerdt, P. 12
virtue 46–7, 54, 137, 186
Vlastos, G. 2

Waterfield, R. 12
Weathers, W. 173, 231
Willock, M. 89
Wisdom 16
Wood, N. 180

Xanthippe 70
Xenophon
   as actor 31, 39, 41, 43, 187–8, 194–9, 203, 204–5
   as narrator 164–5, 188, 191, 194
   Pseudo-Xenophon 9, 209–10

www.ingramcontent.com/pod-product-compliance
Lightning Source LLC
Chambersburg PA
CBHW062132300426
44115CB00012BA/1897